Hands-On Sociology

Third Edition

William Feigelman, Ph.D.
Nassau Community College

Yih-Jin Young, Ph.D.
Nassau Community College

PEARSON

Boston   New York   San Francisco
Mexico City   Montreal   Toronto   London   Madrid   Munich   Paris
Hong Kong   Singapore   Tokyo   Cape Town   Sydney

Senior Series Editor: Jeff Lasser
Series Editorial Assistant: Heather McNally
Senior Marketing Manager: Kelly May
Editorial-Production Service: Omegatype Typography, Inc.
Composition Buyer: Linda Cox
Manufacturing Buyer: JoAnne Sweeney
Cover Coordinator: Joel Gendron
Electronic Composition: Omegatype Typography, Inc.

For related titles and support materials, visit our online catalog at www.ablongman.com.

Library of Congress Cataloging-in-Publication Data

Feigelman, William.
    Hands-on-sociology / William Feigelman, Yih-Jin Young.—3rd ed.
       p.   cm.
    Includes bibliographical references.
    ISBN 0-205-42846-0
       1. Sociology—Research. 2. Sociology—Methodology. 3. Sociology—Statistical methods.
    I. Young, Yih-Jin. II. Title.

HM571F45 2006
302'.01'01'5195—dc22

                                                                    2005048709

Printed in the United States of America
10 9 8 7 6 5 4 3 2 1   10 09 08 07 06 05

Credits: All screen captures from the University of California at Berkeley's SDA site are printed with permission. Additional sources are shown on p. xiv.

CONTENTS

CHAPTER EIGHT
Social Stratification and Social Mobility   118

CHAPTER NINE
Minority/Majority Relations   134

CHAPTER TEN
Marriage and Family in the United States   147

CHAPTER ELEVEN
Aspects of U.S. Political Life   163

PREFACE

FOR THE STUDENT

If there is anything truly exciting about being a sociologist, it is the prospect of doing one's own research and adding to the body of knowledge about society. As you read your textbook and learn about the different parts of society and how they mesh together and change over time, you may feel a sense of wonder about how this knowledge might be applied to different social circumstances or groups. Would research about Americans apply equally to people at different economic levels, to racial or ethnic minorities members, to city dwellers as well as to people living in rural places, and of course, to people in other countries? Usually, you would like to investigate this subject further, if an opportunity to do so is presented. Of course, these investigative urges frequently fall by the wayside as we become involved in other commitments and obligations. Nevertheless, in this volume, we want to offer you as many opportunities as possible to let your sociological imaginations run free, to think imaginatively about social relationships and to examine your ideas carefully and systematically within a scientific framework, with some of the data that professional sociologists rely on.

If you learned anything from your sociology textbooks, it is that doing sociological research is often a very laborious enterprise. First, you must decide on a topic of research interest and then review the existing literature on that topic. Subsequently, you formulate hypotheses to expand the knowledge base or deal with inconsistencies from past findings. Next, you must plan and carry out a data collection process. You must then create data files containing all the necessary data to test your study's principle hypotheses. The most exciting, and fun, part of the whole enterprise is to see how the hypotheses fared. This is what it is all about: Did the analysis support or disprove the hypotheses that guided our investigation? The last step, of course, is to write up all your procedures and findings.

In this volume we will help you "cut to the chase" so to speak. We will show you how professional sociologists apply widely used statistical methods that test hypotheses with survey data. We will also help you find a great deal of archival survey data on mainstream sociological topics: studies on family lifestyles and change, political values and behavior, religious affiliations, crime, drug use, gambling, appreciation of the arts, aging, and so many others that you are sure to find some of personal interest. We will also show you how raw survey data is groomed and readied for analysis, and you won't have to do any time-consuming and messy collection and management of data files yourselves. Your web-based statistical analysis tools will swiftly analyze thousands of cases from census surveys and other professional-quality data sources. All you will need to do is run the tests to see whether your hypotheses were supported. By completing our workbook exercises, you will have the opportunity to practice interpreting sociological data. Of course, you won't only be testing your own hypotheses about social relationships; you will also have to follow some of our practice exercises and examine some of our notions about social relationships. After you complete some of this practice work you will be in a better position to investigate many of your own hypotheses independently. You will also know where to go to explore further many of the survey research studies presented here. Most important, once you have some intimate familiarity with the research process, you'll be able to go wherever you want to explore the vast realm of sociological survey research, and you will be able to make scientifically meaningful conclusions about what data can tell us about our social world.

FOR THE INSTRUCTOR

We are pleased to offer this third edition of *Hands-On Sociology*, which we hope will assume an important place in the array of supplements available for undergraduate sociology classes. We are pleased that an approach offered more than twelve years ago, to a cult of methodologically oriented sociology instructors, still holds up and continues to offer an attractive alternative for teaching entry-level sociology students. Actually, more than ever before, it has become a lot easier to use this approach than it was when this book first appeared. In those early days of computing, most students didn't have personal computers, and many objected to the thought of using their computers for anything other than word processing. At the time, not many people were using e-mail and no one had heard of web browsing; back then, many were intimidated by navigating their computer's directories without the aid of today's user-friendly Windows operating system.

Now, many more of our students enter our classes with a much greater level of computer familiarity than they had a decade ago. Many come to our classes without that fear and trembling that was so often seen in earlier groups of students. Today, more than ever before, we are beginning to find many students who welcome the prospect of using their computers for applications other than word processing, e-mail and web browsing. Some eagerly look forward to the opportunity to use their computers as learning tools and for acquiring data management and data analysis skills. Of course, there are still some who have successfully evaded the computer revolution, but even some of these students are showing a new willingness to put aside their earlier technophobias and become more computer literate.

Our approach to this new edition is different from what was offered in previous editions. In most approaches like ours that emphasize quantitative mastery, students or faculty members must install statistical software, acquire the necessary data files and then make sure they correctly mesh before embarking on any data analysis tasks. If one intends to investigate additional datasets, they must then acquire and install those new datasets before any analysis can be performed with them. In *Hands-On Sociology,* we rely on a fast and easy-to-use web-based statistical software platform—offered freely on the web—to provide a wide variety of professional quality archival data sets. Once students learn how to access the Survey Documentation and Analysis (SDA) statistical software platform at its UC Berkeley website, and once they learn a number of statistical analysis procedures, they can investigate more than 150 archival data sets based on this analysis platform at the University of California, Berkeley; the University of Michigan; Princeton University; the Urban Institute in Washington, D.C.; and many other sites. Through these websites, students can carry out a wide variety of their own investigations on population patterns, family life, crime, aging, education, and a whole host of other subjects.

Our emphasis here is to offer students the least amount of information and instruction needed to enable them to do their own univariate and crosstabular analyses successfully. We also provide two chapters at the end of this volume guiding students through the rudiments of multivariate regression analysis. Once students gain training in data analysis fundamentals, they explore various topics of interest in introductory sociology and social problems courses with archival data from the entire range of General Social Surveys, the 1% Census 2000 PUMS sample, National Election Surveys and a wide variety of other professional quality archival datasets. We have groomed and recoded all data that students will utilize, and we provide easy-to-perform cutting and pasting instructions for students to follow, allowing them to place the necessary command language into their programs to gain their desired data analysis results. Our emphasis is to enhance student empowerment, to enable our classes to experience the thrill and excitement of making their own scientific discoveries. In this volume, we lead students along a path toward acquiring mastery of data analysis fundamentals as we help them overcome their anxieties about dealing with the quantitative realm. Our sets of exercises often lead students to confirm many of the things they read in their general sociology texts. In many cases, students are positioned to extend their knowledge beyond what may have been offered to them in their texts. Most important of all, students acquire critical thinking and data analysis skills. With this supplement, students learn how to more proficiently use the Internet to gather sociological information and to use statistical software to correctly interpret sociological survey data. We also provide a conducive environment for the further exploration of students' sociological questions and interests.

Today, more and more sociology instructors are beginning to discover that traditional teaching approaches utilizing textbooks and readers are less appealing for many of today's television-bred students who want something more exciting and dramatic. And now more than ever before, active learning approaches are being adopted: service learning projects, classroom discussion and presentation groups, Internet and electronic bibliographic searching of sociological materials. We cannot begin to summarize all the many different active learning approaches now in vogue. Among this diverse array of teaching approaches, offering students opportunities to gain quantitative analysis skills assumes an accepted place in undergraduate sociology instruction. Yet, what sets our work apart from the competition is that we offer a wide variety of easy-to-administer multiple-choice tests so that instructors can readily gauge what students are learning from their quantitative analysis enterprises. The bane of many other quantitative learning approaches is the huge amount of time needed to evaluate students' work and learning. *Hands-On Sociology* makes it easy for instructors to challenge their students to learn about quantitative methods, without burying themselves under a mountain of paperwork.

Our approach offers eleven different sets of multiple-choice questions that follow a similar path of subject coverage to that offered in many introductory sociology and social problems textbooks. We lead students along a parallel path of investigations with archival datasets to verify, extend or take exception to the ideas presented in their textbooks. Our multiple-choice test banks make it easy for instructors to see how students are learning to interpret sociological data. We also offer a wide variety of essay problems and more elaborate assignments to satisfy those instructors who want to offer their students longer reportorial assignments. Our workbook tasks can be adapted to fit into a wide variety of pedagogical programs: in-class testing, take-home examinations, term papers and/or practice testing. We also offer most of our materials in electronic form so they can be readily applied to distance learning programs like WebCT or Blackboard.

Once an instructor devotes several classes to demonstrating computer and software use and to reading tables and making interpretations of statistical test results, students should be able to do the workbook's exercises independently. As students begin to grapple with these datasets, many will have fun working with this especially diverse array of archival data offerings, and some will show skill as budding social theoreticians. For some, the opportunity to test systematically their intuitive notions about social relationships will represent a most seductive experience.

We are especially pleased to have such a diverse array of archival data resources available through the UC Berkeley SDA system. Having the entire 30-year history of General Social Surveys at a student's fingertips offers a potent resource for the exploration of change in the United States and in Americans' attitudes to a diverse array of subjects, including homosexuality, gun control, abortion, capital punishment, euthanasia, family and work relationships and countless others. The Census 2000 PUMS data are extremely rich in what they may have to offer for studies of population, urbanization, family and intergroup relations. Throughout this volume, readers will find so many other valuable and important studies of crime, drug use, aging, education, popular culture, and countless other topics, that students and faculty may find it difficult to make choices about which subjects they wish to explore further. Yet these studies will undoubtedly spark interests for further sociological explorations.

THE PLAN OF THIS BOOK

Hands-On Sociology closely follows topics covered in introductory sociology courses: socialization, stratification, intergroup relations, family, crime and deviance, political institutions, population and others. Wherever our archival data resources permit, we follow up on themes that usually appear in introductory texts, giving students opportunities to test for themselves whether textbook theories and prior research are supported by the actual data. For example, in the chapter on socialization, we examine Melvin Kohn's classic work on social class and parental values of child rearing. In the chapter on urbanization, we explore Leo Srole's work on anomia. As we follow the thread of textbooks, we offer an overview for doing social science research: formulating hypotheses, using samples, employing significance tests, and applying statistical controls, among other topics. The effort has been made to draw students so far into the research process that they can begin to do some their own research, without turning them into methodologists. This volume might also serve in an undergraduate research methods course as a useful starting point, as students delve into a variety of research methods, statistical tests, and other methodological issues.

In Chapter 1, a methodological overview, we cover the following subjects: hypothesis testing in social science, applying the scientific method to human behavior, doing survey research, sampling, employing descriptive statistics and tests of statistical significance, and the use of the chi-square statistic. Chapter 2 guides students on how best to use the UC Berkeley SDA statistical software platform and the datasets available there and at other websites. It also teaches students how to copy and paste our data recoding instructions so that they can obtain analytically meaningful results swiftly and with a minimum of difficulty.

Chapter 3 presents a preliminary data analysis exercise, focusing narrowly on the social correlates of abortion attitudes. It walks students through a practice exercise, showing them how to interpret the tabular SDA outputs into analytically meaningful results. At the same time, this chapter shows students the kinds of insights and knowledge that emerge from any specific data analysis enterprise. Chapter 4 focuses on U.S. culture and ethnic diversity, based primarily on General Social Survey data. Chapter 5 explores U.S. urbanization and suburbanization issues, again with data from the General Social Surveys. Both of these chapters are somewhat more elementary than most of the book's later data analysis chapters, emphasizing mastery of univariate frequency distributions and including crosstabular analysis to a limited degree.

In Chapter 6, we cover some of the finer points of crosstabulation: the use of delta values to distinguish between the strength and direction of causal influences and three-way cross-tabulations and their utility to identify spuriousness and to specify the effects of multifold causal influences. Chapters 7 through 14 deal with a variety of subjects—socialization, stratification, minority relations, family, politics, crime, youth problems and population. In these chapters, we bring into play all the crosstabulation elements addressed in Chapters 1–3 and 6. Once the instructor has dealt with the issues covered in these chapters, other chapters can be assigned in almost any order, depending on the instructor's overall topical agenda.

In Chapter 15, students are guided through a variety of statistical methods associated with continuous data analysis, for example means tests and correlation and regression analyses using the SDA software and datasets. In the final chapter, students are presented with a variety of assignments that apply what they learned in Chapter 15 to performing means tests, correlations and multiple and logistic regression analyses problems.

For introductory sociology courses, the particular progression of the first five chapters should work well pedagogically. After coverage of the material in Chapter 6, any of the later chapters can then be offered for assignments. This volume should also be an effective teaching supplement in social problems courses. With all the material contained in this book, there is ample subject matter to complement a typical social problems curriculum. As instructors take an overview of these materials, they will discover no set formula for its successful use. Instead, they will find that many of the modules presented here, in conjunction with other readings and research assignments, will serve well toward the advancement of a wide variety of their academic sociological goals.

ACKNOWLEDGMENTS

A work of this nature, based on the archival research of others, carries a huge debt of gratitude to the many benefactors who generously offered their valuable data to the academic community. At various points in creating this volume, we relied on twelve different studies: The General Social Surveys, the National Election Surveys, the National Survey of Adolescents, the Chicago Homicides Study, Uniform Crime Reports Supplementary Homicide Reports, the Monitoring the Future Surveys, the National Household Surveys of Drug Abuse, the National Gambling Impact Study, the National Survey of America's Families, the Public Use Micro-Data Sample of the 2000 U.S. Census, the Childhood Victimization and Delinquency Study of a Large Urban Northwestern City, and the Multi-Cities Study of Urban Inequality.

Tom Smith and James Davis are the originators of the General Social Surveys (GSS) and deserve particular mention for the rich and wonderful sociological lessons they consistently offer in the GSS and for the timeliness of their surveys. Shamelessly, we have borrowed very heavily from the GSS in creating our data analysis exercises. Whether for the advanced researcher or the beginning student, it is no small wonder the GSS remains one of the most frequently quoted sociological works.

The University of California, Berkeley, has developed a fast, powerful, and easy-to-use SDA statistical analysis platform that is offered freely on the Internet. Without it, this book would have been impossible to create. It is comforting to know that the university's program support people, especially Cathi Walton and Tom Piazza, are always ready to help answer technical questions and are continually making efforts to improve SDA by offering a broader array of statistical outputs and simplifying the ways of accomplishing data analysis tasks. Again, it is no small wonder that the SDA has won an assortment of prizes in the academic community as a teaching tool, and that this system continues to be adopted at an ever-increasing number of academic institutions.

We have also derived many of our research exercises from the Inter-University Consortium for Social and Political Research and their various specialized archives that include such datasets as the Criminal Justice Studies, Substance Use and Mental Health, Aging Datasets, and U.S. Census Studies. The consortium continues to provide an ever-richer array of archival data offerings, with many more freely available on the Internet under the SDA statistical analysis platform. Here too, ICPSR support staff remain most responsive to remedy the few rare instances in which technical problems may emerge in accessing their web-based data analysis system. We are also grateful to the Urban Institute in Washington, D.C., which offers to the academic community the data files of "The National Survey of America's Families" at their organization's web site.

For this third edition of *Hands-On Sociology*, we are deeply appreciative to our many students, who over the past two years were kind enough to offer us much valuable feedback on how to best communicate clearly with students in this volume. They helped to bring us down from the conceptual stratosphere to simplify and to clarify our research exercises into more approachable tasks. At Allyn and Bacon we were especially fortunate to have the wise editorial counsel of Jeff Lasser, who, from the first discussions of this project until its conclusion, acted with continual encouragement and support.

List of Electronic Resources

The following data resources form the basis of the activities in this text. They make use of the online data analysis system called Survey Documentation and Analysis (SDA), developed and maintained by the Computer-Assisted Survey Methods Program (CSM) at the University of California, Berkeley. For more information, visit their web site at: http://sda.berkeley.edu.

Block, Carolyn Rebecca, Richard L. Block, and the Illinois Criminal Justice Information Authority. *Homicides in Chicago, 1965–1995* [Computer file]. 4th ICPSR version. Illinois Criminal Justice Information Authority: Chicago, IL [producer], 1998. Inter-University Consortium for Political and Social Research: Ann Arbor, MI [distributor], 1998.

English, Diana J., and Cathy Spatz Widom. *Childhood Victimization and Delinquency, Adult Criminality, and Violent Criminal Behavior in a Large Urban County in the Northwest United States, 1980–1997* [Computer file]. ICPSR version. State of Washington Department of Social and Health Services, Office of Children's Administration Research: Seattle, WA [producer], 2002. Inter-University Consortium for Political and Social Research: Ann Arbor, MI [distributor], 2003.

Fox, James Alan. *Uniform Crime Reports (United States): Supplementary Homicide Reports, 1976–1999* [Computer file]. ICPSR version. Northeastern University, College of Criminal Justice: Boston, MA [producer], 2001. Inter-University Consortium for Political and Social Research: Ann Arbor, MI [distributor], 2001.

Holzer, Harry, Joleen Kirschenman, Philip Moss, and Chris Tilly. *Multi-City Study of Urban Inequality, 1992–1994: Atlanta, Boston, Detroit, and Los Angeles; Telephone Survey Data* [Computer file]. 2nd ICPSR version. Mathematica: Atlanta, GA; University of Massachusetts, Survey Research Laboratory: Boston, MA; University of Michigan, Detroit Area Study and Institute for Social Research, Survey Research Center: Ann Arbor; University of California, Survey Research Program: Los Angeles, CA [producers]; 1998. Inter-University Consortium for Political and Social Research: Ann Arbor, MI [distributor], 2000.

Johnston, Lloyd D., Jerald G. Bachman, Patrick M. O'Malley, and John E. Schulenberg. *Monitoring the Future: A Continuing Study of American Youth (12th-Grade Survey), 2002* [Computer file]. Conducted by University of Michigan, Institute for Social Research, Survey Research Center. ICPSR ed. Inter-University Consortium for Political and Social Research: Ann Arbor, MI [producer and distributor], 2003.

Kilpatrick, Dean G., and Benjamin E. Saunders. *National Survey of Adolescents in the United States, 1995* [Computer file]. ICPSR version. Medical University of South Carolina: Charleston, SC [producer], 1999. Inter-University Consortium for Political and Social Research: Ann Arbor, MI [distributor], 2000.

National Gambling Impact Study Commission. *Gambling Impact and Behavior Study, 1997–1999: United States* [Computer file]. ICPSR version. National Opinion Research Center: Chicago, IL [producer], 1999. Inter-University Consortium for Political and Social Research: Ann Arbor, MI [distributor], 2002.

U.S. Deptartment of Health and Human Services, Substance Abuse and Mental Health Services Administration, Office of Applied Studies. *National Survey on Drug Use and Health, 2002* [Computer file]. 2nd ICPSR version. Research Triangle Institute: Research Triangle Park, NC [producer], 2004. Inter-University Consortium for Political and Social Research: Ann Arbor, MI [distributor], 2004.

CHAPTER 1

Fundamentals of Sociological Analysis with Archival Survey Data

This book is intended to complement your other sociology textbooks and to increase your competence in doing sociological analysis. The skills introduced here also apply to other realms of scientific inquiry and, especially, to the social sciences. In fact, this work should be relevant to those pursuing practically any field where numbers are important for establishing knowledge—whether it be business, journalism, law, health careers, among countless others.

The aim of this book is to enhance your understanding of how computers are used in the social sciences by actually evaluating sociological data with them. A fundamental goal of these learning activities is to increase your understanding of the ways that scientists acquire and accumulate knowledge and the manner by which scientific conclusions are reached. By working through this book, you will also explore, reinforce, and extend your knowledge of U.S. society and the social issues that trouble our times.

After doing these exercises, you will become a more discerning critic and a capable judge of the persuasiveness of scientific evidence. Although only a minority of this book's readers will want to carry out their own sociological studies, those inclined to do their own research will be better equipped to do so. You should also be more comfortable using computers, more informed of their many uses, and more aware of their advantages for facilitating certain kinds of sociological and other scientific research.

In this first, very crucial, chapter you will encounter some unfamiliar terms and possibly some intimidating numerical concepts (especially if mathematics is not among your stronger subjects), but all of the issues discussed here are essential ones to master. You may want to review this chapter after you have read the material on using the SDA Website in Chapter 2 and worked through the exercises in Chapter 3, "Getting Started: Analyzing the Correlates of Abortion Attitudes." Reviewing should be helpful in reinforcing the ideas and analytic principles presented and should help you feel more confident as you proceed through the remainder of this book.

Our first task will be to explore what it means to know anything in science or in sociology. The most fundamental of all scientific statements is a *hypothesis*, a statement of presumed relationship between two or more things. An example of a hypothesis would be a statement claiming that a community's crime rate is related to its rate of residential turnover. Usually, when we think of a hypothesis we think of it as a statement of relationship between two or more *variables*. (A variable is simply something that can change or vary.) A crime rate is a good example of a variable; one community's crime rate may be higher than another's, or higher or lower than at another point in time.

Scientists also talk about *causation*—how independent variables influence dependent variables. *Independent variables* are the things that precede or influence other things; they make things happen. *Dependent variables* are the scientific problems of study; the results, or the effects of the independent variables. Sometimes the path of scientific causation is clear. If we consider the hypothesis that the age people marry (considered as an independent variable) affects the stability of their marriages (considered as a dependent variable), we can discern a clear temporal sequence of events: People have to get married before they can get divorced.

Frequently in the social sciences, the path of causation is blurry. For example, it is a relatively well established finding that people living in integrated communities are more likely to have interracial and intercultural friendships, compared to people residing in more racially and culturally homogeneous settings. Does living in an integrated community cause one to make more friendships with others from different groups? Or does the possession of friendships with others from different groups make one more receptive to living in an integrated community? Probably there is some truth to both hypotheses, but which is most accurate or important can often remain obscured or uncertain.

In science it is often a worthy enough enterprise simply to establish that two variables are clearly associated. (In scientific jargon this is known as proof of *concomitant variation*.) Of course, it is always desirable, whenever possible, to distinguish "cause" from "effect." At the SDA website you will always be prompted to give your ROW variable choice. Try to think of the row variable as your dependent or problem variable. You will then enter your COLUMN variable. Think of the column variable as the possible causative or independent variable. Remember that dependent variables are the effects and independent variables are the causes or antecedent events. If you consider row variables as the dependent variables and column variables as the independents, you will have fewer difficulties in analyzing the many tables that you will encounter in this book. But, for now, you should remember that in many cases, deeming one variable a cause and another as an effect may be an arbitrary and premature distinction.

You may have heard that in science different types of scientific statements such as facts, laws, theories, postulates, and so on, possess differing degrees of scientific certitude. Although this may be true, it should be understood that all scientific formulations are ultimately hypotheses—statements of presumed relationship—that must be empirically established to be considered valid. *Empirical proofs* are ones that are directly observable; they can be verified by anyone. You do not have to be a wizard or a genius to use the scientific method. You must be willing to use your senses; scientific knowledge must persuade the senses. In the final analysis all scientific knowledge has to be experiential, involving the measurement of directly observable things.

Experimentation is also pivotal to science. Ideally, the scientist wants to employ the *classical experimental design,* in which the scientist has available two similar groups, one designated as an experimental group, the other known as the control. Generally, the scientist will conduct the following steps:

1. Both groups are measured.
2. The experimental group is influenced in some way, while the control group is not manipulated.
3. Both groups are remeasured to assess whether the manipulation of the experimental group has distinguished it from its pre-manipulated state, and from the control group.

The work of Rosenthal and Jacobson (1968) provides a good example of the classical experimental design. They did a study on what is known as the phenomenon of the self-fulfilling prophesy: how people's beliefs come to produce real social consequences. Selecting one school as the site of their experiment, they told the teachers there that certain students in their classes were "potential intellectual bloomers" who would be likely to undergo dramatic intellectual growth. In reality, potential bloomers were chosen randomly. This was the independent variable.

The dependent variable in the experiment was each child's standardized IQ test score. First and second graders were tested, and then retested a year later. The researchers expected that so-called "intellectual bloomer" students would experience IQ test gains because of various advantages afforded them and special encouragement from being regarded as gifted (compared to so-called "ordinary students," the control group). Comparing both groups' test and retest scores, the researchers found that designations of intellectual bloomers did produce significant IQ test gains in the experimental group, and no appreciable changes occurred in the IQ test scores of controls.

Of course, in social science the opportunities to do real-life and laboratory experimentation are not as numerous as they may be in physical science. People's lives are not as readily available for scientific manipulation as chemical compounds, plants, or rocks may be. Yet, there are some limited possibilities for resourceful and inventive researchers to conduct laboratory and real-life experiments with people. If this social experimentation is socially responsible, it will take account of the ethical issues associated with doing the research, and it will avoid doing any harm to its research subjects.

It is imperative to try to approximate the classical experimental design (with before and after conditions and control groups) whenever possible. Very often, in doing social research analysts perform what is known as *correlational analysis,* examining data to find whether change in the amount of one variable is accompanied by comparable change in the amount of another. Such comparative analysis approximates the classical experiment to some extent, comparing those with and without the experimental condition along some dimension. Much of your analyses with the computer program will be of this type, which is a well-established mode of scientific research.

Besides direct experimental interventions, behavioral scientists establish knowledge through a variety of modes; observational studies, surveys, documentary analysis, and content analysis are most important in sociology. Your accompanying texts discuss each of these modes in greater detail.

Surveys, whether by interview or questionnaire, are one of the most commonly used methods for gathering sociological data. In the accompanying set of exercises you will work with several archival survey datasets, including the 2002 General Social Survey that was taken from a representative cross-section of adult Americans.

The General Social Survey has been conducted almost every year since 1972 by the National Opinion Research Center (NORC). Since they first began, GSS surveys have drawn annually on a different respondent population of approximately 1,500 adults from across the country. In recent years, GSS surveys have been released every two years with larger samples of approximately 3,000 respondents. The GSS is a very reliable and professionally reputable data source. It is probably the single most popular data source for describing Americans' behavior. There are conservatively more than 3,000 books, articles or conference presentations based upon the GSS data. You can visit the GSS website (http://webapp.icpsr.umich.edu/GSS) to browse through their online bibliography.

At the GSS website you can also browse through many of the topics that have been investigated at various times in the GSS. There is hardly anything of a controversial nature that hasn't been investigated at one time or another in their annual studies. Your favorite newspapers will often cite GSS based studies, discussing, for example, how attitudes toward euthanasia, capital punishment, and gun control have changed in recent decades. If you have some time, dig around the GSS website to investigate what data exists on any social questions that interest you.

Today, most researchers doing surveys use samples of the populations they study. Interviewing or getting questionnaires from everyone in the population is often neither necessary nor feasible. The most representative sample to have for almost any study would be a *random sample*. In a simple random sample, all units in the total population have an equal chance of being selected. The GSS, for example, uses a multistage probability sample based on a random selection of respondents. In the complex selection process, random assignment is used within each of the various geographical units included—states, counties, census tracts, blocks, and residential units—to arrive at the projected total size of approximately 1500 households annually. For 2002, a single survey was done consisting of a total respondent pool of 2,765 respondents.

Your Berkeley SDA statistical software, as with all statistical software programs will give you various descriptive statistics about any variable in a dataset. Among other statistics, it will provide the following:

- *mean*   the average of all responses
- *median*   the midpoint of all responses
- *mode*   the most frequently appearing response

- *range*   the difference between minimum and maximum values.
- *variance*   the sum of squared differences around the mean divided by the total number of cases minus one.
- *standard deviation*   another measure of dispersion from the mean, in this case the square root of the variance.

Each of these pieces of information is useful for understanding the response of the group as a whole, or of some subpopulation within the total. You may be interested in making comparisons between different subgroups, and these statistics are useful to describe your group's (or subgroup's) central tendencies.

For example, in the 2000 General Social Survey all respondents were asked the highest number of years of schooling they had completed. Figure 1.1 graphically displays the same information you would see if you printed out the distribution for the 2,808 respondents who reported their educational accomplishments in the GSS 2000 survey. This data shows that almost 30 percent of respondents finished their schooling after 12 years as high school graduates with two smaller peaks, corresponding to those who left college after two years and those who completed college. The average or mean educational attainment was 13.3 years. The median or midpoint response for all 2,808 answers was 13 years. The most frequent, or modal, response was 12 years (completion of high school); 823 respondents or 29.3 % completed 12 years of schooling. The range went from a low of 0 years to a high of 20 (or more) years. All these aspects of the graph are probably consistent with your common sense expectations.

According to the formulas given, the variance and standard deviation were, respectively, 8.2 and 2.9. The variance and standard deviation are measures of dispersion based on the mean. On some occasions central

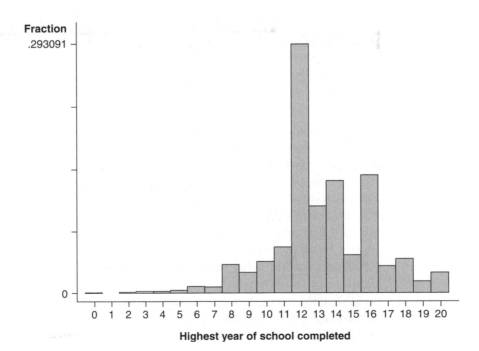

FIGURE 1.1

Highest year of school completed

tendency measures like the mean or mode may fool us and keep us from recognizing important differences about groups. At those times, measures of dispersion like the standard deviation may be the only way that such differences can be identified. As an example, think of two clinics that showed similar mean levels of use. In one, use patterns fluctuated closely around the mean. In the other, frequent use patterns of some users were offset by sparse use patterns among other clinic users. In this latter case, measures of dispersion would be much more useful for describing clinic attendance differences than other central tendency measures such as the mean or mode.

We might make use of this completed schooling data to make comparisons between different subgroups, such as between African Americans and whites, or between men and women. We could also make comparisons over time, such as from the first General Social Survey in 1972 to the most recent in 2002. Measures of central tendency or dispersion can help us to identify social trends such as the narrowing of racial and gender gaps in educational attainments. They could help to show how educational attainments have expanded over the last few decades, perhaps more rapidly in some places than in others, and perhaps more among some subgroups than for others. What is important is that any one of these central tendency or dispersion statistics can give us a handle for pursuing a social analysis.

In dealing with *quantitative analysis,* a universe unto itself, it is very easy to get overwhelmed by all the details. However, you will need to know about means, standard deviations, and some of the other concepts we have identified. For example, suppose we wanted to ascertain whether there is a trend for Americans to marry for the first time at a later age. By looking at the mean ages of marriage, one for older generation groups and another for younger groups, we would be able to see whether there is (or isn't) a change occurring in the age at which people marry.

In later chapters of this book we will cover central tendency statistics in more detail. For now, the most important quantitative measurements we will be relying upon will be raw frequencies and percentages.

Let's plunge directly into an analysis of something that many people, especially the scientifically-minded, might consider totally preposterous: horoscopes. Actually, the General Social Survey helps us in this potentially fruitless enterprise. They collected data on people's birth signs. They also collected data on whether people report finding life "exciting," "routine" or "dull." Knowledgeable horoscope devotees all know that those born under the sign of Virgo are more likely to find life exciting. Most Virgos are thrill-seekers; they like to live at the outer edge, to go skydiving, bungee-jumping, scuba diving and do other adventurous things. Wait a minute are we confusing them with the Capricorns? Yes, it's the Capricorns who are the genuine thrill-seekers. Actually, the truly scientifically-minded would be very skeptical of all of this. They would probably claim that any horoscope-related differences in this respect wouldn't amount to much. But would they be right?

We can use the GSS data to test the scientific community's dismissal of horoscopes. By following the correlational principle mentioned previously—comparing among the diverging subgroups—we can see whether people born under any one birth sign are different from those born under different signs.

First, let's look at the data. Table 1.1 shows the raw frequencies, data and percentages from the 2000 General Social Survey. As we examine this long narrow grid of 36 cells, we might observe that more Libras find life exciting than people born under the sign of Aquarius (84 and 56 respectively, a ratio of 1.5 to 1.0). We might also be impressed to note that almost three times as many Tauruses (14) find life dull when compared to those born under the sign of Aquarius (5). But, if you did that, you would be making your first fatal mistake: *Never judge a crosstabular table by raw frequencies, always compare percentages.* Raw frequency differences don't adjust for the size of each subgroup in the sample, which usually differ from one another. Only by comparing percentages can one adjust for the different sizes of sample subgroups. The only time you will want to examine raw frequencies will be to assess whether there are fewer than 5 cases in each cell. Here, we will find only one case: Cancers who find life dull. Our method of proof suggests this particular cell has too few cases in it to make for any meaningful analysis.

What we should actually do in this scenario is to *compare percentages across the table* to see what we have. Let's focus on one of the potentially more important items, those who find life exciting, a question with a total of 829 respondents. (The total figure appears at the right of the table.) For all birth sign groups, 46 percent found life exciting. And the percentage finding life exciting ranged from a low of 41% for Aquarius people, to a high of 55% among Scorpios. Ordinarily, a 14% difference would seem large enough to be analytically meaningful, but it may not be all that substantial when one considers the extremely large size of this grid with its 36 cells. We could also focus on those who found life dull, 88 cases, showing an average rate of 5 percent for all, with a range from 4 percent for several birth sign groups to a high of 10 percent for Tauruses. Don't these distribution differences seem interesting, perhaps showing Scorpios noticeably higher in finding life exciting, and Tauruses more likely to find life dull?

The question is: How does one know that the observed subgroup differences in percentages are large enough that one may claim one subgroup is higher or lower than another? Are Scorpios really more likely to find life exciting than Aquariuses?

We will always find some variation comparing across our subgroups. In a sample you can usually expect at least 2 to 3 percent differences between subgroups any time measurements are taken. (The difference can sometimes be even more substantial.) These differences are known as *sampling error variation.* To reformulate the question—recognizing that samples will vary, how do we know that the differences between the Scorpios and the Aquariuses in finding life exciting are above and beyond chance or sample variation? (The same would go for the assertion about those who find life dull, with twice as many Tauruses inclined to feel that way as compared to Virgos or Leos.) We will demonstrate this by using the Chi-Square test of statistical significance.

Your SDA statistical software computes the Chi-Square statistics and outputs the all important probability value at the bottom of the grid. This

Variables					
Role	Name	Label	Range	MD	Dataset
Row	**life**	IS LIFE EXCITING OR DULL	1-3	0,8,9	1
Column	**zodiac**	RESPONDENTS ASTROLOGICAL SIGN	1-12	0,98,99	1
Filter	**year(2000)**	GSS YEAR FOR THIS RESPONDENT	1972-2000		1

Frequency Distribution														
Cells contain: -Column percent -N of cases		zodiac												
		1 ARIES	2 TAURUS	3 GEMINI	4 CANCER	5 LEO	6 VIRGO	7 LIBRA	8 SCORPIO	9 SAGITTARIUS	10 CAPRICORN	11 AQUARIUS	12 PISCES	*ROW TOTAL*
	1: EXCITING	**43** 64	**47** 67	**46** 73	**49** 74	**47** 75	**46** 72	**50** 84	**55** 77	**44** 63	**43** 65	**41** 56	**44** 59	*46 829*
life	2: ROUTINE	**52** 78	**44** 63	**47** 74	**49** 74	**50** 80	**50** 78	**46** 77	**40** 56	**50** 71	**53** 81	**55** 75	**50** 67	*49 874*
	3: DULL	**5** 7	**10** 14	**6** 10	**3** 4	**4** 6	**4** 6	**5** 8	**4** 6	**6** 8	**4** 6	**4** 5	**6** 8	*5 88*
	COL TOTAL	*100 149*	*100 144*	*100 157*	*100 152*	*100 161*	*100 156*	*100 169*	*100 139*	*100 142*	*100 152*	*100 136*	*100 134*	*100 1,791*
Means		1.62	1.63	1.60	1.54	1.57	1.58	1.55	1.49	1.61	1.61	1.62	1.62	1.59
Std Devs		.58	.66	.61	.55	.57	.57	.59	.58	.59	.56	.56	.60	.58

Color coding:	<-2.0	<-1.0	<0.0	>0.0	>1.0	>2.0	Z

N in each cell:	Smaller than expected	Larger than expected

Summary Statistics			
Eta* =	.07	Gamma = .01	Chisq(P) = 21.65 (p= 0.48)
R =	.00	Tau-b = .00	Chisq(LR) = 20.50 (p= 0.55)
Somers' d* =	.00	Tau-c = .00	df = 22

*Row variable treated as the dependent variable.

SDA 1.2: Tables

GSS 1972-2000 Cumulative Datafile

Aug 21, 2003 (Thu 07:27 AM PDT)

Variables					
Role	Name	Label	Range	MD	Dataset
Row	zodiac	RESPONDENTS ASTROLOGICAL SIGN	1-12	0,98,99	1

TABLE 1.1

Role	Name	Label	Range	MD	Dataset
Column	**life**	IS LIFE EXCITING OR DULL	1-3	0,8,9	1
Filter	**year(2000)**	GSS YEAR FOR THIS RESPONDENT	1972-2000		1

Frequency Distribution					
Cells contain: -Row percent -N of cases		**life**			
		1 EXCITING	2 ROUTINE	3 DULL	*ROW* *TOTAL*
zodiac	1: ARIES	**43.0** 64	**52.3** 78	**4.7** 7	*100.0* *149*
	2: TAURUS	**46.5** 67	**43.8** 63	**9.7** 14	*100.0* *144*
	3: GEMINI	**46.5** 73	**47.1** 74	**6.4** 10	*100.0* *157*
	4: CANCER	**48.7** 74	**48.7** 74	**2.6** 4	*100.0* *152*
	5: LEO	**46.6** 75	**49.7** 80	**3.7** 6	*100.0* *161*
	6: VIRGO	**46.2** 72	**50.0** 78	**3.8** 6	*100.0* *156*
	7: LIBRA	**49.7** 84	**45.6** 77	**4.7** 8	*100.0* *169*
	8: SCORPIO	**55.4** 77	**40.3** 56	**4.3** 6	*100.0* *139*
	9: SAGITTARIUS	**44.4** 63	**50.0** 71	**5.6** 8	*100.0* *142*
	10: CAPRICORN	**42.8** 65	**53.3** 81	**3.9** 6	*100.0* *152*
	11: AQUARIUS	**41.2** 56	**55.1** 75	**3.7** 5	*100.0* *136*
	12: PISCES	**44.0** 59	**50.0** 67	**6.0** 8	*100.0* *134*
	COL TOTAL	*46.3* *829*	*48.8* *874*	*4.9* *88*	*100.0* *1,791*
Means		6.35	6.47	6.07	6.40
Std Devs		3.32	3.44	3.59	3.39

Color coding:	<-2.0	<-1.0	<0.0	>0.0	>1.0	>2.0	Z
N in each cell:	Smaller than expected		Larger than expected				

Summary Statistics					
Eta* =	.03	Gamma = .01	Chisq(P) =	21.65	(p= 0.48)
R =	.00	Tau-b = .00	Chisq(LR) =	20.50	(p= 0.55)
Somers' d* =	.01	Tau-c = .00	df =	22	

*Row variable treated as the dependent variable.

(CONT.)

is your indicator as to whether subgroup differences are significant or just chance variation. When differences among subgroups are beyond chance variations, we refer to them as being *statistically significant*; when they fall short of the established criteria for sampling differences, we describe the results as being *statistically insignificant*.

The Chi-Square probability value statistic tells you that your grid, with all its particular values in it, had a certain probability of coming out that way by chance alone. The statistician's bottom-line, so to speak, is a probability of .05 or less. In other words, whenever we have a Chi-Square probability of .05 or less, we can say that the differences within the grid subgroups are statistically significant. On the other hand, if the probability is more than .05 then we have insignificant differences. To get back to our horoscope hypothesis, our data's Chi-Square probability statistic came out to be .48. What that means is that from every two out of four grids drawn randomly there will be values in it like the ones we have in ours. This suggests that our results are pretty much like a coin-toss, which is certainly not good enough for a statistical analysis. By using the Chi-Square system, we can easily confirm that the differences between Scorpios and people born under the sign of Aquarius in finding life exciting—and for that matter any other birth sign subgroups—are well within the boundary of chance variations. Birth signs don't mean very much in finding life exciting. Of course, you knew that all along, but we had to go through this elaborate process to get to a result you probably knew intuitively.

One thing you should know about scientists: They take nothing for granted. For any hypothesis we entertain, we initially assume that there will be no association between the hypothetically linked variables. This is what we call the null hypothesis: Assume nothing, but let the data show you if there is a relationship beyond chance variability.

Now let's get serious and consider something more sociological. The month in which a person is born probably has little to do with their attitudes and social relationships. A more promising hypothesis we might entertain could be about people's perceived ideological leanings: whether they feel they are liberals, conservatives or moderates. One might imagine that these ideological sentiments are linked to particular voting preferences. Indeed, party memberships help develop and sustain ideological positions and vice versa. Let's test this hypothesis with the 2002 General Social Survey data. To formally state the hypothesis: we anticipate that political ideologies are associated with voting preferences. Table 1.2 shows the crosstabulation grid from tabulating people's political ideologies and their political preferences.

As we compare the column percentages across each party affiliation group, we see an unmistakable trend showing that people who call themselves 'liberals' vote democratic. Look across the democratic voter subgroup and you see 66% of liberals voting democratic compared to only 25% of conservatives. Similarly, only 12 percent of liberals voted Republican, compared to 60% of self-described conservatives. Somewhat less clear, perhaps, is the possibility that those who claim themselves to be moderates are more inclined to describe themselves as political independents. 23% of moderates considered themselves as independents, which was slightly greater than the 21% of liberals and the 14% of conservatives who felt that way, showing that moderates and liberals were

Variables					
Role	**Name**	**Label**	**Range**	**MD**	**Dataset**
Row	partyid(Recoded)	POLITICAL PARTY AFFILIATION	1-3		1
Column	polviews(Recoded)	THINK OF SELF AS LIBERAL OR CONSERVATIVE	1-3		1
Filter	year(2002)	GSS YEAR FOR THIS	1972-2002		1

Frequency Distribution					
Cells contain: -Column percent -N of cases		polviews			
		1 Liberal	2 Moderate	3 Conservative	*ROW TOTAL*
partyid	1: Democrat	**66.0** 229	**48.9** 251	**25.4** 116	*45.3* *596*
	2: Independent	**21.6** 75	**22.6** 116	**14.2** 65	*19.4* *256*
	3: Republican	**12.4** 43	**28.5** 146	**60.4** 276	*35.3* *465*
	COL TOTAL	*100.0* *347*	*100.0* *513*	*100.0* *457*	*100.0* *1,317*
Means		1.46	1.80	2.35	1.90

Color coding:	<-2.0	<-1.0	<0.0	>0.0	>1.0	>2.0	Z
N in each cell:	Smaller than expected			Larger than expected			

Summary Statistics				
Eta* =	.40	Gamma = .52	Chisq(P) = 224.16	(p= 0.00)
R =	.39	Tau-b = .35	Chisq(LR) = 231.53	(p= 0.00)
Somers' d* = .34		Tau-c = .34	df = 4	

*Row variable treated as the dependent variable.

TABLE 1.2

somewhat more likely to consider themselves as independents than conservatives. Although all of this may seem to make a great deal of sense to us, our statistical formula is not concerned with the names of the categories, and whether the patterns seem logical or sensible. The Chi-Square probability value alone will enable us to ascertain whether the intergroup differences are more significant than simple sampling error variations. The SDA software reported a Chi-Square probability value of .000, meaning that the above grid will show up, by chance, fewer than one in every thousand times. To get this grid by chance alone would be a rare statistical fluke. We can therefore reject the null hypothesis that political ideology is unrelated to political party preferences. Thus, we have supported our hypothesis: Political ideologies are related to party support in the following way—liberals tend to vote democratic, and conservatives tend to vote Republican.

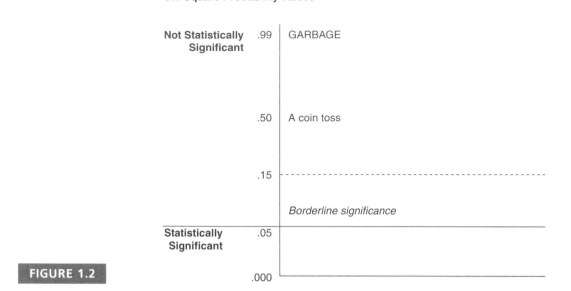

FIGURE 1.2

We're sorry for all the negativity in this discussion. But, keep in mind when the Chi-Square goes below the .05 level we reject the null hypothesis of no association. Figure 1.2 displays the differences in statistical significance by Chi-Square probability values. This graphically shows Chi-Square probability values in terms of their analytic importance.

There is also a borderline situation where the Chi-Square probability hovers close to the .05 level, but falls short of it. Chi-Square probability values falling between .06 and .15 usually cover this borderline area of questionable associations. In cases where you get a Chi-Square probability of, for example, .07 you still may have no association, as a strict interpretation would claim. But, you may have a significant association, too. The Chi-Square statistic is sensitive to the size of the sample and to the number of cells in the grid. Sometimes reconfiguring the number of categories in the grid will make all the difference in making a statistically insignificant result into a significant one.

In the remainder of this chapter we will solidify our understanding of hypothesis testing by examining two additional examples. Consider the hypothetical problem of whether a person's hair color affects his or her likelihood of being left-handed. It may sound odd, and perhaps even ridiculous, that hair color would be associated with the use of one's hands. Actually, we have no reason to suspect that people with one particular hair color are any more likely than others with different hair coloring to be left-handed. Let us say that over all groups in our imaginary population, the chance of being left-handed is .341 (in other words, about one in three). In our contrived distribution, displayed in Table 1.3, we see the rates of being left-handed for people with brown, black, red and blonde hair. We can see that each hair color group's rate of left-handedness is within a few percentage points of the total rate of left-handedness for all groups combined (34.1%). Thus, our provisional interpretation is that none of the different groups are any more left-handed than any of the others. However, we cannot confirm this until we do the Chi-Square signifi-

HAND USE PREFS	Different Hair Color Groups				
	Brown	Black	Blonde	Red	Total
Lefties	130	121	119	130	500
	34.3	31.3	34.1	36.8	34.1
Righties	249	265	230	223	967
	65.7	68.7	65.9	63.2	65.9
Total	379	386	349	353	1467
	100.00	100.00	100.00	100.00	100.00

TABLE 1.3

Pearson chi2(3) = 2.48   Pr = 0.479

cance test, which conceivably could show us that significant differences are noted between the subgroups with different hair colors.

The Chi-Square value for this analysis is .479 (almost like a coin toss, which would be a .50 probability). This result confirms our suspicion that the distribution of the different haired people who are left-handed is within the realm of chance variation. Thus, the final conclusion is what we expected: We cannot reject the null hypothesis of no association as there appears to be no significant relationship between the variables of hair color and left-handedness.

Exploring still another sample hypothesis, let us investigate the association between completing schooling and family income differences. The generalization is as follows: Those who get more schooling are likely to come from homes where there are greater family economic resources (compared to others whose families' economic resources are more limited). You may already be convinced of this hypothesis, knowing many highly educated people who grew up in wealthier families, and many less well educated people who came from economically deprived circumstances.

Of course, as a social scientist, it is not enough simply to "know" something. Rather, you must prove it with a representative sample of the population. Using the GSS database, which comprises such a sample, we want to establish whether the differences of educational attainments and family incomes form an association, instead of displaying random differences that could be attributed to sampling variations. Table 1.4 shows the crosstabulation for educational and family income differences using the 2000 GSS survey data.

Looking across the table, we see the high school dropouts population clustered in poorer homes; 39% came from the lowest income group, compared to only 4% from the richest households. On the lower end of the table, those completing college or more education tend to come from the most wealthy families. Almost half (49%) came from $60,000 or more annual income homes, compared to only about 10% who got that far with their education in homes where total annual income fell below $15,000. We can see from the data that as income levels rose, it becomes progressively more likely that respondents graduated from college.

There does not appear to be a similar relationship for respondents who achieved only a high school level education, except at the highest

Variables					
Role	Name	Label	Range	MD	Dataset
Row	**Educ(Recoded)**	HIGHEST YEAR OF SCHOOL COMPLETED	1-4		1
Column	**income98(Recoded)**	TOTAL FAMILY INCOME	1-4		1
Filter	**Year(2000)**	GSS YEAR FOR THIS RESPONDENT	1972-2000		1

Frequency Distribution

		income98				
Cells contain: -Column percent -N of cases		1 Less than $15,000	2 $15,000-$29,999	3 $30,000-$59,999	4 $60,000 or more	*ROW TOTAL*
educ	1: Less than high school	**39.1** 191	**19.9** 111	**9.9** 78	**3.7** 23	*16.4* *403*
	2: High school	**28.6** 140	**36.4** 203	**31.5** 248	**20.6** 127	*29.3* *718*
	3: Some college	**22.3** 109	**27.4** 153	**34.3** 270	**26.3** 162	*28.3* *694*
	4: College or greater	**10.0** 49	**16.3** 91	**24.4** 192	**49.4** 305	*26.0* *637*
	COL TOTAL	*100.0* *489*	*100.0* *558*	*100.0* *788*	*100.0* *617*	*100.0* *2,452*
	Means	2.03	2.40	2.73	3.21	2.64
	Std Devs	1.01	.98	.94	.90	1.04

Color coding:	<-2.0	<-1.0	<0.0	>0.0	>1.0	>2.0	Z
N in each cell:	Smaller than expected		Larger than expected				

Summary Statistics

N in each cell:	Smaller than expected	Larger than expected

Summary Statistics

Eta* =	.40	Gamma =	.45	Chisq(P) =	481.02	(p= 0.00)
R =	.40	Tau-b =	.34	Chisq(LR) =	460.56	(p= 0.00)
Somers' d* =	.34	Tau-c =	.33	df =	9	

TABLE 1.4 *Row variable treated as the dependent variable.

income level. At the $60,000+ a year level, people are greatly encouraged to get some college or more education. That number rises to over 75 percent overall, and the chance of just finishing high school drops from the 30 percent range to 21 percent at highest income level. Thus, high incomes appear to depress the number of those who only graduate high school because of the widespread likelihood of getting some college among the highest income subgroup.

The percentage differences suggest that the hypothesis is supported. Once again, however, we cannot be fully persuaded until we ascertain that the differences we are seeing exceed those arising from sample variations. The Chi-Square test of significance says that the chance of getting this particular distribution by drawing a different sample would be one in a thousand. Thus, we have established a statistically significant association between the two variables.

One last point before we close. The Chi-Square statistic is not infallible in ascertaining meaningful differences between subgroups; sample sizes must also be taken into account. If you were working with a total sample of 10,000 cases, a difference between subcategory values of 3 percent would show up as a statistically significant one with Chi-Square. But what would it mean to say, for example, that Catholics are 3 percent more likely to have no children than Fundamental Protestants (assuming such a result was found)? Three percent would usually not represent a very meaningful difference between subgroups. With Chi-Square, when one has very large samples, small differences between subcategories will produce statistically significant but sometimes analytically meaningless results.

And at the other end of the numerical spectrum, Chi-Square imposes corresponding limitations with small samples. Performing a 2 by 2 tabular analysis with a sample of under one hundred cases, a difference between subcategories of approximately 30 percent can often be a statistically insignificant one; yet, analytically such a difference could be very meaningful. When working with very small samples, you must be especially careful using the Chi-Square statistic. With a sample of 1,500 cases, these issues will not apply to most of the analytical problems that you will be confronting. However, you should be wary that when sample numbers are low—under 20 for an entire subcategory—Chi-Square reports may not be very reliable.

SUMMARY

This chapter has presented a foundation for interpreting sociological data. Scientific research begins with formulating hypotheses—statements of presumed relationships between two or more variables—which are then subjected to an empirical or objective test. Experimentation is also pivotal to the accumulation of scientific knowledge, as scientists compare changes between experimental and control groups along specified points of research interest. Because they cannot control people's lives in research laboratories, social scientists often base their knowledge upon correlational studies, on associations between social phenomena that unfold in people's everyday interaction.

Survey research is a well-established mode of gathering sociological data. Sampling is generally an essential part of such research, since it is often not possible to interview all persons in a given society. Descriptive statistics—like the mean, median, and standard deviation—enable researchers to summarize the important attributes of groups and populations of scientific interest. Tests of statistical significance make it possible to ascertain whether observed differences between groups merely reflect sampling variations or represent meaningful theoretical divergences. The Chi-Square statistic—explained at length in this chapter, and to be relied upon throughout most of this volume—is one such useful test for distinguishing between sampling and theoretically important differences.

We are now ready to move onto our next task, learning to use the SDA statistical software program proficiently at your computer.

CHAPTER 2

Using SDA at Home or in Campus Computer Labs

INTRODUCTION

As we've observed students using personal computers in our lower level undergraduate sociology classes for the last several years, we've learned they vary a great deal in their previous exposure to computers. Some are very familiar and comfortable with PCs and are already skilled at word processing and other computer applications. Others haven't had much experience, and some among this latter group fear they may never master the PC.

Some of the things we discuss in this chapter might seem to be old hat to experienced computer users; people who feel very much at ease with computers might want to skip over those parts. However, there are many things offered in this chapter pertaining to the guidelines for doing your on-line data analyses at the Berkeley SDA Website with their statistical analysis software. If you want to do your online data analysis with the least amount of difficulty, read this chapter carefully, and come back to it, if necessary, if you are finding any problems in completing later chapter exercises.

USING THE LABS OR YOUR OWN COMPUTER

Notwithstanding whether you'll be doing our assignments at your home computer or at a workstation in one of your campus' computer labs, much of what we say here will have relevance for both environments. If you expect to be doing your online data analysis assignments in campus computer labs, pay attention to the hours of lab availability. Don't wait for the last minute to do your assignments. Try to avoid coming into the labs during peak usage periods. And try to follow all instructions given by lab technicians regarding the appropriate usage of their machines. To do our assignments you will want to use your preferred web browser to take you to the SDA Berkeley Website at: http://sda.berkeley.edu.

If the start-up and menu system at your lab is not clear, ask for technical assistance to get a browser running and then type in the above SDA address into the Web address box and press the Enter key. Remember, please do not ask lab technicians how to do the online analysis problems. Their expertise will help you to use their equipment, and little else. After you have read and understood all the principles for doing statistical analyses and understood how to navigate around at the SDA Website and how to use its data files and software, you should be ready to complete our analysis problems correctly.

If you are fortunate enough to have your own personal computer, and we're finding the overwhelming majority of students today have access to computers at home, you'll be able to do our assignments whenever you can use your home machine. You won't need a very fast computer to do your work at the SDA Website. A Pentium II type machine with a 56K telephone modem should provide all the necessary computing power for accessing the SDA Website and for doing your online data analyses with efficiency. Most newer computers available at the time of this writing have a Pentium IV chip, and many people now have DSL or cable modem lines for faster home Internet access. If you have these things, fine. But if your machine is older and you rely on a 56K dial-up modem, not to worry: you still will be able to do our analysis problems relatively speedily. The SDA Website does all your data analysis on its supercomputer, then gives you the results almost immediately—even on a late-1990s type machine. You will have to have Internet access, but if you don't want to have the regular expense of paying for an AOL account (or similar), there are plenty of free Internet providers around. In addition, you will need to have a recent web browser installed on your computer (Internet Explorer and Netscape are the most popular, but Firefox and Safari would work just as well), which are also available free of charge. Finally, you will need to have a printer.

If you haven't had much experience using computers before, you'll probably want to read the next several paragraphs carefully. Although computers can be damaged in certain ways, they are not much more fragile than a typewriter. The keyboard itself needs little special attention, although you should protect it from dust, food, moisture and any foreign objects to keep it working smoothly. Keep the computer away from extremes of temperature and magnets. It is also wise to keep the computer in a fairly dust-free environment, covering it (or at least the keyboard) when not in use. It does no harm to leave a desktop computer on for extended periods of time; however, when not in use the monitor should be turned off to avoid "burn-in" resulting in screen "ghosts." Laptop users are advised never to leave their machines on when not in use.

Before you start, make sure that your monitor, keyboard, mouse and printer are all properly connected to the central processing unit (where you insert your diskettes). If you don't have a printer available, you can still proceed; but you'll have to copy your results to disk. If you are using your home personal computer it is also advisable to have a surge protector on the electrical line between your computer's plug and the wall outlet. This will prevent the computer from being damaged in the event of a power surge.

Many newer users of computers have heard about the dreadful possibility of losing their work because their machine suddenly went off. There are any number of reasons why your work could get lost on a personal computer, including:

- The electrical power could go off as sometimes happens during an electrical storm.

- During operation you could accidentally kick or pull out the plug from the wall socket.
- You could have an equipment failure, such as the system itself, a bad disk drive, or a bad disk.
- You could press the wrong combination of keys and cause your program to abort.

If you use a computer for long enough any or all of these things are likely to happen. You don't have to worry too much about having devastating losses doing your online data analyses. With the SDA statistical analysis software, the worst loss you could ever suffer might be to have to retype three or four analysis selection choices, less than a minute or more of work. However, there could be considerable losses from lost word processing work. Be sure to save your text writings to disk regularly, to avoid that dreadful experience of losing an entire afternoon's work. Also, it is a good idea to make separate disk backups of your word processed project files. You can never tell when your computer may crash and you wouldn't want all your precious written work to go down with it.

Although your computer can take a certain amount of punishment, your diskettes are fragile. Most of the time you will probably be working with the commonly used 3½-inch hard plastic diskettes, although Zip Disks, CD-ROMs and even small "Flash Drives" are becoming increasingly common. Never touch the hub of the diskette or the thin metal covering, protecting the soft plastic surface of the disk where the computer's disk drive writes to it. Always handle the disk by its label. Carefully insert the disk into the diskette drive, metal side inserted first, and disk hub facing down. To release the disk from the drive, press the drive ejector button. If you see that the disk's metal covering is misshapen in any way, carefully make a back-up of it (we will describe how to do this in the next paragraph) and discard the damaged original. Spending less than $2 for one of those small plastic boxes to prevent diskettes from getting banged around in your brief case or knapsack is a worthwhile investment. And, of course, never leave disks exposed to great heat or cold; nor subject them to magnetic forces.

Making regular back-ups of your work can cut your losses—due to machine or operation errors—to no more than a few minutes of lost work. Backing up your diskettes is a simple process, although the process might vary slightly, depending upon which edition of Windows you are using, whether it is Windows 98 Second Edition, Windows 2000, ME, XP or another edition:

1. Format the disk you intend to place your valued work on. It often says on the diskette box that the disks are preformatted but that is not always true. Formatting a disk is rather simple.
   a. Place the disk to be formatted in the drive that accommodates your hard plastic 3½-inch diskettes. This is usually configured as the "A" drive.
   b. Double click the "**My Computer**" icon.
   c. Select the "A" drive by clicking the icon once.

    d. Click the icon with the right button of your mouse to get the pullout list of operations choices.

    e. Select format with the left mouse button.

    f. Press **Start** to initiate the formatting process. A light usually will shine while formatting is taking place and will go off once it is done.

2. Copying files from your hard drive (usually known as the "C:\" drive) to the diskette drive is done fairly easily.

    a. Double click the "**My Computer**" icon.

    b. Navigate your way to the folder containing the file you wish to copy. If your view of the screen contents is too small or too large you can use your mouse to pull out or push in the top, bottom or sides of the window showing the file(s) you want to copy. Make sure to keep your window small enough so that you can also click on your "My Computer" icon again.

    c. Now, make a second window showing your "A" drive contents.

    d. Drag and drop the desired file(s) from the folder in your "C" drive to the "A" drive. Your Windows software will copy the file from first location to the second one.

    e. Close these windows by pressing the **X** button in the upper right corner of the window.

You are now ready to resume another computing activity.

At the time of this writing more and more people are beginning to use USB flash card or jump drive devices for backing up their important files. These are more durable than floppy disks, are so small they can be attached to people's key chains and hold much more information than floppy disks. Once you attach one of these devices to one of the USB ports on your computer, it will be automatically recognized, and you can copy files to it much as you would to a floppy disk drive, as described above.

USING THE SDA STATISTICAL ANALYSIS SOFTWARE AT THEIR WEBSITE

Before we get into the mechanics of using the SDA Website, it is important to understand conceptually what you are doing. The SDA Berkeley Website has a variety of social science archival data sets at its site and it also offers its powerful and fast SDA statistical software to analyze their data. As you go through the exercises in this book you will also visit other websites that have different data sets and which also offer the SDA software to analyze their data. Now let's talk about survey data. Before you can do any meaningful analyses of it, data often has to be cleaned and recoded. You will find, for example, that every time questions are asked to people, there are always some respondents who "don't know" or "refuse" to answer a given question. When we are doing data tabulations, we will usually want to delete those useless cases from the analyses. We will sometimes give you recoding statements to include, telling the software to omit tabulating those observations with missing or useless data entries. Another problem is that the data often has to be "groomed" for our data analyses techniques. Take a variable such as years of education completed.

As you observed in the previous chapter, this variable has a distinct value for each additional year of education completed. It would be unwieldy to do an analysis with it. Imagine, for example, doing an analysis of gender differences in educational attainments. We would end up with a confusing, gigantic grid showing the differences between men and women in completed education with two sets of 20 different points on the education scale shown, one set of 20 categories for males, another for females. With 40 categories to compare with one another, it would be analytical chaos. In a case like this, it makes sense to recode the data by collapsing categories. (Throughout this book we will supply you with all the recoding statements necessary to tell the program how we want a variable regrouped.) In the original data collection of the GSS "years of school completed" was formatted into a series of categories running from 0 to 20. We will recode the education completed variable into the following five categories:

1. less than a high school education (0–11 years)
2. high school graduate (12 years)
3. some college (13–15 years)
4. college graduate (16 years)
5. postgraduate (17–20 years)

Recoded this way, it will be a great deal easier to discern whether there are any differences in educational attainment between men and women—or for that matter between any other groups' educational attainments that we might be interested in (e.g. between different races, or the foreign-born vs. Native born, etc.). Don't worry, we will be making all the necessary data transformations for you to facilitate your analyses. Another important item, especially in the General Social Surveys, are in the "Selection filter" choices to apply. With 24 separate surveys already completed in its 31-year history, it is important to specify which time frame your analyses of General Social Surveys will embrace. Selection filters delineate a specific subgroup or time frame that your analysis will be conducted within. If we were interested, for example, in whether there were any gender differences in the acceptance of abortion, and if we didn't specify a selection filter, we would get an analysis of the question based on nearly 40,000 cases. Such an analysis would not be very useful to us for several reasons. For one, it would not tell us whether at the present time men and women think any differently about abortion. Secondly, we would not be able to see whether there had been any changes in men and women's attitudes toward abortion over the 30 year history of GSS surveys. Finally, it would render the tests of statistical significance useless. With such an enormously large sample of over 40,000 cases, virtually any differences would become statistically significant.

Therefore, we will usually want to apply selection filters to ensure that we only consider the most recently available GSS survey. Actually, there is a more recent GSS survey than the 2002 survey. One was completed in 2004. However, at the time of writing, the GSS administrators are still processing the data. This dataset will eventually be added to their master file sometime in 2005. Thereafter, there will be a slight time lag before the

Berkeley SDA group installs this updated file on their server. Therefore, we are presently unable to include any more recent GSS surveys beyond the one done in 2002.

Another point worth mentioning now is that in the diagrams presented throughout this book there may be slight discrepancies between what we show you in this text and what you will see at the Berkeley SDA website. There are several reasons for this. For one, the Berkeley site is regularly being upgraded and revised. At the time of this writing, a new feature for making bar charts was added to SDA. With this new feature, the data entry screen has been revised to permit users to input information about desired features sought in chart outputs. However, all relevant data entry points for us remain the same as shown here. All data analysis output displays should remain constant as well. Another reason why data entry screens may vary slightly is because you will be visiting different websites when you do your SDA analyses. If you do an analysis of the General Social Survey data, you will use versions of the program installed at the UC Berkeley campus. If you utilize the Chicago Homicides Study data or the National Household Survey of Drug Use data, you will be using the supercomputer and SDA programs installed at the University of Michigan. At Michigan they have a slightly earlier version of the SDA software installed than they do at Berkeley. At other sites, you will find still different versions of the SDA software. Despite these differences between websites and software versions, they will all be essentially identical in their input and output display screens.

GENERATING FREQUENCY DISTRIBUTIONS

When you are doing our online data analysis exercises, you will usually be doing one of two different analytic tasks—frequency distributions and crosstabulation. A *frequency distribution* is a report of how often each of the score values of a variable occur. For example, how often does "male" and "female" occur for the variable SEX(GENDER) in the data set? The answer will tell us how many males and females we have in the sample.

Let's do it now for educational attainments. In the GSS the variable label for educational attainments is EDUC. If you ever want to do library research on any GSS variable, knowing a variable label will be helpful to track down any past GSS-based research in which scholars have used this variable. You can go to the GSS Website, mentioned in the last chapter, and do any number of searches on how researchers may have employed the variable EDUC in earlier studies. For now, however, let us try to generate a frequency distribution for the educational attainments of respondents to the 2000 GSS survey. The following steps will guide you through the process of doing this:

1. Go to the SDA Website at http://sda.berkeley.edu.
2. At their homepage, select **SDA Archive**.
3. Click **GSS Cumulative Datafile 1972-2002 - Full Analysis**.
4. Select the "Frequencies or crosstabulation" option and press **Start**.
5. Enter **educ** in the row variable box (SDA entries should always be made in lower case text).

6. Type year(2000) in the selection filter box.
7. Select the "Statistics" option in the box labeled "Table Options."
8. Press the button marked **Run the Table**.

Variables					
Role	**Name**	**Label**	**Range**	**MD**	**Dataset**
Row	**educ**	HIGHEST YEAR OF SCHOOL COMPLETED	0-20	97,98,99	1
Filter	**year(2000)**	GSS YEAR FOR THIS RESPONDENT	1972-2002		1

Frequency Distribution				
Cells contain: -Column percent -N of cases		**Distribution**	**Cells contain:** -Column percent -N of cases	**Distribution**
educ	0	.0 / 1	**educ** 11	5.4 / 153
	2	.1 / 3	12	29.3 / 823
	3	.2 / 6	13	10.3 / 290
	4	.2 / 6	14	13.3 / 374
	5	.3 / 9	15	4.5 / 127
	6	.8 / 22	16	14.0 / 393
	7	.7 / 20	17	3.2 / 90
	8	3.4 / 95	18	4.1 / 114
	9	2.5 / 69	19	1.4 / 39
	10	3.8 / 106	20	2.4 / 68
			COL TOTAL	**100.0** / 2,808

Summary Statistics					
Mean =	13.26	Std Dev =	2.87	Coef var =	.22
Median =	13.00	Variance =	8.23	Min =	.00
Mode =	12.00	Skewness =	-.13	Max =	20.00
Sum =	37,247.00	Kurtosis =	.78	Range =	20.00
Inference about the mean:					
Std Err =	.05	CV(mean) =	.00		

TABLE 2.1

Table 2.1 shows the output that you should have obtained when you ran this analysis and matches Figure 1.1, with the highest category for 12 years of education or high school graduates (with 823 cases) and two other bulges for those with 16 years of school (college grads), 393 cases; and those with 14 years of school, those with some college or junior college degrees, 374 cases. Overall, 2,808 respondents answered the education question. The summary statistics box shows years completed ranged from 0 to 20, with a mean of 13.3, the median was 13, a mode of 12, a standard deviation of 2.9 and a variance of 8.2.

As useful as this information may be, we will probably be better off having the education variable collapsed, as we had regrouped it before. Using the following recode language, type **educ(r:0-11 "less than hs"; 12 "hs"; 13-15 "somecoll"; 16 "collgrad"; 17-20 "postgrad")** as the new collapsed education variable and **year(2000)** in the selection filter box. You should get the distribution shown in Table 2.2. Note that the SDA software is rather unforgiving. If you omit anything as insignificant as an end of quote for a new label, the analysis won't go forward. But don't worry too much about this as we will provide you with all the correct recoding language for each chapter. All you will need to do is correctly cut and paste these recoding statements into the appropriate boxes. We will guide you through this process later in this chapter.

Table 2.2 shows that nearly three-fifths of all respondents had high school diplomas or at least some college education. It also shows that college graduates and postgraduates outnumbered high school dropouts, 25 percent to 18 percent. With information like this, we can, for example, readily discern how well educated U.S. citizens presently are.

Frequency distributions are a very important procedure and we will be regularly doing them on different variables of interest. We usually do a frequency distribution at an early stage of our analysis, to understand how responses are concentrated, and before we would begin to formulate a hypothesis. To make sure you fully understand frequency distributions, we will examine the age distribution of 2000 GSS respondents:

1. Type **age** in the "Row" variable box.
2. Type **year(2000)** as the "Selection Filter" choice and again select "Statistics" from "Table Options."
3. Click **Run the Table.**

The result will be a rather long output displaying the number of people and percentage at each age level. We haven't reproduced this here as it is five pages long when printed. (Later in this chapter we will show you how to print or save your SDA tables.) If you did your age table correctly you will find that the mean age for all 2,809 GSS 2000 respondents was 46 years, with a median of 43, a mode of 32, a standard deviation of 17.4, and a variance of 301.6. Two things in the age distribution should stand out:

1. There was no one younger than 18 years of age. In all GSS surveys respondents must be 18 years of age or older to be included.
2. There was also no one older than 89 years of age. The GSS uses "top-coding" for age. Anybody older than 89 who participated in the sur-

Variables					
Role	**Name**	**Label**	**Range**	**MD**	**Dataset**
Row	**educ(Recoded)**	HIGHEST YEAR OF SCHOOL COMPLETED	1-5		1
Filter	**year(2000)**	GSS YEAR FOR THIS RESPONDENT	1972-2002		1

Frequency Distribution		
Cells contain: -Column percent -N of cases		**Distribution**
educ	1: less than hs	**17.5** 490
	2: hs	**29.3** 823
	3: somecoll	**28.2** 791
	4: collgrad	**14.0** 393
	5: postgrad	**11.1** 311
	COL TOTAL	*100.0* *2,808*

Summary Statistics					
Mean =	2.72	Std Dev =	1.22	Coef var =	.45
Median =	3.00	Variance =	1.50	Min =	1.00
Mode =	2.00	Skewness =	.34	Max =	5.00
Sum =	7,636.00	Kurtosis =	-.77	Range =	4.00

Inference about the mean:

Std Err =	.02	CV(mean) =	.01

TABLE 2.2

vey was coded at the 89 year mark. If you want to get a more useful indicator of age variability, you would probably want to regroup and collapse the ages of all respondents.

Table 2.3 shows the age distribution for the 2,809 respondents grouped into 5 categories: 18–25 year olds; 26–35 year olds; 36–50 year olds; 51–64 year olds; and 65–89 year olds. The mean age was 46 when the data was ungrouped and it seems that grouping hasn't changed the overall pattern much. Table 2.3 shows a third of all respondents were aged between 36 and 50. When the data is grouped in this way, it shows more elderly respondents (17 percent) than younger ones aged between 18 and 25 (11 percent). However, the more interesting analytical questions revolve around comparing different subgroups. For example, are women outliving men? Are there differences in life expectancy between whites,

Variables					
Role	**Name**	**Label**	**Range**	**MD**	**Dataset**
Row	**age(Recoded)**	AGE OF RESPONDENT	1-5		1
Filter	**year(2000)**	GSS YEAR FOR THIS RESPONDENT	1972-2002		1

Frequency Distribution		
Cells contain: -Column percent -N of cases		**Distribution**
age	1: 18-25	**11.4** 320
	2: 26-35	**20.0** 562
	3: 36-50	**33.4** 939
	4: 51-64	**18.0** 505
	5: 65-89	**17.2** 483
	COL TOTAL	*100.0* *2,809*

Summary Statistics					
Mean =	3.10	Std Dev =	1.23	Coef var =	.40
Median =	3.00	Variance =	1.51	Min =	1.00
Mode =	3.00	Skewness =	.00	Max =	5.00
Sum =	8,696.00	Kurtosis =	-.88	Range =	4.00

Inference about the mean:

Std Err =	.02	CV(mean) =	.01

TABLE 2.3

African Americans, Hispanics or Asians? To examine these questions we will need to move on to a much more complicated part of data analysis: crosstabular comparisons.

TESTING HYPOTHESES BY CROSSTABULAR ANALYSIS

With crosstabular analyses we can test hypotheses. Usually we will employ the Chi-Square test of significance, discussed in the last chapter, to see whether the observed differences we are finding between categories would exceed the range expected by sampling error variability. In crosstabular analysis, we want to see whether the differences in one variable are linked to change or differences in another. The Chi-Square statistic tells us whether observed differences across variable categories are substantial enough that we can claim the two variables are associated. Although it will get more complicated than this, this is a good beginning.

Let's do an analysis of political behavior to see whether it is linked in any way to people's social class. We've all heard of "high" and "low" class people. In the General Social Survey people were asked what social class they thought they belonged to: whether it was upper class, middle class, working class or lower class. For now, without getting into the specifics of what it means to be member of a social class, we'll accept the respondents' suppositions of their own class membership and see whether they are associated with any differences in their political behavior. Remember what we said in the last chapter: We will assume that an independent variable influences a dependent variable. This means that social class will be the independent variable and that the political behaviors we are examining will be the dependent variables. To do this, you will need to perform the follow steps:

1. Go to the GSS cumulative file at the SDA Website and again select the "Frequencies or crosstabulation" option.
2. We will begin with voting—did you or did you not vote in the 1996 presidential election (**VOTE96**)? This will be our dependent variable, which means that it will go in the "Row" variable box.
3. Type **year(2000)** as your selection filter, confining our analysis to the 2000 GSS survey. Note that if you do a frequency distribution for **VOTE96**, you will see that there were four responses to this question:
   i. voted
   ii. did not vote
   iii. ineligible
   iv. refused
4. We will now need to prepare this variable for our crosstabular analysis. We will exclude those who refused to answer (about .3 percent of all cases) and those who were ineligible (7.4 percent of cases). Perhaps a claim could be made to include the "ineligibles" with those who "did not vote," but we will simply exclude these cases, too.
5. Type the following syntax into the "Row" variable box: **vote96 (r: 1 "voted"; 2 "did not vote")**.
6. In the "Column" variable box enter **class**.
7. Select "Statistics" from the Table Options box.
8. Click **Run the Table** and see whether it matches Table 2.4.

If you look at the Chi-Square *p* value down near the end of the output, under "Summary Statistics," you will see p=0.00, which means that a grid with these numbers in it would come up by chance in fewer than one in a hundred times. This low number goes below our statistician's bottom line of the .05 percent test criteria, exceeding the criteria needed for asserting that there is a significant association. This means that class and voting are unmistakably related to one another. And you can also see the association between the two by carefully examining the column percentages; three-fourths of the middle and upper class members voted,

Variables					
Role	Name	Label	Range	MD	Dataset
Row	vote96(Recoded)	DID R VOTE IN 1996 ELECTION	1-2		1
Column	class	SUBJECTIVE CLASS IDENTIFICATION	1-5	0,8,9	1
Filter	year(2000)	GSS YEAR FOR THIS RESPONDENT	1972-2002		1

Frequency Distribution

Cells contain: -Column percent -N of cases		class				
		1 LOWER CLASS	2 WORKING CLASS	3 MIDDLE CLASS	4 UPPER CLASS	ROW TOTAL
vote96	1: voted	56.2 / 68	62.2 / 708	75.2 / 874	76.2 / 77	68.4 / 1,727
	2: did not vote	43.8 / 53	37.8 / 431	24.8 / 289	23.8 / 24	31.6 / 797
	COL TOTAL	100.0 / 121	100.0 / 1,139	100.0 / 1,163	100.0 / 101	100.0 / 2,524
Means		1.44	1.38	1.25	1.24	1.32
Std Devs		.50	.49	.43	.43	.46

Color coding: <-2.0 <-1.0 <0.0 >0.0 >1.0 >2.0 Z
N in each cell: Smaller than expected | Larger than expected

Summary Statistics

Eta* =	.15	Gamma =	-.28	Chisq(P) =	56.27 (p= 0.00)
R =	-.14	Tau-b =	-.14	Chisq(LR) =	56.41 (p= 0.00)
Somers' d* =	-.12	Tau-c =	-.14	df =	3

*Row variable treated as the dependent variable.

TABLE 2.4

compared to only half among lower class people and three-fifths among working class people. And, of course, those not voting are much more likely to be concentrated in the lower social categories. Of course, with only two categories in a dependent variable, the responses of the second category must be the reciprocals of the first.

Let's take a look at another hypothesis about class and political behavior: people's political ideologies, whether they feel they are "liberals," "moderates," or "conservatives." We will examine whether this aspect of political thinking is related to one's class position. This time your row variable choice will be POLVIEWS. We will use the following recode language to compress extremely, moderately and slightly liberals into a single "liberal" category, and an analogous compression for conservatives. Type polviews (r:1-3 "liberal"; 4 "moderate"; 5-7 "conservative") into the "Row"

Variables					
Role	**Name**	**Label**	**Range**	**MD**	**Dataset**
Row	**polviews(Recoded)**	THINK OF SELF AS LIBERAL OR CONSERVATIVE	1-3		1
Column	**class**	SUBJECTIVE CLASS IDENTIFICATION	1-5	0,8,9	1
Filter	**year(2000)**	GSS YEAR FOR THIS RESPONDENT	1972-2002		1

Frequency Distribution						
Cells contain: -Column percent -N of cases		**class**				
		1 LOWER CLASS	2 WORKING CLASS	3 MIDDLE CLASS	4 UPPER CLASS	*ROW TOTAL*
polviews	1: liberal 1-3	**24.6** 30	**23.8** 284	**29.0** 353	**30.0** 30	*26.5* *697*
	2: moderat 4	**44.3** 54	**45.0** 537	**35.3** 430	**29.0** 29	*39.9* *1,050*
	3: conserv 5-7	**31.1** 38	**31.2** 373	**35.7** 435	**41.0** 41	*33.7* *887*
	COL TOTAL	*100.0* *122*	*100.0* *1,194*	*100.0* *1,218*	*100.0* *100*	*100.0* *2,634*
Means		2.07	2.07	2.07	2.11	2.07
Std Devs		.75	.74	.80	.84	.77

Color coding:	<-2.0	<-1.0	<0.0	>0.0	>1.0	>2.0	Z
N in each cell:	Smaller than expected		Larger than expected				

Summary Statistics

Eta* = .01 Gamma = .01 Chisq(P) = 29.95 (p= 0.00)

R = .00 Tau-b = .00 Chisq(LR) = 30.12 (p= 0.00)

Somers' d* = .00 Tau-c = .00 df = 6

*Row variable treated as the dependent variable.

TABLE 2.5

variable field. Next, enter **class** as the column choice, **year(2000)** as the selection filter, and select the "Statistics" option box. After you run the table, your output should look like Table 2.5.

Again, if you look at the Chi-Square *p* value down near the end of the output, under "Summary Statistics" you will see p=0.00, meaning a grid with these numbers would come up by chance in less than one in a hundred times. The low number again goes below our statistician's bottom line of the 5 in a 100 chance test criteria, making for a significant association, meaning that class and political ideologies are related to each other. You can also see the association between the two by carefully examining the column percentages. 41 percent of upper class people consider themselves conservatives, compared to only 31 percent among lower or working class respondents. Secondly, at least 9 to 16 percent more lower and working class respondents considered themselves to be political moderates than those among middle and upper class respondents. And finally, six percent more of the upper class respondents thought of themselves as political liberals, compared to their working class affiliates. The Chi-Square statistic tells us that these differences (upper class people thinking of themselves as conservatives; lower classes considering themselves to be moderates) wouldn't come up by chance in fewer than one in a hundred instances.

Before we get lulled into the idea that everything we do is related to our social class standing, let's look at something else: The relationship of social class to attitudes about capital punishment, specifically whether people favor or oppose the death penalty for murder. We might think that upper or lower class members would think differently about the death penalty than the lower classes. To test this hypothesis, run a new table

Variables					
Role	**Name**	**Label**	**Range**	**MD**	**Dataset**
Row	**cappun**	FAVOR OR OPPOSE DEATH PENALTY FOR MURDER	1-2	0,8,9	1
Column	**class**	SUBJECTIVE CLASS IDENTIFICATION	1-5	0,8,9	1
Filter	**year(2000)**	GSS YEAR FOR THIS RESPONDENT	1972-2002		1

Frequency Distribution						
Cells contain: -Column percent -N of cases		**class**				
		1 LOWER CLASS	2 WORKING CLASS	3 MIDDLE CLASS	4 UPPER CLASS	*ROW TOTAL*
cappun	1: FAVOR	**67.2** 86	**69.8** 814	**68.0** 788	**68.6** 70	*68.8* *1,758*
	2: OPPOSE	**32.8** 42	**30.2** 352	**32.0** 371	**31.4** 32	*31.2* *797*
	COL TOTAL	*100.0* *128*	*100.0* *1,166*	*100.0* *1,159*	*100.0* *102*	*100.0* *2,555*
Means		1.33	1.30	1.32	1.31	1.31
Std Devs		.47	.46	.47	.47	.46

Color coding:	<-2.0	<-1.0	<0.0	>0.0	>1.0	>2.0	Z
N in each cell:	Smaller than expected			Larger than expected			

Summary Statistics					
Eta* =	.02	Gamma =	.02	Chisq(P) =	1.07 (p= 0.79)
R =	.01	Tau-b =	.01	Chisq(LR) =	1.07 (p= 0.79)
Somers' d* =	.01	Tau-c =	.01	df =	3

*Row variable treated as the dependent variable.

TABLE 2.6

inserting **cappun** into the row variable box, **class** in the column variable, **year(2000)** as the selection filter, and check off the box for getting the statistics. Your results should look like Table 2.6.

If we look at the Chi-Square p value we see that it is at 0.79, a very high value that suggests there is no relationship between the two variables. That is to say, it doesn't matter what social class people belong to, their sentiments about capital punishment won't be any different because of it. Look at this table carefully to see that 69 percent overall favored capital punishment; and the variability in capital punishment approval changed only 1 percentage point across the different social class categories. Social class is clearly not related to people's attitude toward capital punishment.

We will now review all the procedures necessary to do crosstabular analyses correctly:

1. Enter your problem or result variable in the "Row" variable box. (Remember this is your dependent variable).
2. Enter your presumed causative variable in the "Column" variable box. (This is your independent variable).
3. Specify your selection filter variable(s) and category(ies), if any.
4. Select the "Statistics" option in the "Table Options".
5. Press the **Run the Table** button.

Once you have the data in a tabular format, examine the Chi-Square probability statistic. Is it below the .05 significance criteria? If yes, then the relationship is clearly significant statistically. If no, is it a borderline significance value (between .06 and .15)? Borderline values suggest that with larger samples the differences might have been significant. Also, when Chi-Square probabilities fall below the .15 mark, a regrouping of the variable categories might be all that is needed to make statistical significance. Such differences can sometimes be reported as a *possible association* between variables, for which there may be need for further study.

You should also check to see that there are no cells with fewer than 5 cases in them, and none where fewer than 20 cases were found in the entire subcategory. We would be extremely hesitant to make generalizations about a variable where we had too few cases of that group in our sample. However, Chi-Square results for the other remaining cell differences in the table can often be meaningful, especially when the other subcategory numbers and percentage differences are substantial.

Carefully examine the crosstabulation table itself. Never compare cell frequency differences. They always result from subgroup size differences. Only compare column percentages and compare them across from each other. If subcategory differences are about 10 percent or greater than each other; this could mean a statistically significant association with a larger sample. Forget about column percentage differences of three percent or less; even with very large samples and achieving statistical significance, these wouldn't be likely to amount to meaningful differences unless we were dealing with a very rare event behavior. To sum up, there are many considerations to take into account before one may say there is a significant relationship between two variables. When all of the above significance conditions are met, we can usually speak of a relationship with confidence.

However, we might also speak of the chance of a possible association (or at least the need of further study of the hypothesis) when the conditions are as follows:

1. There are differences of at least 10 percentage points between comparable subcategories.
2. The Chi-Square probability level is around the .10 probability level.
3. There are only a few instances in a very large crosstabulation grid of cell values falling below 5.

Results obtained under these conditions could be suggestive, and even more worthy of consideration, when they coincide with other analogous significant differences between variables or with findings from other researchers.

One final important tip to guide in your crosstabular investigations is to pay attention to the color-coding of the SDA results screens. We'll try to keep this explanation as simple as possible, since this is not a math class and we are not trying to turn you into mathematicians. Simply put, the Chi-Square test statistic we are employing is built around how the inner cell values of the crosstabulation grid will be distributed, when the outer values are known. If any one or more of the inner grid values are greater or smaller than within a range of expectations, then statistical significance can occur. When greater clusters of responses are found together in any one of the cells of the crosstabulation grid, the SDA program will show this with bright vivid colors. Higher value response clusters are shown in bright red and lower value response clusters are shown in bright blue. When responses are within the more expected and normal range of responses (and are less clustered together) the program will generate less vivid colors. The reds showing high clusters will become pinks, and the blues showing lower value clusters will turn pale blue. Go back and review the tables you created in this chapter and you will see the differences right away. Where statistical significance occurs you will see more vivid colors; in cases of non-significance the colors are more pale and subdued. Always check a grid's probability values, but examining the colors gives you important clues about what the results are and of which subgroup(s) in the grid are the most important ones in generating the statistical significance of the grid as a whole.

In Chapter 6, "Some Finer Points in Doing Crosstabular Analysis," there will be a discussion of more complex crosstabulations with control variables, which are called three-way crosstabulations. For the time being though, we will confine our attention to two-variable analyses. You are now almost ready to begin doing the exercises in the remaining chapters of this book. Your next task will be to complete the practice exercise in Chapter 3 on analyzing the correlates of abortion attitudes. However, before you proceed with your analyses, there are several other important things you should know.

SDA SHORTCUTS, PRINTING, AND SAVING SDA OUTPUT FILES

Throughout this text you will be asked to solve various analytical problems (mostly at the Berkeley SDA Website, but sometimes at several other websites) where you will use the SDA statistical software. Recoding of original data categories will frequently be needed to facilitate your analyses. For each chapter in this volume, you will find all the recodes you need for your analyses at **www.ablongman.com/feigelman3e** and **www.ncc.edu/ users/feigelb/sda.htm**. Make sure to consult either of these websites before you try to answer each of the series of questions for each chapter. At both of these sites you will find a hypertext list of the chapters in this book where we have offered workbook exercises that necessitate using recoded variables. Pick the chapter you are working on and the list of recoded variables will appear. The list is presented in alphabetical order in two parts: one for the variables that need to be recoded, and the other for those where no recoding is needed. Once you have obtained the recoded variable list for the chapter exercises you are working on, "minimize" the list of recodes (by pressing the "_" button in the top right corner of your browser window) and go to the SDA web site at **http://sda.berkeley.edu/ cgi-bin/hsda?harcsda+gss02**. As your assignments call for the insertion of different variables into the row, column or control variable boxes, it is a simple task of copying the relevant recodes and pasting them into the required boxes for your analysis.

That's all there is to it. You can toggle back and forth between the SDA Website and the SDA Recode Source Website to fill in all necessary command boxes before you run an analysis.

After you execute a job, it is often helpful to print out that table or tables before you begin answering our questions. Printing is a cinch. Simply go to **File**, **Print** to print out the last table you tabulated. There are some exercise questions where you will need to compare several different tables with each other. In those instances, having printed output will be absolutely necessary.

If you don't have a printer or want to conserve your paper supply, you can also save your SDA output results to disk. However, saving to disk doesn't work with all word processors and Internet access tools. After extensive testing we have found that the only combination of Internet access tools and word processing programs that work reliably together are Internet Explorer and Microsoft Word. Netscape does not appear to save the graphics. And if you convert your Word files into WordPerfect files, the graphic formatting will not be transferred. To transfer your information from Internet Explorer to Microsoft Word, perform the following steps:

1. Assuming that you have just viewed a results screen you wish to retain, go to **Edit**, **Select All**. As you can probably guess, this will select all of the information on your screen.
2. You will now need to copy this by going to **Edit**, **Copy**.
3. Minimize Internet Explorer and start Microsoft Word.
4. Go to **Edit**, **Paste** on the top tool bar. This will copy the table from Internet Explorer into your new document.

5. Go to **File, Save** to save the table in this new document. Try to give it a name that will enable you to easily find it again!

SUMMARY

This chapter has demonstrated how to use your computer to do the analysis problems that appear throughout this book at the SDA Website most efficiently. We have shown you how to use the SDA statistical analysis software to do:

1. *Frequency distributions*   analyses of single variables.
2. *Crosstabular analyses*   hypothesis testing of two potentially related variables with the Chi-Square statistic.

We have also demonstrated how to cut and paste recoding statements into the SDA Website so that you can do your analyses more expeditiously. You are now ready to begin your own analyses of sociological data and draw your own conclusions about the scientific merit of given hypotheses. With SDA and the large array of archival datasets provided there and elsewhere, you can imagine a wide range of possible associations between social attributes. Then, you can submit these speculations to careful and systematic examination.

CHAPTER 3

Getting Started: Analyzing the Correlates of Abortion Attitudes

Let's begin by looking at attitudes toward an issue that remains controversial in our society: abortion. GSS (General Social Survey) respondents are asked annually a number of questions about their attitudes toward abortion. They are asked whether they would approve of abortion under a variety of circumstances, including:

- If the baby is likely to have a serious birth defect.
- If the mother's health is jeopardized by having the baby.
- If the mother was raped.
- If the mother is unmarried and not inclined to marry the baby's father.
- In cases of poverty.

The GSS surveys seem to indicate that, depending upon the particular circumstances, abortion has differing levels of acceptability. For example, well over 80 percent of respondents consistently indicate support for abortion when the mother's health is endangered by the pregnancy. Somewhat fewer, but still a majority, however, give support for it when the pregnancy was caused by rape.

This is a good subject to start with to illustrate how to use the SDA to make interpretations of the General Social Survey data. In this practice exercise, you will be guided through the SDA procedures and tabulation results to choose the most appropriate answers to the forthcoming series of multiple-choice questions. Let's look at people's willingness to approve of abortion for any reason, which happens to be the least generally approved circumstance:

1. Open your web browser (Internet Explorer or Netscape), and go to the SDA (Survey Documentation and Analysis) website at the University of California, Berkeley: http://sda.berkeley.edu.
2. Click on **SDA Archive** on the upper left corner of the page.
3. Under the subtitle "National Omnibus Surveys," click on **GSS Cumulative Datafile 1972–2002**.
4. You will see the layout shown in Figure 3.1.

5. Select the option "Frequencies or crosstabulation" and click **Start**.

6. The layout of the page that opens is shown in Figure 3.2.

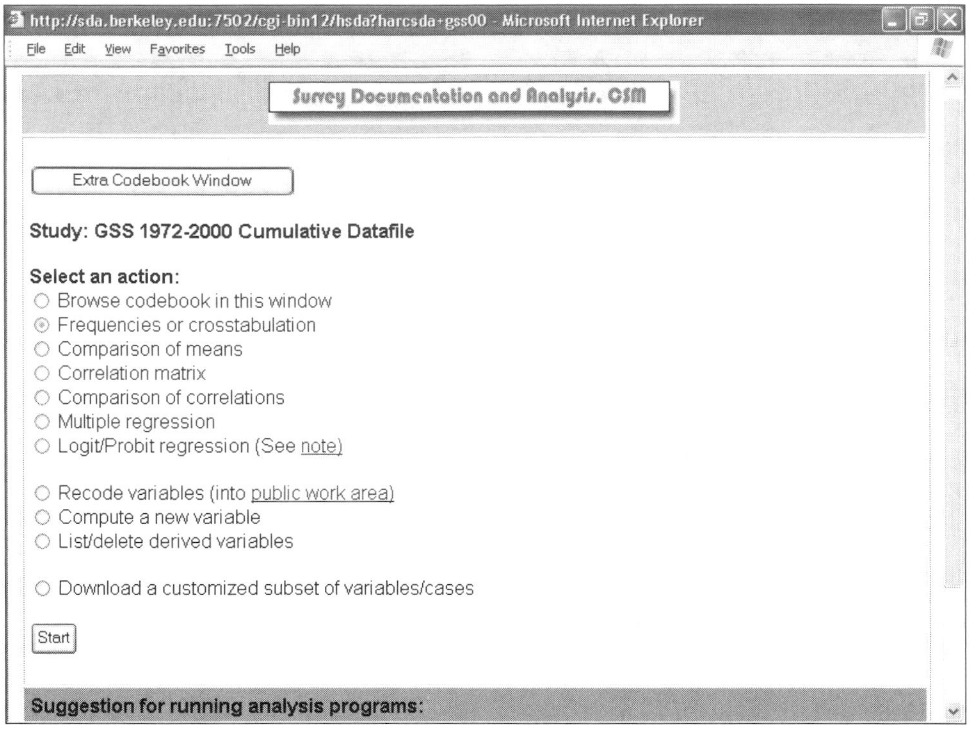

FIGURE 3.1

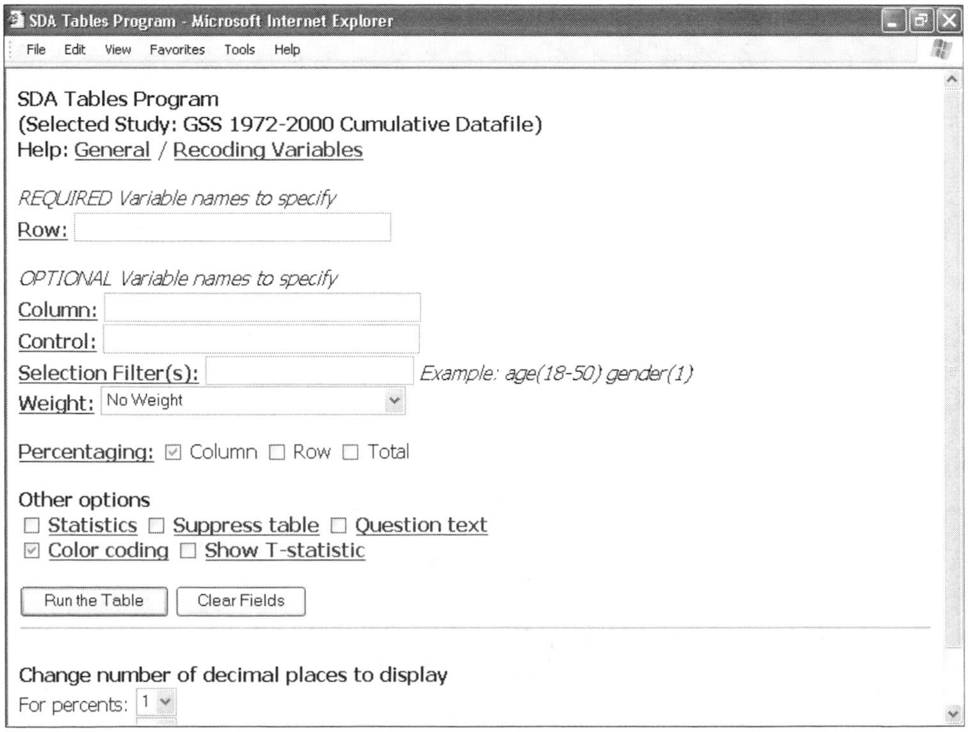

FIGURE 3.2

7. On this page, we will need to enter the variable names and other commands needed to get the tables we need.
   a. To create a table for abortion attitude (**ABANY**), type **abany** into the box labeled "Row".
   b. Type **year(2000)** into the box "Selection Filter(s)." This will limit our analysis to only the responses from the 2000 survey.
   c. Note that you should always enter the variable names you will be using in your SDA analyses in lower case type. If you use upper case, you will sometimes receive an error message.
   d. Select the "Column" option under "Percentages."
   e. Under "Other options," select "Statistics," "Question text," and "Color coding."
   f. Finally, click **Run the Table**.
   g. If you are still confused about to what to do, Figure 3.3 shows this page with all of the correct options filled in. Simply follow what you see and you should be able to complete the task.
8. The result screen should have generated the first table shown in Table 3.1. Compare your results with this one; if your table is different, redo your work.

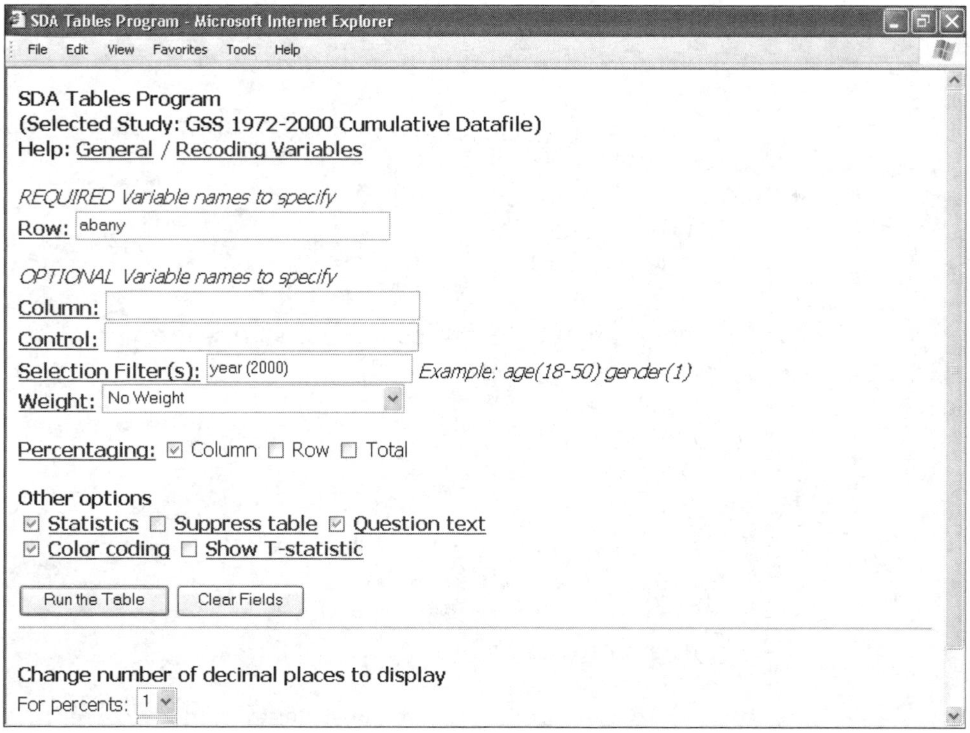

FIGURE 3.3

TABLE 3.1

SDA 1.?: Tables - Microsoft Internet Explorer				
File Edit View Favorites Tools Help				

Frequency Distribution

Cells contain: -Column percent -N of cases		Distribution
abany	1: YES	39.9 705
	2: NO	60.1 1,063
	COL TOTAL	100.0 1,768

Summary Statistics

Mean =	1.60	Std Dev =	.49	Coef var =	.31
Median =	2.00	Variance =	.24	Min =	1.00
Mode =	2.00	Skewness =	-.41	Max =	2.00
Sum =	2,831.00	Kurtosis =	-1.83	Range =	1.00

Inference about the mean:

Std Err =	.01	CV(mean) =	.01

Statistics exclude missing-data and out-of-range values.

You are now ready to answer the following three questions about abortion attitudes:

1. What percentage of respondents approves of abortion for any reason?
   a. 40 percent
   b. 60 percent
   c. 70.5 percent
   d. 35 percent
2. What percentage of respondents disapproves of abortion for any reason?
   a. 40 percent
   b. 60 percent
   c. 70.5 percent
   d. 35 percent
3. From this data alone, would you say that the majority of Americans:
   a. Approve of abortion
   b. Are evenly divided on the abortion issue
   c. Disapprove of abortion

Your answers to these three questions should have been: 1. a; 2. b; 3. c.

GENDER AND ATTITUDES TOWARD ABORTION

We will now attempt to probe the correlates of abortion attitudes, to see whether they may have anything to do with patriarchal or male chauvinistic attitudes. If we think historically about the subject, we might suspect men to be more inclined to assume restrictive views on abortions. In the United States, children typically carry their father's name and inherit their father's property. Furthermore, in some subcultures, a man's worth is measured by the number of children he fathers. Consequently, there may be a basis to expect that men (rather than women) are more willing to have women bear children, despite the possible adverse consequences of pregnancy. In addition, since men do not directly assume any of the physical risks of childbearing, it may also make it easier for them to expect women to carry their pregnancies to term.

Mothers, by contrast, are at physical risk by having children; and have also historically assumed a disproportionally greater burden in providing childcare. Reproductive freedom has also become an important part of the feminist social consciousness, emerging during the revival of feminism from the late 1960s. It seems logical to assume that there would be more female feminists than male feminists. We may therefore have reason to expect women to be more accepting of the right to have abortions than men. Now, let's try to test the hypothesis.

1. Go to the SDA website at http://sda.berkeley.edu.
2. Click **SDA Archive**, and then click **GSS Cumulative Datafile 1972–2000**. Select "Frequencies or crosstabulation" and click **Start**.
3. Enter **abany** in the "Row" box; **sex** in the "Column" box; and **year(2000)** in the "Selection Filter(s)" box.
4. Select "Column" from the "Percentage" option list.
5. Under "Other options," select "Statistics," "Question text," and "Color coding."
6. Keep in mind that **ABANY** is the dependent (or row) variable and **SEX** is the independent (or column) variable. The layout of these instructions is shown in Figure 3.4.
7. Check that the figure matches what you have typed and selected and click **Run the Table**.

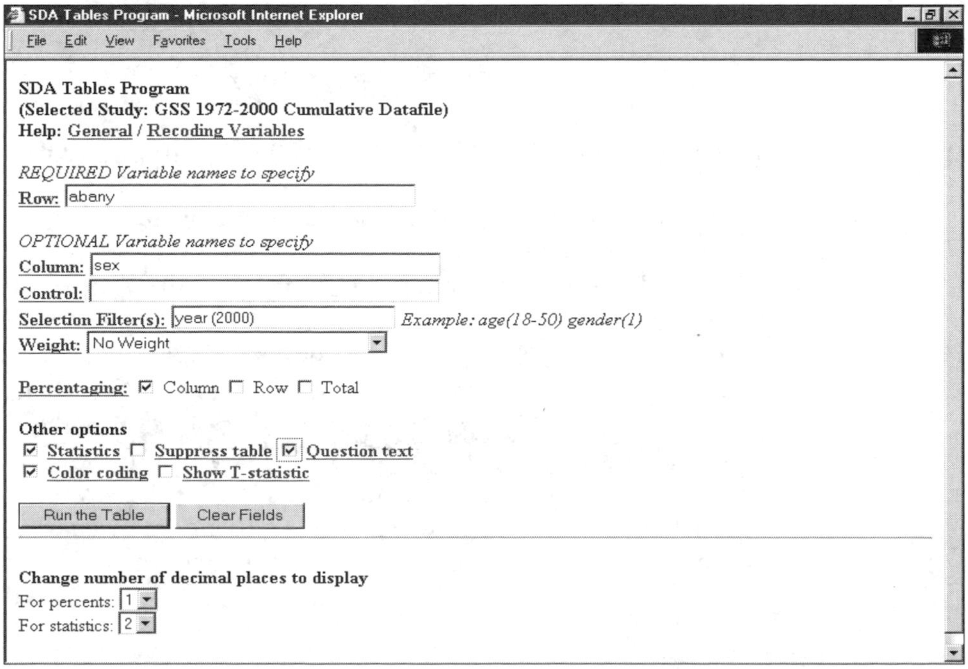

FIGURE 3.4

The bivariate relationship between gender and abortion attitudes is shown in Table 3.2.

Frequency Distribution				
Cells contain: -Column percent -N of cases		**sex**		
		1 MALE	2 FEMALE	*ROW TOTAL*
abany	1: YES	**39.9** 309	**39.8** 396	*39.9* *705*
	2: NO	**60.1** 465	**60.2** 598	*60.1* *1,063*
	COL TOTAL	*100.0* *774*	*100.0* *994*	*100.0* *1,768*
	Means	1.60	1.60	1.60
	Std Devs	.49	.49	.49

Color coding: <-2.0 <-1.0 <0.0 >0.0 >1.0 >2.0 T

N in each cell: Smaller than expected | Larger than expected

Summary Statistics

Eta* =	.00	Gamma =	.00	Chisq(P) =	.00 (p= 0.97)
R =	.00	Tau-b =	.00	Chisq(LR) =	.00 (p= 0.97)
Somers' d* =	.00	Tau-c =	.00	df =	1

*Row variable treated as the dependent variable.

TABLE 3.2

Before answering questions from this information, we need to learn how to interpret our results. Among males, 39.9% of respondents approve of abortion for any reason. That is, the number of males who approve abortion for any reason divided by total number of male respondents, or:

$$(309 \div 774) \times 100\% = 39.9\%$$

Among females, 39.8% approve abortion for any reason. That is:

$$(396 \div 994) \times 100\% = 39.8\%$$

The above results indicate virtually no difference between men and women on the abortion issue. There is only 0.1 percentage point difference between the two subgroups (39.9% − 39.8% = 0.1%). This difference of 0.1% suggests that men and women do not differ in their attitudes toward abortion. As a general rule of thumb, a relationship may exist if the percentage difference is 10% or higher. In our case, it is clear that no gender difference in abortion attitudes is found.

Although percentage difference analysis is an easy and useful technique to explore a relationship between two variables, it is not considered scientific. A more scientific measure is the Chi-Square analysis. In Table 3.2, look at the section "Summary Statistics." You will find "Chisq(P) = .00 (p=.97)". This means that the Pearson Chi-Square value is 0 and the probability level is .97. In social science research, a significant relationship between two variables exists when the probability level is .05 or less. The p value of .97 in this table is considerably higher than the .05 percent probability level needed for statistical significance. We can therefore conclude that the relationship between gender and abortion attitudes is a statistically insignificant one. Another way you can detect meaningful links between independent and dependent variables is to examine carefully the color coding of your SDA table output. Bright and vivid colors suggests a significant relationship; dull color differences, as you will see on your screen, suggest no meaningful differences or association.

With the above knowledge, let's answer the following questions.

4. Which gender is more accepting of abortion?
   a. Women.
   b. The answer is unclear; it could be men or there could be no differences between the sexes. This is a case of borderline significant differences.
   c. Men definitely.
   d. Men and women show similar and undifferentiated abortion attitudes.
5. What does the Chi-Square statistic suggest?
   a. Differences are not very profound between the two groups and could be due to chance
   b. Differences are statistically significant
   c. Substantial differences between the groups are noted
   d. Both b and c
6. Do the findings support the claim that men think differently about the abortion issue than women?
   a. This data supports it
   b. This data contradicts it
   c. This data doesn't provide any clues either way

The most appropriate answers for these three questions are: 4. d; 5. a; 6. b.

ECONOMIC FACTORS IN DETERMINING ATTITUDES TOWARD ABORTION

Another factor that could influence people's attitudes on abortion is their economic (or social class) position. We often read in our newspapers about the higher and problematic-rates of abortions among the poor and among racial minority members. If we think about this for a moment, we might be inclined to suspect that the poor and members of racial minorities would be among those more likely to favor abortion. Because they appear to have a greater abortion rate to deal with problems such as unwanted pregnancies, they may accept or tolerate this behavior more readily than members of other social groups. They could also be more inclined to favor it because of their greater personal acquaintance with others who have had abortions.

To examine the hypothesis that class and race are related to abortion attitudes, we will need to first tabulate abortion attitudes (**ABANY**) by family income differences (**INCOME98**); and then by race differences (**RACE**).

1. Go to the SDA website at http://sda.berkeley.edu.
2. Click **SDA Archive**, and then select the **GSS Cumulative Datafile 1972–2002**. Select "Frequencies or crosstabulation" and click **Start**.
3. Enter **abany** in the "Row" box.
4. Carefully type the following into the "Column" box:
      income98(r: 1-10 "less than 15K"; 11-16 "15K-35K"; 17-19 "35K-60K"; 20-21 "60K-90K"; 22-23 "90K and higher")

   This syntax simply means we are collapsing categories of family income into five groups. Alternatively, the recodes can be copied and pasted into the appropriate boxes by operning a new browser window and following the instructions given on pages 33–34 to find the correct recodes for this chapter.
5. Type **year(2000)** in the "Selection Filter(s)" box.
6. Select "Column" from the "Percentage" option list.
7. Under "Other options," select "Statistics," "Question text," and "Color coding."
8. Click **Run the Table**. Table 3.3 shows the relationship between family income and abortion attitudes.

SDA 1.2: Tables - Microsoft Internet Explorer

File   Edit   View   Favorites   Tools   Help

Frequency Distribution

		income98					
Cells contain: -Column percent -N of cases		1 less than 15K	2 15K - 35K	3 35K - 60K	4 60K - 90K	5 90K and higher	*ROW TOTAL*
abany	1: YES	**36.5** 116	**36.1** 171	**40.3** 157	**45.1** 105	**52.9** 83	*40.2* *632*
	2: NO	**63.5** 202	**63.9** 303	**59.7** 233	**54.9** 128	**47.1** 74	*59.8* *940*
	COL TOTAL	*100.0* *318*	*100.0* *474*	*100.0* *390*	*100.0* *233*	*100.0* *157*	*100.0* *1,572*
	Means	1.64	1.64	1.60	1.55	1.47	1.60
	Std Devs	.48	.48	.49	.50	.50	.49

Color coding:	<-2.0	<-1.0	<0.0	>0.0	>1.0	>2.0	T
N in each cell:	Smaller than expected		Larger than expected				

Summary Statistics

Eta* =   .11   Gamma = -.14   Chisq(P) =   17.96 (p= 0.00)

TABLE 3.3

Now answer the following questions.

7. What does the "abortion attitudes-by-income" table show?
   a. More rich people favor abortion
   b. More poor people favor abortion
   c. No differences between the two income groups
8. What does the Chi-Square statistic suggest?
   a. Differences are not very profound between the four income groups and could be due to chance
   b. Differences between the groups are statistically significant and considerable
   c. Unclear results

We will now examine the link between race and abortion attitudes.

1. Go to the SDA website at http://sda.berkeley.edu.
2. Click **SDA Archive**, and then select the **GSS Cumulative Datafile 1972–2002**. Select "Frequencies or crosstabulation" and click **Start**.
3. Enter **abany** in the "Row" box; **race(1,2)** in the "Column" box; and **year(2000)** in the "Selection Filter(s)" box.
4. Select "Column" from the "Percentage" option list.
5. Under "Other options," select "Statistics," "Question text," and "Color coding."
7. The layout of the above instructions is shown in Figure 3.5. Check that the figure matches what you have typed and selected and click **Run the Table**.
8. Table 3.4 shows the output for the relationship between race and abortion attitudes.

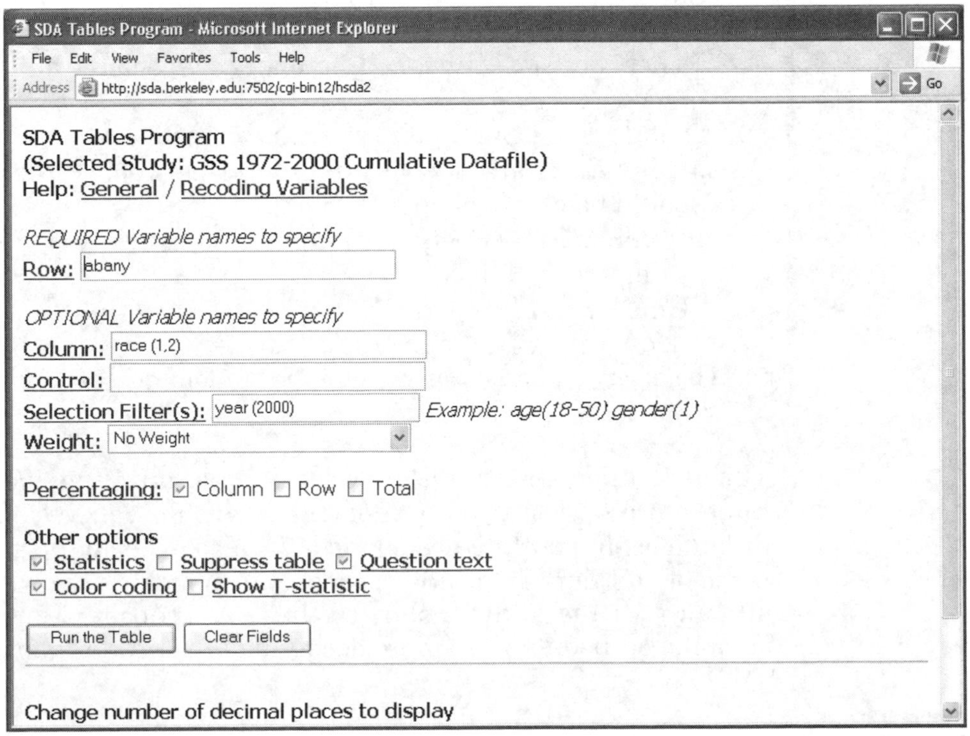

FIGURE 3.5

SDA 1.2: Tables - Microsoft Internet Explorer

File   Edit   View   Favorites   Tools   Help

Frequency Distribution

Cells contain: -Column percent -N of cases		race		
		1 WHITE	2 BLACK	ROW TOTAL
abany	1: YES	40.8 577	36.8 96	40.2 673
	2: NO	59.2 836	63.2 165	59.8 1,001
	COL TOTAL	100.0 1,413	100.0 261	100.0 1,674
	Means	1.59	1.63	1.60
	Std Devs	.49	.48	.49

Color coding:	<-2.0	<-1.0	<0.0	>0.0	>1.0	>2.0	T
N in each cell:	Smaller than expected			Larger than expected			

Summary Statistics

Eta* =	.03	Gamma =	.09	Chisq(P) =	1.51	(p= 0.22)
R =	.03	Tau-b =	.03	Chisq(LR) =	1.52	(p= 0.22)
Somers' d* =	.04	Tau-c =	.02	df =	1	

TABLE 3.4

You are now ready to answer the following questions:

9. What does the "abortion attitudes-by-race" table show? (Hint: Pay particular attention to the probability level; remember, even if there are percentage differences between subgroups, if the probability level is above .05, then the differences aren't meaningful and statistically significant ones.)
   a. More whites accept abortion
   b. More African Americans accept abortion
   c. There are no significant differences between the attitudes of the two races
10. What does the Chi-Square statistic suggest?
   a. Differences are not very profound between the two groups and could be due to chance
   b. Differences between the groups are statistically significant and considerable
   c. Unclear results

   The most appropriate answers for the last four questions are: 7. a; 8. b; 9. c; 10. a.

Thus far, all of our findings may seem rather puzzling. We expected men to be more opposed to abortion than women, yet we found no gender differences in abortion acceptance. We also expected to see more acceptance of abortion among lower income respondents than among the more affluent, yet the findings showed the very opposite: More economically advantaged people were more accepting of abortion than poorer respondents. We expected that African Americans would show more acceptance of abortion than whites, yet the racial gap in abortion acceptance was only about four percentage points, a non-significant difference. All these results suggest that good common sense may fail us if we think it will usually lead us to the right answer.

In fact, common sense can often be mistaken and may be inconsistent with sound sociological theorizing, which may not be so widely known or understood. You should also be prepared to accept that many questions may not be readily known or easily predicted. There are many open questions and only when one carefully examines the empirical evidence (the actual survey data results) can one arrive at a truer picture of the pattern of causal relationships. An additional factor that must be taken into account is the cumulative record of findings. Sometimes a mere quirk in the wording of a question or a sample selection bias may be all that it takes to produce an anomalous result in research findings that would wash away under the long-term cumulative evaluation of testing and re-testing of research hypotheses. In short, doing social science is no cinch.

RELIGION AND ATTITUDES TOWARD ABORTION

Let's return to the task of trying to unravel the correlates of abortion attitudes. So far, we haven't established much positive information about it. We have only demythologized the question somewhat, which can be an important and worthy enough enterprise in itself. We have also established another important distinction between having an abortion and thinking about it in general terms. This appears to be the case in the failure to confirm race and class differences in having abortions with the differences in the attitudinal acceptance of abortion. They are very different as a person may disapprove of abortion in terms of their general attitudes but still have one if certain needs or circumstances arise. We found the pattern between abortion behavior and attitudes simply didn't match up. We'll return to this point later in this chapter. For now, let's investigate something that everyone knows is related to abortion acceptance: religion and differences in religious beliefs. We will use **RELIG** here, signifying all major religious categories.

Go to the SDA website at **http://sda.berkeley.edu**. Click **SDA Archive**, and then select the **GSS Cumulative Datafile 1972–2002**. Select "Frequencies or crosstabulation" and click **Start**. The correct command syntax to use is given in the following list (if an option isn't listed, leave it blank or at the default setting):

- "Row": abany
- "Column": relig(r: 1 "Protestant"; 2 "Catholic"; 3 "Jewish"; 4 "None"; 5-9 "Other")
- "Selection Filter(s)": year(2000)
- "Percentaging": Select "Column"
- "Other options": Select "Statistics," "Question text," and "Color coding."

Table 3.5 shows the correct output.

SDA 1.2: Tables - Microsoft Internet Explorer

File Edit View Favorites Tools Help

Frequency Distribution

Cells contain: -Column percent -N of cases		relig					
		1 Protestant	2 Catholic	3 Jewish	4 None	5 Other	ROW TOTAL
abany	1: YES	35.2 337	33.3 142	76.1 35	57.3 141	68.3 28	39.8 683
	2: NO	64.8 621	66.7 284	23.9 11	42.7 105	31.7 13	60.2 1,034
	COL TOTAL	100.0 958	100.0 426	100.0 46	100.0 246	100.0 41	100.0 1,717
	Means	1.65	1.67	1.24	1.43	1.32	1.60
	Std Devs	.48	.47	.43	.50	.47	.49

Color coding:	<-2.0	<-1.0	<0.0	>0.0	>1.0	>2.0	T
N in each cell:	Smaller than expected			Larger than expected			

Summary Statistics

Eta* =	.22	Gamma = -.26	Chisq(P) =	86.67	(p = 0.00)
R =	-.19	Tau-b = -.14	Chisq(LR) =	85.53	(p = 0.00)
Somers' d* = -.13		Tau-c = -.15	df =	4	

TABLE 3.5

Now, answer the following multiple-choice questions:

11. Which two religious subgroups show the least support for abortion?
    a. Protestants and Catholics
    b. Jews and the religiously nonaffiliated
    c. Protestants and Jews
    d. Catholics and Jews
    e. Protestants and the religiously nonaffiliated
12. Which two subgroups show the most support for abortion?
    a. Protestants and Catholics
    b. Jews and other religions
    c. Jews and Catholics
    d. The religiously nonaffiliated and Protestants
    e. Protestants and Jews
13. What does the Chi-Square statistic suggest?
    a. Differences are not very profound between the subgroups represented here and could be due to chance
    b. Differences are statistically significant
    c. Unclear results
14. How would you describe the viewpoints of Catholics on the abortion issue from this data?
    a. Generally permissive
    b. Generally restrictive
    c. The data doesn't suggest any particular conclusion on the Catholic response

The correct answers for these questions are: 11. a; 12. b; 13 b; 14. b.

Attitudes of Protestants to Abortion

Besides religious affiliation, it is well known that fundamental Protestants, such as adherents of various Baptist Churches and other evangelical churches (such as Assembly of God affiliates, Seventh Day Adventists, Jehovah Witnesses, among others) are strong advocates of pro-life campaigns. This religious affiliation to Protestant fundamentalism may be pivotal in explaining their anti-abortion attitudes. We will empirically compare fundamental Protestants to moderate Protestant affiliates (such as Methodists and Lutherans) and to liberal Protestants (such as Unitarians and Episcopalians). To answer this question, we need to use FUND as our independent variable and ABANY as our dependent variable.

1. Go to the SDA website at http://sda.berkeley.edu.
2. Click **SDA Archive**, and then select the **GSS Cumulative Datafile 1972– 2002**. Select "Frequencies or crosstabulation" and click **Start**.
3. Enter abany in the "Row" box; fund in the "Column" box; and year(2000) in the "Selection Filter(s)" box.
4. Select "Column" from the "Percentage" option list.
5. Under "Other options," select "Statistics," "Question text," and "Color coding."
7. The layout of the above instructions is shown in Figure 3.6. Check that the figure matches what you have typed and selected and click **Run the Table**.
8. Table 3.6 shows the correct output for this analysis.

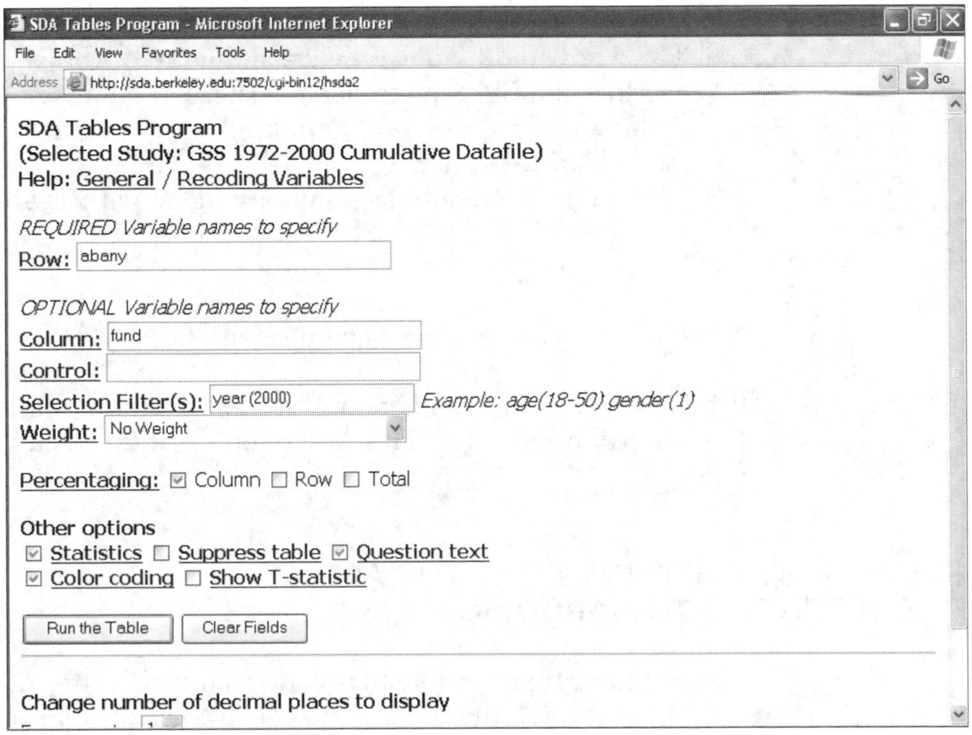

FIGURE 3.6

Frequency Distribution				
Cells contain: -Column percent -N of cases	**fund**			
	1 FUNDAMENTALIST	2 MODERATE	3 LIBERAL	ROW TOTAL
abany 1: YES	30.2 151	36.6 238	50.5 259	39.0 648
2: NO	69.8 349	63.4 412	49.5 254	61.0 1,015
COL TOTAL	100.0 500	100.0 650	100.0 513	100.0 1,663
Means	1.70	1.63	1.50	1.61
Std Devs	.46	.48	.50	.49

Color coding:	<-2.0	<-1.0	<0.0	>0.0	>1.0	>2.0	T
N in each cell:	Smaller than expected			Larger than expected			

Summary Statistics					
Eta* =	.17	Gamma =	-.27	Chisq(P) =	46.30 (p= 0.00)
R =	-.16	Tau-b =	-.15	Chisq(LR) =	46.14 (p= 0.00)
Somers' d* =	-.13	Tau-c =	-.17	df =	2

TABLE 3.6

You are now ready to answer the following questions:

15. What does the "abortion attitudes-by-fund" table show?
    a. More liberals favor abortion
    b. More moderates favor abortion
    c. More fundamentalists favor abortion
    d. There are no differences between the three groups
16. What does the Chi-Square statistic suggest?
    a. Differences are not very profound between the two groups and could be due to chance
    b. Differences between the groups are statistically significant and considerable
    c. Unclear results

The correct answers to these questions are: 15. a; 16. b.

All this suggests that fundamentalist identification is a powerful correlate to abortion attitudes. This is something you probably suspected all along.

EDUCATIONAL ATTAINMENT AND CAREERS AND ATTITUDES TOWARD ABORTION

Another interesting variable that may affect one's attitudes toward abortion is educational attainment. We might expect more highly educated respondents to be more liberally minded and hence more accepting of abortion. To test this hypothesis, we'll use **EDUC** as the independent variable and **ABANY** as the dependent variable.

1. Go to the SDA website at http://sda.berkeley.edu.
2. Click **SDA Archive**, and then select the **GSS Cumulative Datafile 1972–2002**. Select "Frequencies or crosstabulation" and click **Start**.
3. Enter **abany** in the "Row" box; **educ(r:0-11;12;13-15;16-20)** in the "Column" box; and **year(2000)** in the "Selection Filter(s)" box.
4. Select "Column" from the "Percentage" option list.
5. Under "Other options," select "Statistics," "Question text," and "Color coding."
7. The layout of the above instructions is shown in Figure 3.7. Check that the figure matches what you have typed and selected and click **Run the Table**.
8. Table 3.7 shows the correct output for this analysis.

FIGURE 3.7

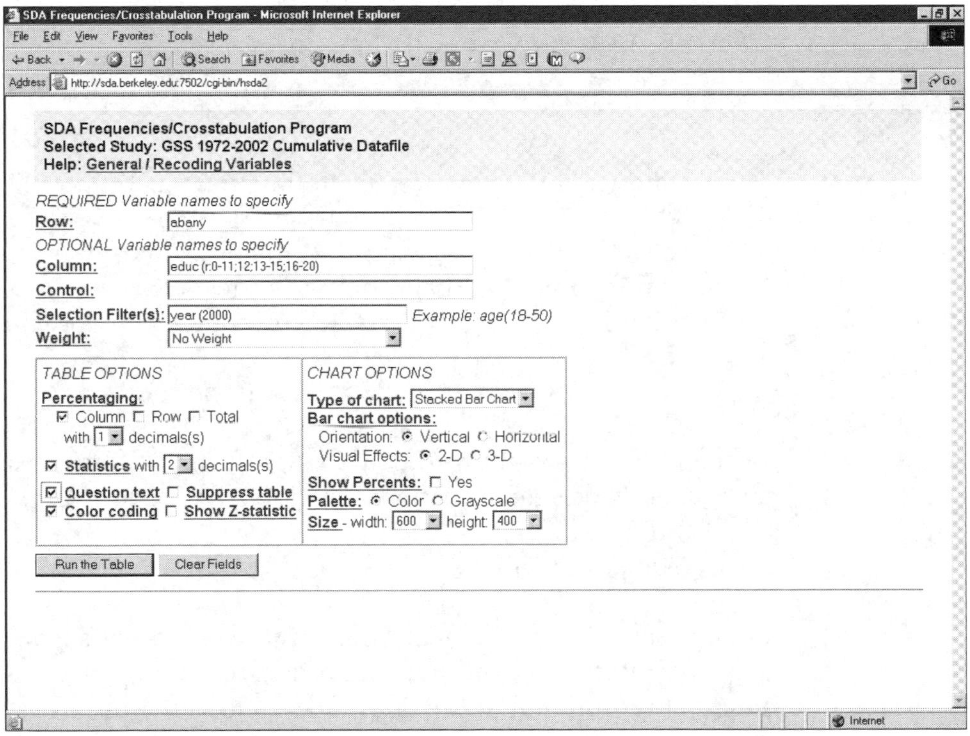

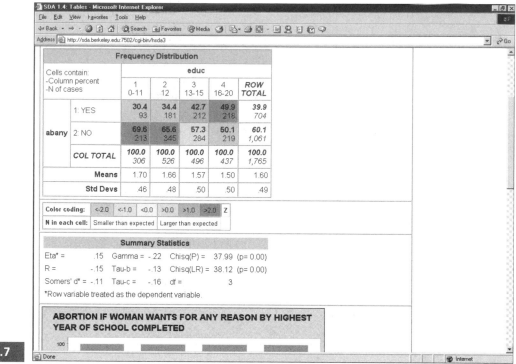

TABLE 3.7

You are now ready to answer the following question:

17. What does the data show about the association between educational accomplishment and abortion attitudes?
    a. Slightly more highly educated respondents favor abortion than high school drop-outs
    b. Those with less education tend to be more favorably disposed to abortion
    c. There are substantial and significant differences, showing the highly educated more inclined to accept abortion than the less well educated
    d. None of the above

Seeing the pattern of education and income level or social class level suggests an interesting and important question for your further exploration. Essay Question 3–B at the end of this chapter deals with this topic. Also think about the following: Why should one's attitudes about abortion differ when one views their work as a career rather than as a job? If you can answer this question fully, you'll be well on your way to understanding the class and education correlations with abortion attitudes.

Let's run another cross-tabulation: abortion attitudes by a woman's work status. To create a table examining the relationship between women's work status and abortion attitudes, go to the SDA website at **http://sda .berkeley.edu**. Click **SDA Archive**, and then select the **GSS Cumulative Datafile 1972–2002**. Select "Frequencies or crosstabulation" and click **Start**. The correct command syntax to use is given in the following list (if an option isn't listed, leave it blank or at the default setting):

- "Row": abany
- "Column": wrkstat(r: 1 "Work F/T"; 2,6 "Work P/T/School"; 5; "Retired";7 "Keep House")
- "Selection Filter(s)": year(2000) sex(2)
- "Percentaging": "Column"
- "Other options": Select "Statistics," "Question text," and "Color coding."

In the Selection Filter Box, we typed year(2000) sex(2) to ensure that we only examine information from the female respondents surveyed in 2000. The output table is shown in Table 3.8.

TABLE 3.8

Now answer each of the following multiple-choice questions.

18. Which two groups of women are least accepting of abortion?
    a. Full-time workers and housewives
    b. Part-time workers and housewives
    c. Housewives and retired workers
    d. Full and part-time workers
19. Which groups of women are the most accepting of abortion?
    a. Other workers and housewives
    b. Full-time workers and the unemployed
    c. Full-time workers, part-time workers, and students
    d. Housewives and part-time workers

20. What does the Chi-Square statistic suggest?
   a. Differences are not very profound between the subgroups represented here and could be due to chance
   b. Differences are statistically significant and considerable
   c. Unclear results

The correct answers for questions 17–20 are: 17. c; 18. c; 19. c; 20. b.

Another very important line of sociological theorizing has investigated the differences in women's roles and their attitudes about abortion. Look at the writings of Kristen Luker to explore this body of knowledge. You may want to try answering Essay Question 3–D at the end of this chapter to see if you can explain why working women are more likely to hold different abortion attitudes than retired women or housewives.

AGE AND ATTITUDES TOWARD ABORTION

Another interesting variable that may affect one's attitudes toward abortion is age. Many believe that the elderly are more conservatively inclined on many social issues like abortion. Is this hypothesis supported? To test it, let's use age as the independent variable and abany as the dependent variable. As we have done before, go to the SDA website at http://sda.berkeley.edu. Click **SDA Archive**, and then select the **GSS Cumulative Datafile 1972–2002**. Select "Frequencies or crosstabulation" and click **Start**. The correct command syntax to use is given in the following list (if an option isn't listed, leave it blank or at the default setting):

- "Row": abany
- "Column": age(r:0-24 "less than 25"; 25-39 "25-39"; 40-64 "40-64"; 65-110 "65 and older")
- "Selection Filter(s)": year(2000)
- "Percentaging": "Column"
- "Other options": Select "Statistics," "Question text," and "Color coding"

Table 3.9 shows the table generated from this series of commands.

```
SDA 1.2: Tables - Microsoft Internet Explorer
File   Edit   View   Favorites   Tools   Help
```

Frequency Distribution

Cells contain: -Column percent -N of cases		1 less than 25	2 25-39	3 40-64	4 65 and older	*ROW TOTAL*
abany	1: YES	37.8 65	43.2 231	41.2 308	32.3 101	*39.9* *705*
	2: NO	62.2 107	56.8 304	58.8 440	67.7 212	*60.1* *1,063*
	COL TOTAL	*100.0* *172*	*100.0* *535*	*100.0* *748*	*100.0* *313*	*100.0* *1,768*
	Means	1.62	1.57	1.59	1.68	1.60
	Std Devs	.49	.50	.49	.47	.49

Color coding:	<-2.0	<-1.0	<0.0	>0.0	>1.0	>2.0	T
N in each cell:	Smaller than expected			Larger than expected			

Summary Statistics

Eta* =   .08   Gamma = .08   Chisq(P) =   10.83 (p= 0.01)

TABLE 3.9

Now, answer the following multiple-choice question:

21. What does the "abany-by-age" table show?
    a. Those who are under age 25 are more opposed to abortion than other age groups
    b. Those who are between 25 and 39 are more opposed to abortion than other age groups
    c. Those who are between 40 and 64 are more opposed to abortion than other age groups
    d. Those who are 65 years and older are more opposed to abortion than other age groups
    e. No significant differences can be found between the four age groups.

    The answer to this question is: d.

Among those who are between the ages of 25 and 39, about 43% approve of abortion for any reason. For those who are 65 years old and older, it is only 32%. The percentage difference between the above two groups is about 11%. Most importantly, the probability level for the Chi-Square value (10.83) is .01, indicating a significant relationship exists between age and abortion attitudes.

However, we may wonder whether it is age or the lower educational attainments that is more common among the elderly that is the primary reason why elderly persons are more opposed to abortion than younger folks. This brings us to a more complex level of analysis that we will be examining more fully in a later chapter. We will suggest it now; it is called a *control variable analysis*. A control variable is a potential confounder; it, rather than the presumed cause, may be the real influential force behind the changes we are observing in the dependent variable.

To clarify this question, whether it is age or educational differences that are related to differences in support or opposition to abortion, we will create two separate tables to observe the age/abortion attitudes hypothesis. One will show those with high school degrees or less education, the other, those with some college or more education. If education is the true cause of the attitude towards abortion, the age/abortion attitudes hypothesis will no longer remain statistically significant when the groups are subdivided in this way. If on the other hand, age is itself an influential force, then the age/abortion attitudes hypothesis will be sustained. Try doing this analysis and then answer the question that follows. If you are very uncertain about what you are doing here, don't worry: We will be explaining this in greater detail in a later chapter. Now, however, it should be simply understood that there can be multiplicity of causal forces. And sometimes coincidental things can pose as causal influences, when they are merely offshoots of other genuinely causative forces.

Go to the SDA website at http://sda.berkeley.edu. Click **SDA Archive**, and then select the **GSS Cumulative Datafile 1972–2002**. Select "Frequencies or crosstabulation" and click **Start**. The correct command syntax for doing a control variable analysis with education (**DEGREE**) as the control variable, **AGE** as the independent variable, and **ABANY** as the dependent variable is given in the following list (if an option isn't listed, leave it blank or at the default setting):

- "Row": abany
- "Column": age(r:0-24 "less than 25"; 25-39 "25-39"; 40-64 "40-64"; 65-110 "65 and older")
- "Control": degree(r: 0-1 "High School or Less"; 2-4 "Some College or More")
- "Selection Filter(s)": year(2000)
- "Percentaging": "Column"
- "Other options": Select "Statistics," "Question text," and "Color coding."

Tables 3.10 and 3.11 shows the tables generated from this series of commands.

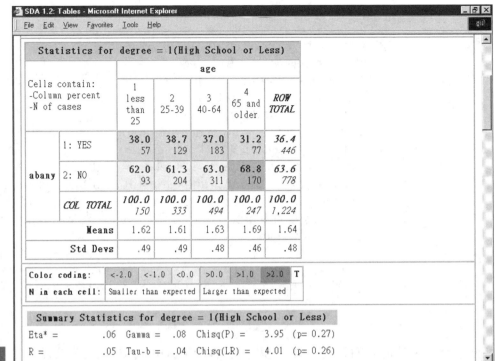

Statistics for degree = 1(High School or Less)

Cells contain: -Column percent -N of cases		age				
		1 less than 25	2 25-39	3 40-64	4 65 and older	*ROW TOTAL*
abany	1: YES	**38.0** 57	**38.7** 129	**37.0** 183	**31.2** 77	*36.4* *446*
	2: NO	**62.0** 93	**61.3** 204	**63.0** 311	**68.8** 170	*63.6* *778*
	COL TOTAL	*100.0* *150*	*100.0* *333*	*100.0* *494*	*100.0* *247*	*100.0* *1,224*
	Means	1.62	1.61	1.63	1.69	1.64
	Std Devs	.49	.49	.48	.46	.48

Color coding: | <-2.0 | <-1.0 | <0.0 | >0.0 | >1.0 | >2.0 | T
N in each cell: | Smaller than expected | Larger than expected

Summary Statistics for degree = 1(High School or Less)

Eta* =   .06   Gamma =   .08   Chisq(P) =   3.95   (p= 0.27)
R =   .05   Tau-b =   .04   Chisq(LR) =   4.01   (p= 0.26)

TABLE 3.10

Statistics for degree = 2(Some College or More)

Cells contain: -Column percent -N of cases		age				
		1 less than 25	2 25- 39	3 40-64	4 65 and older	*ROW TOTAL*
abany	1: YES	**37.5** 6	**50.5** 101	**49.2** 124	**34.9** 22	*47.6* *253*
	2: NO	**62.5** 10	**49.5** 99	**50.8** 128	**65.1** 41	*52.4* *278*
	COL TOTAL	*100.0* *16*	*100.0* *200*	*100.0* *252*	*100.0* *63*	*100.0* *531*
	Means	1.62	1.50	1.51	1.65	1.52
	Std Devs	.50	.50	.50	.48	.50

Color coding: | <-2.0 | <-1.0 | <0.0 | >0.0 | >1.0 | >2.0 | T
N in each cell: | Smaller than expected | Larger than expected

Summary Statistics for degree = 2(Some College or More)

Eta* =   .10   Gamma = .09   Chisq(P) = 5.65 (p= 0.13)

TABLE 3.11

Now, answer the following multiple-choice question:

22. The control variable analysis of age and abortion acceptance with education as the control shows:

a) Age and abortion attitudes are still highly significantly related to one another, suggesting that age itself is a powerful influence on abortion attitudes

b. Age and abortion attitudes are no longer significantly related to one another, suggesting that educational differences rather than age is a more powerful influence on abortion attitudes

c. Age and abortion attitudes are still significantly related to one another, especially among less well educated respondents, suggesting that age is still a powerful influence on abortion attitudes

d. None of the above

The correct answer to Question 22 is b. If you didn't get this, don't worry as we'll be offering a more detailed explanation of this type of analysis in a later chapter.

CHANGES IN ATTITUDE TOWARD ABORTION OVER TIME

To conclude this preliminary exercise it will be necessary to run a time–series analysis. Do you think abortion attitudes have changed over the years? Doesn't it seem that we now live in a more permissive society? Let's check this out.

1. Go to the SDA website at http://sda.berkeley.edu.
2. Click **SDA Archive**, and then select the **GSS Cumulative Datafile 1972–2002**. Select "Frequencies or crosstabulation" and click **Start**.
3. Enter **abany** in the "Row" box.
4. Type **year(r: 1975-1979 "1975-79"; 1980-1984 "1980-84"; 1985-1989 "1985-89"; 1990-1994 "1990-94"; 1995-2000 "1995-2000")** in the "Column" box.
5. Select "Column" from the "Percentage" option list.
6. Under "Other options," select "Statistics," "Question text," and "Color coding."
7. Click **Run the Table**.
8. Table 3.12 shows the table generated from this series of commands.

		Frequency Distribution					
		year					
Cells contain: -Column percent -N of cases		1 1976- 79	2 1980- 84	3 1985- 89	4 1990- 94	5 1995- 2000	*ROW* *TOTAL*
abany	1: YES	**35.5** 1,052	**38.1** 2,323	**38.2** 1,963	**44.8** 2,139	**42.0** 2,252	*40.0* *9,729*
	2: NO	**64.5** 1,911	**61.9** 3,778	**61.8** 3,173	**55.2** 2,633	**58.0** 3,115	*60.0* *14,610*
	COL TOTAL	*100.0* *2,963*	*100.0* *6,101*	*100.0* *5,136*	*100.0* *4,772*	*100.0* *5,367*	*100.0* *24,339*
	Means	1.64	1.62	1.62	1.55	1.58	1.60
	Std Devs	.48	.49	.49	.50	.49	.49

Color coding:	<-2.0	<-1.0	<0.0	>0.0	>1.0	>2.0	T
N in each cell:	Smaller than expected			Larger than expected			

Summary Statistics

Eta* =	.06	Gamma = -.07	Chisq(P) = 96.02 (p= 0.00)
R =	-.05	Tau-b = -.05	Chisq(LR) = 95.86 (p= 0.00)
Somers' d* = -.04		Tau-c = -.06	df = 4

TABLE 3.12

You are now ready to answer this final question:

23. Overall, how has abortion attitudes changed over the years?
    a. It has not changed at all
    b. Respondents in the late 1990s are more approving of abortion than those who responded in the 1970s
    c. Respondents in the late 1990s are less approving of abortion than those who responded in the 1970s
    d. Abortion attitudes among respondents in the late 1980s tend to be much more approving of it than their counterparts in late 1990s

    The correct answer to this question is b.

SUMMARY

The above analyses should provide a good idea of what will be expected of you in coming exercises. In subsequent chapters, you'll be required to use the SDA command language to execute an analysis with one of the various datasets provided; then, you will make the most appropriate and correct interpretation of results. At the same time, you will become proficient with SDA syntax. Moreover, you will also master a sociological content area. All of the SDA variable titles and recoding syntax needed to complete the chapter exercises in this book can be found in the following locations:

1. at the end of each chapter (printed format)
2. at: www.ncc.edu/users/feigelb/sda.htm (electronic format)
3. at: www.ablongman.com/feigelman3e (electronic format)

In this chapter we have investigated abortion attitudes. Some of what we found probably confirmed ideas you already had on the subject. Findings showing that Christian Fundamentalists and Catholics are more against abortion than non-Christians and the non-affiliated, probably comes as no surprise. Other findings, however, may have been inconsistent with your expectations. In some respects, we may have shattered several myths about abortion. For example, we questioned the myth holding that men are more opposed to abortion than women; that lower income respondents are more in favor of it than the rich; and that African Americans are more supportive of abortion than whites. Each of these beliefs failed to gain any confirmation with the 2000 General Social Survey data. This analysis also suggested some other hypotheses about abortion that you may not have thought about before. For example, why housewives are more opposed to abortion than women who work; and why the more highly educated and wealthier members of society are more accepting of abortion than the less well-educated and affluent members.

Your instructor may wish for you to further investigate these questions. For each chapter, we provide several essay questions for students to investigate research issues further, to prod them to examine the professional research literature on the subject, to place their research findings within the larger body of social scientific knowledge. Any of the following essays questions would make excellent topics for term papers.

ESSAY QUESTIONS

3–A   Reviewing some of the considerable number of other studies available on male and female attitudes toward abortion and toward feminism generally, discuss how these findings on abortion attitudes and gender converge with past evidence. Elaborate on what the evidence shows about how the sexes feel about feminism and abortion.

3–B   Offer an explanation for the findings on the associations between abortion attitudes with income and education. Why are highly educated and wealthier members of society more likely to favor abortion than the poor and the educationally deprived? Cite evidence from previous research findings on this hypothesis.

3–C   How do you explain the pattern of relationships between abortion attitudes and race? Review the findings obtained here and compare and contrast these results with previous published studies.

3–D   Explain why different groups of women (working women, housewives, and retirees) hold different attitudes on abortion. Consult and cite other sociological studies in preparing your answer.

3–E   From the entire dataset, select an independent variable of your own choosing (and different from those analyzed here) and relate it to the dependent variable of abortion attitudes. Interpret your findings and discuss whether there is a statistically significant association between the variables or subgroups in your hypothesis.

3–F   Based on all the answers given in this group of crosstabulations, develop an overview of why people are inclined to assume different attitudes on the abortion issue.

CHAPTER PROJECT

In addition to the **ABANY** variable, the GSS also asked a variety of questions about abortion acceptance. For this project, you will need to prepare a graph displaying any trends in the various abortion attitudes that may have taken place over the history of GSS surveys from 1972 to 2002. You can either prepare one graph showing all six different dimensions of abortion acceptance over the nearly 30 year history of GSS surveys, or you can prepare six separate graphs showing a single trend in each. The horizontal axis will show the different survey periods: 1972–1974; 1975–1979; 1980–1984; 1985–1989; 1990–1994; 1995–2002. The vertical axis will show the percentage approving of abortion under the indicated condition. If you assemble all the variables into a single graphic, you will need to use different colored inks to distinguish one variable from another. You can then draw interconnecting lines on each variable's measurements, joining each time period percentage of acceptance to show the trends. After you prepare the graph(s), discuss all trends of increasing, decreasing, stable patterns of the different manifestations of abortion acceptance over the 30 year period of surveys. The goal of this assignment is to understand whether there have been any clear patterns of changes in people's attitudes toward abortion over the past few decades. The original GSS questions on abortion attitudes was:

Please tell me whether or not you think it should be possible for a pregnant woman to obtain a legal abortion if . . .

the woman wants it for any reason? [Variable Name: **ABANY**]
there is a strong chance of serious defect in the baby? [Variable Name: **ABDEFECT**]
she is married and does not want any more children? [Variable Name: **ABNOMORE**]
the woman's own health is seriously endangered by the pregnancy? [Variable Name: **ABHLTH**]
the family has a very low income and cannot afford any more children? [Variable Name: **ABPOOR**]
she became pregnant as a result of rape? [Variable Name: **ABRAPE**]

For each of the above six variables, you need to run a time–series analysis. In other words, you will need to run six separate tables. Here is a sample set of instructions for completing the trend analysis for the variable ABDEFECT:

1. Go to the SDA website at http://sda.berkeley.edu.
2. Click **SDA Archive**, and then select the **GSS Cumulative Datafile 1972–2002**. Select "Frequencies or crosstabulation" and click **Start**.
3. Enter **abdefect** in the "Row" box.
4. Type **year**(r: 1972-1974 "1972-74"; 1975-1979 "1975-79"; 1980-1984 "1980-84"; 1985-1989 "1985-89"; 1990-1994 "1990-94"; 1995-2002 "1995-2002") in the "Column" box.
5. Select "Column" from the "Percentage" option list.
6. Under "Other options," select "Statistics," "Question text," and "Color coding."
7. Click **Run the Table**.
8. Print the result or save it on your computer.
9. Now repeat the above procedures for each of the other five variables. Make sure to enter a new abortion measure in the Row box (e.g., ABNOMORE, ABANY, etc.).

Answer the following questions and give them to your instructor, along with your graph(s):

1. Respondents are most sympathetic to abortion under which conditions? Which variable gets the least support? Can you offer an explanation for these differences in acceptance?
2. Which variable shows the most dramatic change over time? Why do you think this is the case? Give your own explanation and then consult the social science literature to see what the arguments are.
3. Which variable shows the least amount of change over time? Why do you think this is the case? Try to explain the lack of change in people's attitudes and then consult social science literature to see what the experts argue.
4. By looking at the trends of the six variables, how would you describe the trends in abortion attitudes in the United States over the past few decades? Is there a clear pattern? Discuss.

SYNTAX GUIDE

Go to: http://sda.berkeley.edu/cgi-bin12/hsda?harcsda+gss02
Select "Frequencies or crosstabulation"
Click **Start**

Recodes

Please note that all recodes can also be copied and pasted from either www.ncc.edu/users/feigelb/sda.htm or www.ablongman.com/feigelman3e.

If you type the recode syntax in, make sure that you type *exactly* what is shown below.

age (r:0-24 "Less than 25"; 25-39 "25-39"; 40-64 "40-64"; 65-89 "65 and older")

degree (r:0-1 "high school or less"; 2-4 "some college or more")

educ (r:0-11 "Less than high school"; 12 "HS grad."; 13-15 "Some College"; 16-20 "College or higher")

income98(r:1-10 "Less than 15K";11-16 "15K-35K";17-19 "35-60K";20-21 "60-90K"; 22-23 "90K and higher")

race (r:1 "White"; 2 "Black")

relig (r:1 "Protestant"; 2 "Catholic"; 3 "Jewish"; 4 "None"; 5-9 "Other")

wrkstat (r:1 "Work F/T"; 2,6 "Work P/T/School"; 5 "Retired"; 7 "Keep house")

year (r:1975-1979 "1975-1979"; 1980-1984 "1980-1984"; 1985-1989 "1985-1989"; 1990-1994 "1990-1994"; 1995-2002 "1995-2002")

No recode needed: ABANY; FUND.

CHAPTER 4

Culture and Ethnic Diversity

In this chapter, we will use the GSS database to help unravel the connections between locales and some of the ideas and behavior patterns of Americans. *Culture,* as your textbook states, is the total way of life of a people. It has to do with how people adapt to their environment, their collective solutions to confront environmental challenges, and the totality of their beliefs and behavior patterns for dealing with one another and the world outside them.

Students of culture are intrigued by how climate and geography influence the patterns of human association and the progression and development of cultures. Speculating on the development of American culture, we might surmise that peoples already familiar with living in forestland settings and the geographic characteristics associated with them—temperate climates, regular rainfall, and rich soils—would become successful farmers sooner than those unfamiliar with such places. They might eventually consider the possibilities of raising large quantities of grains such as wheat, corn, and barley, as they converted forestland into farms. This was the fate of many of this country's early settlers, who migrated here from such countries as England and Germany. They had long histories of successful farming back in their European homelands and they were already familiar with the geographical conditions they encountered in the colonies and eastern parts of the United States. During the 1700s, many of these immigrants adapted readily to the American continent and to the ample opportunities available here to acquire fertile farmlands.

Others, however, especially those who migrated from rocky, subtropical, arid settings around the Mediterranean Sea, may have encountered greater difficulties in adapting to early agrarian America. Unless they engaged in herding or maritime occupations—familiar livelihoods back in their European homelands—they would have encountered more uncertainty and difficulty in the interior of North America. It is no wonder that most Mediterraneans (Italians, Greeks, Spaniards) have remained in the Northeastern region, clustered in coastal cities; few have ventured forth to the Midwest heartland of America. Many can still be found concentrated in the country's maritime industries.

Thus, geographical differences exert an impact on our cultural patterns. First, we will consider place of origin—reflected in one's ethnicity or ancestry—an important component of culture. Yet, place by itself is not that clear a determinant. Anthropologists tell us repeatedly that many peoples living in similar locales develop vastly different cultures. We make it a point to differentiate ourselves from others.

Religion and the values that people cherish to identify themselves by are other very important dimensions of culture that we must consider.

Different groups have their distinctive gods and their own special ways of expressing reverence to them. Hindus unite with each other—and draw boundaries between themselves and rivals. They worship their own deities, adhere to their particular norms, food preferences, habits of dress, and so forth. Similarly, Christians and Jews possess their own distinctive ideas, and modes of complying to their particular divine expectations. As part of their observances, members of each group share common perspectives which help to establish the group's own special identity and to differentiate their members from outsiders. Each group exhorts its members to abide by its own particular conceptions of spiritual purity. Although people may inhabit similar locales, because of their diverging religious and other group memberships, they ultimately may become vastly different from one another in how they coordinate their lives.

First, let us assess our ancestries. The 2002 GSS asked people where their families came from. The original responses were coded into 42 different categories. To make it easier to work with, we regrouped the responses into 13 new categories, based on the number of replies, geographical similarities, and cultural affinities. The regrouped categories are as follows:

- *Hispanics* (Spanish, Mexican, Puerto Rican, Other Spanish, West Indian and South and Central American)
- *Eastern European* (Austrian, Czech, Hungarian, Polish, Russian, Lithuanian and Romanian)
- *English* (English, English Canadian, Scottish, and Welsh)
- *Scandinavian* (Danish, Finnish, Swedish, and Norwegian)
- *Western European* (French, Dutch, French Canadian, Swiss, and Belgian)
- *German*
- *Irish*
- *Italian*
- *African*
- *Asian* (Chinese, Japanese, Indian, Filipinos)
- Owing to their limited numbers, respondents of diverging national origins were included among *Others*

It is no surprise to see that we are a nation of immigrants. Only 118 of GSS 2002 respondents (out of 2,135 or 5.5%), identified themselves as *American Indians* or as natives. 65 respondents (3%) identified themselves as *Americans*. The majority of GSS respondents identified themselves as belonging to a single ethnic group.

In this section and following the lead of James A. Davis (1987), we will work primarily with three overlapping variables: *ethnicity*, *religion*, and *race*. Before you begin, be sure to review the procedures documented in Chapter 3. For most of this chapter, we will be using the GSS 2002 dataset. Thus, be sure to enter **year(2002)** in the "Selection Filter(s)" box (there are some exceptions in which you will use other years). The recoded variable list is presented at the end of this chapter and can also be found at: **www.ncc.edu/users/feigelb/sda.htm** and **www.ablongman/feigelman3e**.

Do a frequency distribution on the variable **ETHNIC** (or to put it in SDA command language: Tabulate **ETHNIC**) and then answer the following questions.

1. Which country or ethnic subgroup seemed to provide the highest percentage of immigrants?
   a. England
   .b. Germany
   c. Ireland
   d. Spain
2. What percentage of immigrants did this country account for?
   a. 7 percent
   b. 10 percent
   c. 12 percent
   • d. 16 percent
3. Which country or ethnic subgroup was second?
   . a. England and Wales 15.4
   b. Germany
   c. Ireland 12.5
   d. France

Now, tabulating **RACECEN1** (race) as your analysis selected variable, answer:

4. What percent of U.S. adults identified themselves as Blacks?
   a. 7 percent
   ⤺ b. 15 percent
   c. 21 percent
   d. 28 percent

With **BORN** as your tabulated variable, answer:

5. What percentage of U.S. adults were foreign born?
   ⟨ a. 2 percent
   b. 9 percent
   c. 11 percent
   d. 21 percent

To answer questions 6 and 7, you will have to perform the following steps:

1. Go to the U.S. Census website (**www.census.gov**) and click on **Gateway to Census 2000.**
2. Click on **American Factfinder** to go to the section that will provide tables and charts for Census 2000 data.
3. Select the table for the entire U.S., showing social characteristics, education and ancestry, etc. from the STF 3 file. (Hint: you will find your answer on Quick Table-P14, QT-P14; search for that table).

Now answer questions 6 and 7.

6. According to the Census 2000 data, what percentage of the U.S. population is foreign born?
   a. 2 percent
   . b. 7 percent
   · c. 11 percent
   d. 21 percent

7. Are there any discrepancies between these two surveys in enumerating the foreign born percentage?
   a. There are no discrepancies—the figures from the two surveys match almost perfectly
   b. There is a 2 percent difference between both, which could be due to population differences: the GSS only included adults; the Census included everyone.
   ; c. There is a big discrepancy of at least 8 percent, suggesting that either the GSS or the Census, or both, may have made some serious measurement problems.
   d. None of the above.

Now, reverting again to the GSS, with **PARBORN** as your tabulated variable, answer:

8. What percentage of U.S. adults have one or more parents who were foreign born?
   • a. 5 percent
   ✗ b. 12 percent
   c. 17 percent
   d. 28 percent

With **GRANBORN** as your tabulated variable, answer:

9. What percentage of U.S. adults have one or more grandparents who were foreign born?
   a. 20 percent
   b. 38 percent
   c. 50 percent
   d. 69 percent

With **REGION** as your tabulated variable, answer:

10. Which region of the country has the largest number of respondents?
   a. Northeast
   • b. South
   c. Central
   d. West

11. Which region of the country has the fewest number of respondents?
   a. Northeast
   b. South
   c. Central
   • d. West

Now, using **RELIG** as your tabulated variable, answer:

12. Which subgroup has the greatest number of adherents?
    a. Catholics
    •b. Protestants
    c. Buddhists
    d. Jews
    e. The religiously unaffiliated
13. What percentage of Americans are affiliated with the two leading religious subgroups?
    a. 29 percent
    b. 38 percent
    c. 59 percent
    ‹ d. 78 percent
14. Who are more numerous, Jews or the religiously unaffiliated?
    a. Jews
    . b. The religiously unaffiliated

Your next task will be to run several crosstabulations and answer the questions pertaining to each association. First, run **REGION** by **ETHNIC** and answer Questions 15 through 17. Then, run **REGION** by **RELIG** and answer Questions 18 and 19. Finally, run **REGION** by **RACECEN1** and answer Question 20.

Answer the following set of questions about where each of the subcultural groups are concentrated:

15. Which ethnic subcultural group is most heavily concentrated in the Midwest (Central) region?
    a. Scandinavians   36.5
    b. Eastern Europeans 25.5
    c. Western Europeans 23.9
    ‹ d. American Indians 39
    e. Germans   37
16. In which region are most Hispanics found?
    a. Northeast
    b. South
    c. Central
    . d. West
17. Which following subgroup has the biggest concentration of its members in the Northeast?
    a. Scandinavians
    b. Eastern Europeans
    • c. Italians
    d. Hispanics
    e. Germans
18. Where are Jews most heavily concentrated?
    •a. Northeast
    b. South
    c. Central
    d. West

19. Where are most Protestants located?
    a. Northeast
    ✓ b. South
    c. Central
    d. West
20. In what region does one find most African Americans?
    a. Northeast
    • b. South
    c. Central
    d. West

Your next task will be to crosstabulate **REGION** as the dependent variable, with **BORN** as the independent variable.

Now, answer the following set of questions:

21. In what part of the country are the foreign born most likely to be living?
    a. Northeast
    ✗ b. South
    c. Central
    d. West
22. Which area of the country seems to possess the greatest amount of residential stability? In other words, which area shows the highest percentage of people who continue to live in same area they lived in when they were 16? (Hint: Crosstabulate **REGION** by **REG16**.)
    a. Northeast
    • b. South
    c. Central
    d. West

Now, let us investigate which ethnic subgroups are most and least well established in the United States. Run **PARBORN** as your dependent variable by **ETHNIC** to determine the variations among ethnic subgroups who have parents that were born abroad.

23. Which ethnic subgroup is most likely to have parents born abroad?
    a. Scandinavians
    b. Eastern Europeans
    • c. Asians
    d. Hispanics
    e. Germans
24. Which subgroup is the most well established (most likely to have their parents born here)?
    a. Irish 92.✓
    b. Italians 78.9
    • c. Germans 95.4
    d. Africans 86.5
    e. English 88.1

Run **BORN** as the dependent variable against **ETHNIC** to confirm which groups have migrated here most and least recently and answer the following question:

25. Which group shows the highest percentage of its members being born outside the U.S.?
    a. Scandinavians 5.2
    b. Eastern Europeans 14.9
    • c. Asians   73.6
    d. Hispanics   41.2
    e. Germans   2.7

Run **RELIG** as the dependent variable by **ETHNIC** to determine what religious beliefs the various ethnic subgroups are likely to have and answer the following questions:

26. Which ethnic subgroup has the lowest percentage of Catholics?
    a. Scandinavians
    b. Eastern Europeans
    c. Italians
    d. Hispanics
    e. Africans
27. From what part of the world do most American Jews appear to originate?
    a. Scandinavia
    b. Eastern Europe
    c. Italy
    d. Germany
    e. France
28. What is the predominating faith among people of Hispanic descent?
    a. Catholic
    b. Protestant
    c. Jewish
    d. Religiously unaffiliated
    e. None of the above

Ethnicity is very important in determining many things about how people conduct their everyday life, such as the foods they eat, their social customs like when they encourage their members to marry, and a great many of their daily living habits. One such matter ethnicity may effect is the structure of the household unit, whether a family may be inclined to take in boarders, whether households are multigenerational (or whether they consist only of parents and their young children). Of course, these things are shaped by many other factors, as well. They may also be influenced by religious differences, economic factors, among many other things.

Generate the crosstabulation between UNRELAT (whether a family has non-kin members living within it) and ETHNIC and answer the following question:

29. Which group shows the greatest inclination to live among non-kin family members?
    a. Africans
    b. Asians
    c. Italians
    d. Germans
    e. The differences between the groups could be due to chance

Now crosstabulate having a multigenerational family by ethnicity to see if these cultural groupings differ in their pattern to live in three generation families (or in having adult children and parents live together). Crosstab FAMGEN by ETHNIC and answer questions 30 and 31. Note: Be sure to type year(1998) in the "Selection Filter(s)" field for this crosstabulation.

30. Which group shows the least inclination to have three generational families?
    a. Scandinavians
    b. Eastern Europeans
    c. Hispanics
    d. Irish
    e. Africans
31. Which group shows the greatest inclination to have three-generation families?
    a. Scandinavians
    b. Eastern Europeans
    c. Hispanics
    d. Asians
    e. American Indians

Another factor possibly related to one's ethnicity is the timing of the decision to get married. Of course, this could also be related to the amount of education obtained, social class status, and other factors. Crosstabulate AGEWED with ETHNIC and answer the following question. Note: Be sure to type year(1998) in the "Selection Filter(s)" field for this crosstabulation.

32. Which group shows the greatest inclination not to marry until after age 25?
    a. Asians
    b. Eastern Europeans
    c. Italians
    d. Hispanics
    e. Africans

Now, crosstabulate MARITAL with ETHNIC and answer the following question. Note: Be sure to type year(2002) in the "Selection Filter(s)" field for this crosstabulation.

33. Which groups shows the greatest inclination to marry?
    a. Scandinavians
    b. Eastern Europeans
    c. Italians
    d. Hispanics
    e. English

In the final section of this chapter, we will look at Americans' appreciation and participation in the arts, an important aspect of culture. Culture extends beyond the arts and letters into all man-made products and ideas. In the 1998 General Social Survey, respondents were asked if they had done any of the following activities during the course of the preceding twelve months:

- attended any dance or ballet performances (**DANCE**)
- went to a stage play (**DRAMA**)
- went to a classical music or opera performance (**GOMUSIC**)
- made any art or crafts objects (**MAKEART**)
- took part in any music, dance or theatrical performance (**PERFORM**)
- played any musical instruments (**PLYMUSIC**)
- attended any popular music performances (**POPMUSIC**)
- read any works of fiction (**READFICT**)
- seen any films in a movie theatre (**SEEMOVIE**)
- went to any art museums or galleries (**VISITART**)

Tabulate each of the following variables: **DANCE, DRAMA, GOMUSIC, MAKEART, PERFORM, PLYMUSIC, POPMUSIC, READFICT, SEEMOVIE,** and **VISITART.** Remember to run 10 separate tables and be sure to type **year(1998)** in the "Selection Filter(s)" field. You may need to print them out or record the results on a piece of paper.

Now answer the following five questions.

34. Which of the ten activities was the most popular?
    a. Seeing movies
    b. Reading fiction
    c. Attending popular music concerts
    d. Making art or crafts objects
35. Which was the second most popular activity?
    a. Seeing movies
    b. Reading fiction
    c. Attending popular music concerts
    d. Making art or crafts objects
36. Which was the least popular one?
    a. Going to dance performances
    b. Attending dramatic theater performances
    c. Performing in theatrical events
    d. Going to classical music concerts
    e. Visiting art galleries

37. What percentage of respondents engaged in the most popular activity?
   a. 68
   b. 45
   c. 85
   d. 38
   e. 54

38. Does arts participation (MAKEART; PERFORM; PLYMUSIC) exceed being an art consumer (DANCE; DRAMA; GOMUSIC; POPMUSIC; READFICT; SEEMOVIE; VISITART)? (Hint: Calculate the mean for the three art participation items and compare it to the mean for the seven participation items one notes.)
   a. There are substantially higher rates for arts participation than for arts consumption
   b. There are substantially higher rates for arts consumption than for arts participation
   c. The average differences fall below five percent of each other, suggesting similarity between the two

Now, we'll be looking at some bivariate relationships. Keep in mind that you need to select "Statistics" from "Other options" on the SDA's "Frequencies or crosstabulation" screen. Run READFICT as the dependent variable against SEX to determine whether there is a gender difference in reading fiction.

39. Which gender reads more fiction?
   a. Men read more than women
   b. Women read more than men
   c. There were no significant differences in reading fiction

Now, run PERFORM as the dependent variable against RACE to determine whether there is a race difference in giving music, dance or theatrical performances.

40. Are there race differences in giving music, dance or theatrical performances?
   a. African Americans give performances more than whites
   b. Whites give performances more than African Americans
   c. There were no significant race differences in giving music, dance or theatrical performances.

41. Do younger people play musical instruments (PLYMUSIC) more than middle-aged or older ones? (Hint: Use AGE as your independent variable.)
   a. Younger people play musical instruments more than the middle-aged or elderly
   b. Middle-aged people play musical instruments more than older people
   c. There were no significant age differences in playing musical instruments

42. Are there significant ethnic differences in going to theatrical events? (Hint: Run DRAMA by ETHNIC)
    a. Western Europeans go to theaters most often
    b. The English and Germans are the most inclined to attend theaters
    c. There were no significant ethnic differences in theater attendance
    d. Hispanics and African Americans go to the theaters least often
    e. None of the above choices are correct
43. Are there regional differences in movie attendance? (Hint: Run SEEMOVIE by REGION)
    a. Westerners go to movies most often
    b. Northeasterners are the biggest moviegoers
    c. Southerners go to movies the most
    d. There are no significant regional differences in movie attendance

ESSAY QUESTIONS

4–A   Explain why the groups mentioned in questions 30 and 31 differ in their inclinations to live in three-generational families. You may review previous research literature in developing your answer.

4–B   Explain why the groups mentioned in your answer to question 32 may be inclined to marry late. Review previous research literature in your answer.

4–C   From this dataset, select another dependent variable of your own choosing and relate it to the independent variable ETHNIC. Interpret your findings and discuss whether there is a statistically significant association between the variables or subgroups in your hypothesis. Cite previous research evidence.

4–D   Focusing on any one of the ten groups covered here, and reading published research about that group, discuss some of their distinctive behavior patterns, values, and aspects of life style. Demonstrate with the GSS 2002 database how they differ from other ethnic groups in the United States along some of these selected dimensions.

4–E   In the 1998 GSS Culture Module, respondents were asked whether they felt that local, state or the federal government should assist arts organizations.(LOCALART; NATLART; STATEART) Analyze these responses and prepare a table showing which government branch is the most preferred one for supporting the arts. Make another table showing whether any forms of arts participation or consumption is related in any way to the belief that government should help support the arts.

CHAPTER PROJECT

From the ten varieties of arts participation and consumption covered in the 1998 GSS Culture Module, see if you can create a social profile of arts enthusiasts. Do they come from any particular regional, ethnic, social class, gender or age group? Present all tables that support your conclusions.

REFERENCES

Davis, James A. 1987. *Social Differences in Contemporary America,* Orlando, FL: Harcourt, Brace, Jovanovich.

SYNTAX GUIDE

1. Go to: http://sda.berkeley.edu/cgi-bin12/hsda?harcsda+gss02.
2. Select "Frequencies or crosstabulation".
3. Click **Start**.
4. Enter the **DEPENDENT** variable in the "Row" box.
5. Enter the **INDEPENDENT** variable in the "Column" box.
6. Select the "Column" option under "Percentages."
7. In the "Selection Filter(s)" box, enter **year(2002)**. Note that there are some exceptions. See AGEWED, FAMGEN, and MARITAL for details.
8. Under "Other options," select "Statistics," "Question text," and "Color coding."
9. Click **Run the Table**.

RECODES

Please note that all recodes can also be copied and pasted from either www.ncc.edu/users/feigelb/sda.htm or www.ablongman.com/feigelman3e. If you type the recode syntax in, make sure that you type *exactly* what is shown below.

age(r: *-39 "Less than 40 years old"; 40-60 "40-60 years old"; 61-* "More than 60 years old")

agewed(r: *-20 "less than 21"; 21-25 "21-25"; 26-* "26 and older")
   Note: When using AGEWED, type year(1994) in the "Selection Filter(s)" box.

ethnic(r:1,39 "Af";4,8,24 "En";14 "Iri";15 "Ita";2,6,13,21,23,33-35 "EEu";11 "Ger";7,9,19,26 "Sca";17,22,25,28,38 "His";3,10,18,27,36 "WEu";5,16,20,31,37,40 "As"; 97 "US"; 30 "AIn";12,29,32,41 "Otr")

famgen(r: 1-4 "One or two-generation families"; 5-6 "Three-generational families")
   Note: When using FAMGEN, type year(1998) in the "Selection Filter(s)" box.

marital(r: 5 "Never married"; 1-4 "Ever-married")
   Note: When using MARITAL, type year(1994) in the "Selection Filter(s)" box.

parborn(r: 0 "Both born in U.S."; 1-2 "One parent foreign born"; 8 "Both parents born overseas")

race(r: 1 "White"; 2 "Black")

reg16(r: 0 "Foreign-born"; 1-2 "Northeast"; 3-4 "Central"; 5-7 "South"; 8-9 "West")

region(r: 1-2 "Northeast"; 3-4 "Central"; 5-7 "South"; 8-9 "West")

unrelat(r: 0 "None"; 1-8 "1 or more are not related")

The following variables can be used directly (no recode is necessary):
   BORN; DANCE; DRAMA; GOMUSIC; GRANBORN; LOCALART; MAKEART; NATLART; PERFORM; PLYMUSIC; POPMUSIC; RACECEN1; READFICT; RELIG; SEEMOVIE; SEX; STATEART; VISITART

CHAPTER 5

Urbanization and Suburbanization

Approximately a century ago, the French sociologist Emile Durkheim wrote a book, entitled *The Division of Labor in Society*, which described how his contemporary urban society represented a distinct contrast from all past societies. For Durkheim, the urban order brought forth a new cohesion in society that he called organic solidarity, meaning that people were united to each other by their complementary roles in the production process. In the modern urban–industrial order, each person needed other members of society for their diverging and interrelated production activities. This represented a sharp break from the agrarian past, where society was united by an almost tribal-like togetherness based on social similarities, which Durkheim called mechanical solidarity.

Durkheim acknowledged that the new order afforded unprecedented opportunities for creative expression and individualism. Yet, it also fostered an anonymous atmosphere, in which almost anyone could become prey to anyone else, who wanted to "use" them. In the less regulated social environment of the city, crime would become a more commonplace occurrence. We will now examine Durkheim's hypotheses about urban crime with the GSS 1994 data. To get started:

1. Go to the SDA website: http://sda.berkeley.edu.
2. Click on **SDA Archive** on the upper left corner of the page.
3. Under the subtitle "National Omnibus Surveys," click on **GSS Cumulative Datafile 1972–2002**.
4. Select the option "Frequencies or crosstabulation" and click **Start**.
5. The layout of the page that opens is shown in Figure 5.1.

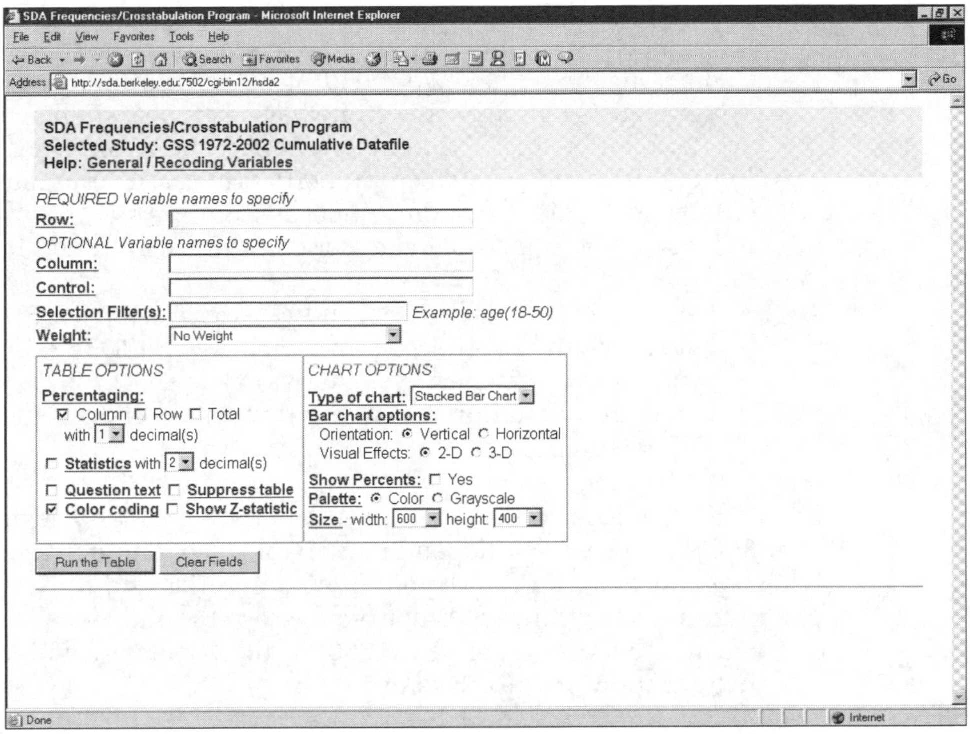

FIGURE 5.1

6. Put the **DEPENDENT** variable in the "Row" box and **INDEPENDENT** variable in the Column box.
7. Since we are working on the 1994 GSS file, be sure to type **year(1994)** in the "Selection Filter(s)" Box.
8. Select the "Statistics" and "Question text" option from the "Table Options" box.
9. *Don't forget to apply the correct recode language for each question.*

Begin by tabulating being afraid to walk at night in your neighborhood (**FEAR**) as the dependent variable by community of residence (**SRCBELT**) as the independent variable and answer the following questions.

1. Being afraid to walk at night in the local neighborhood appears to be highest in which type of community?
   a. Urban
   b. Suburban
   c. Small cities
   d. Rural areas
   e. Fear of walking at night in neighborhood does not appear to vary much by community
2. Type of community displays what kind of association with fear of walking at night in the local neighborhood?
   a. Below the level of statistical significance
   b. Statistically significant
   c. Unclear or uncertain
   d. None of the above

Although there may be a variation in people's fear of crime depending upon the type of communities they live in, they could be mistaken when it comes to the actual likelihood of being criminally victimized. Many criminologists classify crimes into various types, such as "index" crimes, "white collar" crimes, "victimless" crimes, and so on. One popular distinction that is made is between property crimes, like burglary or auto theft, and crimes against persons, such as murder, rape, or robbery. Several dimensions of crime-related experiences were included in the GSS:

- being a victim of a burglary in the past year (**BURGLR**)
- being a victim of a robbery in the past year (**ROBBRY**)
- ever being threatened by a gun (**GUN**)
- personal acquaintance with a murder victim in the last year (**CIDEKNEW**)

Using each of these as dependent variables, and type of community (**SRCBELT**) as your independent variable, see whether there is any correspondence between the types of communities and the real risks of being criminally victimized. When you assess the murder victim-hypothesis, you will have to enter **year(1990)** in the "Selection Filter(s)" Box, since that question was not asked in 1994.

3. Burglary appears to be highest in which type of community?
   a. Urban
   b. Suburban
   c. Small cities
   d. Rural areas
   e. Though there appear to be differences in burglary experiences by type of community, they fall short of statistical significance
4. Robbery appears to be highest in which type of community?
   a. Urban
   b. Suburban
   c. Small cities
   d. Rural areas
   e. Though there appear to be differences in robbery experiences by type of community, they fall short of statistical significance
5. Being threatened with a gun appears to be highest in which type of community?
   a. Urban
   b. Suburban
   c. Small cities
   d. Rural areas
   e. Being threatened with a gun does not appear to vary much by community
6. Knowing someone who was murdered appears to be highest in which type of community?
   a. Urban
   b. Suburban
   c. Small cities
   d. Rural areas
   e. Knowing someone who was murdered does not appear to vary much by community

Another line of sociological theorizing about cities is that with their many different and competing groups (especially in the largest cities), an uncaring atmosphere is fostered with every person for himself or herself. Few people care about their community's welfare, and many develop attitudes of cynicism and pessimism. Sociologists refer to *anomie* as the condition where society displays a state of normlessness—a state where no rules apply or where the rules contradict each other. Intergroup urban competition and conflict are believed to inspire anomie. Some sociologists have developed the term *anomia* to refer to the individual's sense of being anomic—of being cut off from meaningful affiliations in society, as well as harboring attitudes of fatalism, cynicism, and a generally negative outlook.

The GSS included three attitude questions about anomia in its 1994 survey. It asked respondents whether they agreed or disagreed with the following statements:

- "In spite of what some people say, the condition of the average man is getting worse." (**ANOMIA5**)
- "It is hardly fair to bring a child into this world with the way things look for the future." (**ANOMIA6**)
- "Most people in public office are not interested in the problems of the average man." (**ANOMIA7**)

If we add these three responses together we can establish an anomia scale. You will have to make your own anomia scale, **TOTANOMA**, based on the sum of positive responses to these three questions. To create the scale, carry out the following instructions:

1. Go to: http://sda.berkeley.edu/cgi-bin12/hsda?harcsda+gss02.
2. Select "Compute a new variable".
3. Click **Start**.
4. Type: **totanoma=anomia5+anomia6+anomia7** into the box labeled "EXPRESSION TO DEFINE THE NEW VARIABLE".
5. Select "Yes" for the option "Replace that variable, if it already exists?".
6. Click **Start Computing**.

The newly created anomia scale (**TOTANOMA**) has a few categories. Those respondents who showed greatest level of anomia on all three questions will have a score of 6. The higher the number, the lower the level of anomia. For the next few questions, be sure to use the recoded syntax for **TOTANOMA** when you perform crosstabulation tasks.

If this sociological theorizing about urban residents is correct, then urbanites should show higher levels of anomia than those living in less densely populated places.

Now, answer the following questions. (Remember to enter **year(1994)** in the "Selection Filter(s)" Box.)

7. Anomia (**TOTANOMA**) appears to be highest in which types of community (run **TOTANOMA** by **SRCBELT**)?
   a. Urban
   b. Suburban
   c. Small cities
   d. Rural areas
   e. Anomia does not appear to vary much by community
8. Type of community displays what kind of an association with anomia?
   a. Below the level of statistical significance
   b. Statistically significant
   c. Unclear or uncertain
   d. None of the above

Now let's see the trends for **TOTANOMA**. Run **TOTANOMA** by **YEAR** (as the independent variable). Be sure to leave the "Selection Filter(s)" Box empty for this question. Then answer the following question.

9. Respondents in what years reported the greatest level of **TOTANOMA**?
   a. 1975–79
   b. 1980–84
   c. 1985–89
   d. 1990–94

One might also conclude that people who display high levels of anomia would be more apathetic and unconcerned about their communities. To verify whether anomia has any real behavioral consequences, try running several other variables that display whether people actually are involved and care about their communities:

- whether they regularly read newspapers (**NEWS**)
- whether they belong to any voluntary associations (**MEMNUM**)
- whether they vote in elections (**VOTE92**)

Try to verify if **TOTANOMA** is associated with each of these variables. (Hint: Make **TOTANOMA** the independent variable.) Be sure to enter **year(1994)** in the "Selection Filter(s)" Box for questions 10 through 21.

10. The crosstabulation between **TOTANOMA** and newspaper reading (**NEWS**) shows:
    a. Anomia may be linked to less newspaper reading
    b. Anomia is definitely not linked to newspaper reading
    c. The relationship is statistically significant
    d. The relationship falls way below the level of statistical significance
    e. b and d only

11. The crosstabulation between **TOTANOMA** and voluntary associational membership (**MEMNUM**) shows:
    a. Anomia is linked to fewer organizational memberships
    b. Anomia is not linked to organizational memberships
    c. The relationship is statistically significant
    d. Anomia is linked to more organizational memberships
    e. a and c only

12. The crosstabulation between **TOTANOMA** and voting (**VOTE92**) shows:
    a. Anomia is linked to lower voting rates
    b. Anomia is not linked to voting rates
    c. The relationship is statistically significant
    d. The relationship falls below the level of statistical significance
    e. a and c only

13 Is it also true that urban residents are less likely to read newspapers than people living in other types of communities? Tabulate newspaper reading (**NEWS**) by type of community (**SRCBELT**) to verify this hypothesis.
    a. Big city residents are the least likely to read newspapers daily
    b. Suburban residents are the most likely to read newspapers daily
    c. Small city residents are the most likely to read newspapers daily
    d. It is unclear whether there are any differences here

14. Can you also conclude that urban residents are less likely to belong to organizations than people living in other types of communities? (Tabulate the number of voluntary organizational memberships (**MEMNUM**) by type of community (**SRCBELT**) to verify this hypothesis.)
    a. Yes
    b. No
    c. It is unclear whether there are any differences here

15. Can you also conclude that urban residents are less likely to vote than people living in other types of communities? (Tabulate voting in a presidential election (**VOTE92**) by type of community (**SRCBELT**) to verify this hypothesis.)
    a. Yes
    b. No
    c. It is unclear whether there are any differences here

Another assertion made by some sociologists about city living is that it tends to atomize people. Self-centered urbanites, pursuing their ambitions and personal goals, have little time for socializing and especially for deep attachments to their extended families. Many analysts have speculated that urbanites (and suburbanites as well, for that matter) are driven so completely by their success and career ambitions that family and community participation is likely to assume a secondary place in their lives. The GSS asked people how frequently they socialized with family and friends. Five questions were asked of respondents in reporting their frequency of socializing with:

- parents (**SOCPARS**)
- brothers and sisters (**SOCSIBS**)
- any relatives (**SOCREL**)

- neighbors (SOCOMMUN)
- friends (SOCFREND)

Investigate each of these crosstabulations (with SRCBELT as the independent variable) and then answer the following questions.

16. Examining each of the five crosstabulations shows that, in at least one instance, urbanites and suburbanites are *more* inclined to frequent socializing than those living in other kinds of communities. This applies to socialization with:
    a. Parents
    b. Brother and sisters
    c. Any relatives
    d. Neighbors
    e. Friends

17. The crosstabulation between socializing with neighbors (SOCOMMUN) and community type (SRCBELT) shows:
    a. Urbanization may be linked to less socializing with neighbors
    b. Urbanization is not linked to less socializing with neighbors
    c. The relationship is statistically significant
    d. The relationship falls substantially below the level of statistical significance
    e. b and d

18. The crosstabulations between socializing with different groups of family members (SOCREL, SOCPARS, SOCSIBS) and type of community (SRCBELT) shows:
    a. Urbanization may be linked to less socializing with some groups of extended family members
    b. Urbanization does not seem to be linked to different (and reduced) frequencies of kin association
    c. Urbanites and suburbanites show great differences in their patterns of socializing with extended family members
    d. All of the above
    e. Only a and c

Some have claimed that urban living is associated with the fragmentation of family life. Investigate this hypothesis by crosstabulating getting divorced (EVDIV) with type of community (SRCBELT).

19. The crosstabulations between getting divorced (EVDIV) and type of community (SRCBELT) shows:
    a. Urbanization seems clearly linked to higher divorce rates
    b. Urbanization does not seem to be linked to higher divorce; more divorces are found among suburbanites
    c. The relationship is statistically significant
    d. The relationship is statistically insignificant
    e. None of the above

Why people have close or infrequent associations with their kin is an important issue that should also be examined. A factor that could explain whether people have frequent or infrequent contact with extended kin is whether they moved from where they grew up. Those who moved are probably less likely to see their relatives as often as those who have remained in the same communities. Tabulate mobility from where one lived at age 16 (**MOBILE16**), as the dependent variable, by type of community (**SRCBELT**), as the independent variable, to see whether there is any association between these two factors.

20. Are there any differences in mobility in the different types of communities?
    a. Yes, suburbanites show the most movement and rural residents the least, and the differences are significant
    b. Yes, small town and rural residents show the most mobility and differences are significant
    c. The differences between the different types of communities are small and statistically insignificant
    d. No, the differences between types of communities, though apparent, fall below the level of statistical significance

It has also been claimed that race is another factor correlated with the frequency of visiting kin.

21. Which race appears to visit all groups of extended kin most often (run **SOCREL** by **RACE**)?
    a. Whites
    b. African Americans
    c. Visiting is similar in both groups
    d. The relationship between **socrel** and **race** is not significant.
    e. Only c and d

Now, let's investigate the predominating patterns of residence in the United States and see how they may be shifting at the present time. Begin by tabulating type of community alone (**SRCBELT**) and answer the next question. Make sure to use **year(2002)** in the "Selection Filter(s)" Box.

22. In which type of community does it appear that most Americans now live?
    a. Large cities (the 100 largest urban places in the U.S.)
    b. Suburban areas (of the 100 largest cities)
    c. Small cities (in counties having towns with over 10,000 population, but not among the top 100 urban places)
    d. Rural places (in counties with no towns of greater than 10,000 population)
23. Crosstabulate types of communities (**SRCBELT**) by **YEAR** (as the independent variable). Be sure to leave the "Selection Filter(s)" Box empty. Which of the following statements is true?
    a. The number of respondents living in rural areas has been increasing since 1970s
    b. Since the 1970s, the number of respondents living in small cities has remained highest
    c. The relationship between **SRCBELT** and **YEAR** is not significant
    d. The number of respondents living in large cities has been increasing since 1970s
    e. None of the above

For questions 24 through 36, be sure to enter **year(2002)** in the "Selection Filter(s)" Box.

24. Using one's residence at age 16 (**RES16**) as your selected variable, where did the greatest percentage of Americans live when they were aged 16?
    a. Large cities
    b. Suburban areas
    c. Small cities
    d. Rural places
25. Looking at the particular percentages for **RES16** and **SRCBELT** side by side, what does it suggest about which communities have been growing the most in recent years?
    a. Large cities
    b. Suburban areas
    c. Small cities
    d. Rural places
26. Looking at this same display, what does it suggest about which communities have been diminishing the most in recent years?
    a. Large cities
    b. Suburban areas
    c. Small cities
    d. Rural places

Now, run **AGE** by **SRCBELT** and speculate on future growth and decline. (Hint: A high percentage of younger age segments could suggest a growing population, while high percentages of older, past-child-bearing-age persons could mean eventual population decline.)

27. What does this crosstabulation suggest about which communities will see the most growth in the future?
    a. Large cities and suburbs
    b. Small cities
    c. Rural places
    d. There are no significant differences between age and community type
28. What does this crosstabulation suggest about which communities will be declining?
    a. Large cities
    b. Suburban areas
    c. Small cities
    d. Rural places

Now let us try to identify the demographic correlates of residence. (Hint: In this last set of questions you will want to use the type of community (**SRCBELT**) as the dependent variable and each of the potential demographic correlates as independent variables.)

29. Running type of community (SRCBELT) by marital status (MARITAL), what does it suggest about where the greatest concentrations of the never married are likely to live?
   a. In large cities
   b. In suburbs
   c. In small cities
   d. In rural places
   e. No particular concentrations are noted
30. Tabulating type of community (SRCBELT) by age differences (AGE) where are young people most likely to live?
   a. Large cities and suburban areas
   b. Small cities
   c. Rural places
   d. No particular concentrations are noted
31. Based upon the same crosstabulation, compared to other age groups, where are the majority of older folks likely to reside?
   a. Large cities
   b. Suburban areas
   c. Small cities
   d. Rural places
   e. There are no significant differences noted between age and type of community
32. Tabulating type of community (SRCBELT) by ethnic differences (ETHNIC), which race/ethnic group is most overrepresented in the cities?
   a. Hispanics
   b. Africans
   c. Scandinavians
   d. English
   e. Eastern Europeans
33. Based upon the same crosstabulation, which ethnic groups is most overrepresented in the rural regions?
   a. Hispanics
   b. Africans
   c. Irish
   d. English
   e. American Indians
34. Tabulating type of community (SRCBELT) by regional differences (REGION), which part of the country has the greatest proportional rural population?
   a. East
   b. Central
   c. South
   d. West
   e. There are no statistically significant differences in community residence patterns by regional differences

35. Tabulating type of community (**SRCBELT**) by religious differences (**RELIG**), which religious group is proportionally the most urbanized?
    a. Catholics
    b. Protestants
    c. Other religion
    d. Jews
    e. Those unaffiliated with religion
36. Which religious group is proportionally the most inclined to live in rural areas?
    a. Catholics
    b. Protestants
    c. Other religion
    d. Jews
    e. Those unaffiliated with religion

ESSAY QUESTIONS

5–A   Read Chapter 6 on how to apply control variables and re-examine questions 7, 10, 11 and 12 in this chapter. Apply the control variable of social class differences. First sort the data into two separate prestige groups using **prestg80(r:17-39;40-86)** as the control variable. With this recode, you will be able to split the sample into two prestige groups: low prestige workers (blue collar occupations) and higher prestige workers (white collar workers). Re-run each of the five crosstabulations in questions 7, 10, 11 and 12, controlling for prestige differences. Present all the tabular results and discuss what your findings show about differences in **TOTANOMA** by type of community, and whether newspaper reading, voluntary associational membership and voting are associated with differences in **TOTANOMA** scores when prestige differences are controlled.

5–B   Referring to some sociological literature of your choice, write an essay on the diverging patterns of kinship, friendship, and organizational participation found today in American communities of differing sizes. Reflect on how the GSS data supports or takes exception to the notions investigated.

5–C   Selecting any dependent variable in the GSS database as your dependent variable, develop a hypothesis (not already mentioned here) on how urbanization is likely to affect that variable. Review previous literature on this hypothesis. Run the crosstabulation, and discuss and evaluate your results. Suggest reasons for any discrepancies between your findings and the results of prior studies.

5–D   Develop your own theory of how urbanization could act as a control variable—where it mediates or changes the association in another bivariate relationship. (Look at the example cited in Chapter 6, where gender influenced the association between marital status and general happiness.) Investigate an association that you think would be altered depending upon whether people lived in densely populated places or less densely populated ones. (For this analysis combine urban and suburban residents into a new single category, and also combine small city and rural residents together, too. Use srcbelt (r: 1-4 "urban"; 5-6 "Rural and small city") as your urbanization variable.) Explain why changes would be expected to occur in the bivariate association when your control variable is applied. Compare and contrast your prediction on how the association differed in the densely populated and less densely populated places with the actual results.

CHAPTER PROJECT

As sociologists frequently recognize, sociology often produces evidence that takes sharp exception to the conventional wisdom shared by members of society. Referring to any of the data trends presented in this chapter, discuss how this notion could be true in a particular case. What are the commonsense understandings about the trend or relationship? How do these GSS findings take exception to it? What are the theoretical dimensions to the issue that many lay people may be overlooking. Discuss.

SYNTAX GUIDE

RECODES

Please note that all recodes can also be copied and pasted from either www.ncc.edu/users/feigelb/sda.htm or www.ablongman.com/feigelman3e. If you type the recode syntax in, make sure that you type *exactly* what is shown below.

age(r: 18-29 "18-29"; 30-39 "30-39"; 40-49 "40-49"; 50-64 "50-64"; 65-* "65 or higher")

cideknew(r: 0 "0"; 1 "1"; 2-9 "2 or more")
>   *Note: Enter* year(1990) *in the "Selection Filter(s)" Box when* CIDEKNEW *is analyzed.*

ethnic(r:1,39 "Af";4,8,24 "En";14 "Iri";15 "Ita";2,6,13,21,23,33-35 "EEu";11 "Ger";7,9,19,26 "Sca";17,22,25,28,38 "His";3,10,18,27,36 "WEu";5,16,20,31,37,40 "As"; 97 "US"; 30 "AIn";12,29,32,41 "Otr")

evdiv(1,2)

memnum(r: 0 "None"; 1 "One"; 2 "Two"; 3-* "3 or more")

prestg80 (r:17-39; 40-86)

race(1,2)

region(r: 1-2 "Northeast"; 3-4 "Central"; 5-7 "South"; 8-9 "West")

relig(r:1 "Protestant"; 2 "Catholic"; 3 "Jewish"; 4 "None"; 5-9 "Other") res16(r: 6 "Large city"; 4-5 "Suburbanite"; 3 "Small city"; 1-2 "Rural and farm")

socfrend(r: 1-3 "Weekly"; 4-7 "Once a monthly or less")

socommun(r: 1-3 "Weekly"; 4-7 "Once a monthly or less")

socpars(r: 1-3 "Weekly"; 4-7 "Once a monthly or less")

socrel(r: 1-3 "Weekly"; 4-7 "Once a monthly or less")

socsibs(r: 1-3 "Weekly"; 4-7 "Once a monthly or less")

srcbelt(r: 1-2 "Large city"; 3-4 "Suburbanite"; 5 "Small city"; 6 "Rural and farm")

totanoma(r:3 "High"; 4 "Moderate"; 5-6 "Low")

vote92(1,2)

year(r: 1972-1974 "1972-74"; 1975-1979 "1975-1979"; 1980-1984 "1980-84"; 1985-1989 "1985-89"; 1990-1994 "1990-94"; 1995-2000 "1995-2002")

No recode needed: BURGLR, FEAR, GUN, NEWS, MOBILE16; ROBBRY

CHAPTER 6

Finer Points of Crosstabular Analyses

Thus far, all the clear-cut and precise answers we have obtained about significant and insignificant relationships may suggest that doing scientific analysis can be a rather simple and straightforward task; just key in the variable names, select the significance tests, let the computer do the calculations, and then write up the results.

But it isn't nearly that simple. An important concern of the scientist is to integrate present findings into the established body of results that have been obtained by previous studies. Sometimes, present findings confirm or extend previous evidence. Frequently, however, results are enigmatic or inconsistent with the body of findings obtained by past research. Scientists are obliged to explain why certain findings have presently emerged; what theoretical factors underlie the observed patterns; what the particular features associated with the time, place, and conditions of the study (such as the wording of the particular questions given to survey respondents) make such findings now occur; and what could account for any inconsistencies between these data and previous scientific evidence. Often, the many fragments of research evidence form a puzzling and confused total picture.

Present scientific findings must inevitably be reconciled with those obtained by previous studies. One of the problems associated with integrating scientific results is distinguishing between spurious associations and theoretically meaningful ones. *Spurious associations* are not causally appropriate; they are simply coincidental relations. Tests of significance do not protect researchers from obtaining associations that are theoretically unintelligible or absurd. Scientific analysts must be able to detect spurious associations from relationships that are causally significant ones.

If a claim were to be made that storks bring babies, nonsensical as it may seem, it may not be such a simple task for the scientist to discredit this hypothesis by examining it through observation alone. Observers going out into communities would note a high volume of stork sightings in places with more births per household; and lower rates of stork sightings in the communities with fewer births. Thus, provisionally at least, the scientist would be unable to dispose of the storks-bring-babies hypothesis on empirical grounds until a different order of observations were undertaken.

Control variables become important to the scientist to help detect spuriousness. A *control variable* is another variable introduced into an analysis between two other variables to see whether it affects their association. In the case of the storks-bring-babies hypothesis, urbanization might be a useful control variable. Assuming we found an association between stork sightings and the number of births, we might then subdivide the sample into urbanized and rural subsamples. Our contention would be that urbanization—rather than storks—affects the birth rate. We could claim that urban communities, with the high prices levied there for living space, tend to discourage people from raising large families. (Cities also discourage storks from establishing nests and finding food, amidst their hostile environments of pervasive concrete and steel.) By contrast, we might also argue that in the countryside, where space is far less costly, people find it easier to have larger families (and storks, too, can nest and forage more readily in such open, pastoral settings).

The crucial test for spuriousness would be to examine whether the statistically significant association between storks and birth rates found in the undifferentiated population disappears when it is examined within each of the two subpopulations of urban and rural residents. Now the association should disappear, suggesting that it was urbanization, rather than storks, that affected the birth rate variations. It is important that associations between variables not only be observationally valid; they must jibe with preexistent scientific knowledge.

Let us offer an example from the General Social Surveys, showing how an apparent relationship between two seemingly linked variables could be dissolved with the application of a crucial control variable.

1. Go to the SDA website at http://sda.berkeley.edu.
2. Click **SDA Archive**, and then select the **GSS Cumulative Datafile 1972–2000**. Select "Frequencies or crosstabulation" and click **Start**.
3. Enter **abany** in the "Row" box.
4. Type the following text into the "Column" box: **race(r:1 White"; 2 "Black")**. This will recode **RACE** into a two category response of "Whites" and "Blacks," and omit the diverse category of "Others."
5. Type **year(1994)** in the "Selection Filter(s)" box.
6. Select "Column" from the "Percentage" option list.
7. Under "Other options," select "Statistics," "Question text," and "Color coding."
8. Click **Run the Table**.

When you tabulate the results, you should find an 8 percent difference between whites and black in accepting abortion for any reason; you will also note that this is significant with Chi-Square at the .03 level. It therefore seems clear that African Americans are more opposed to abortion for any reason than whites. In Table 6.1 you will see the two-way table showing abortion attitudes and race.

However, some analysts might be skeptical that skin color differences alone could be that important in shaping abortion attitudes. For those

Frequency Distribution				
Cells contain: -Column percent -N of cases		Race		
		1 Whites	2 Blacks	*ROW TOTAL*
abany	1: YES	**47.7** 763	**40.2** 101	*46.7* *864*
	2: NO	**52.3** 835	**59.8** 150	*53.3* *985*
	COL TOTAL	*100.0* *1,598*	*100.0* *251*	*100.0* *1,849*
Means		1.52	1.60	1.53
Std Devs		.50	.49	.50

Color coding:	<-2.0	<-1.0	<0.0	>0.0	>1.0	>2.0	Z
N in each cell:	Smaller than expected			Larger than expected			

Summary Statistics					
Eta* =	.05	Gamma = .15	Chisq(P) =	4.91	(p= 0.03)
R =	.05	Tau-b = .05	Chisq(LR) =	4.95	(p= 0.03)
Somers' d* = .08		Tau-c = .04	df =	1	

*Row variable treated as the dependent variable.

TABLE 6.1

thinking this way, it might seem that the distinctive religious affiliations shared among African Americans, rather than their skin color, would be the more important factor behind their abortion opposition. It should be noted that African Americans are widely affiliated with various Protestant churches with many linked to the Baptist Churches, Jehovah Witnesses, the Assembly of God, and other Evangelistic Churches. All these churches are known as fundamentalist ones. And these so-called "Bible-belt" churches have generally shown a strong condemnation toward abortion. Thus, it may well be that racial differences have less to do with abortion disapproval than with religious fundamentalism.

We'll examine the two separate tables showing abortion attitudes and race among the Fundamentalists (Table 6.2) and Non-Fundamentalists (Table 6.3). Note how the statistically significant race differences between abortion attitudes and race shown in the two-way table changes when the control variable is applied. The racial differences in abortion attitudes have faded and the statistical significances have dropped. These tables therefore show that it was religious fundamentalism, rather than race, that explains these differences in abortion opposition.

An additional value of applying control variables is for a better understanding of the nature of an association. It can help us to identify within which subpopulations a relationship may be strengthened or weakened; it can help us to distinguish the conditions under which the two-way

Statistics for fund = 1(Fundamentalists)

Cells contain: -Column percent -N of cases		race		
		1 Whites	2 Blacks	*ROW TOTAL*
abany	1: YES	**33.1** 149	**34.4** 52	*33.4* *201*
	2: NO	**66.9** 301	**65.6** 99	*66.6* *400*
	COL TOTAL	*100.0* *450*	*100.0* *151*	*100.0* *601*
Means		1.67	1.66	1.67
Std Devs		.50	.50	.50

Color coding:	<-2.0	<-1.0	<0.0	>0.0	>1.0	>2.0	Z
N in each cell:	Smaller than expected			Larger than expected			

Summary Statistics for fund = 1(Fundamentalists)

Eta* =	.01	Gamma =	-.03	Chisq(P) =	.09	(p= 0.77)
R =	-.01	Tau-b =	-.01	Chisq(LR) =	.09	(p= 0.77)
Somers' d* =	-.01	Tau-c =	-.01	df =	1	

*Row variable treated as the dependent variable.

TABLE 6.2

Statistics for fund = 2(Other Religous Groups)

Cells contain: -Column percent -N of cases		Race		
		1 Whites	2 Blacks	*ROW TOTAL*
abany	1: YES	**53.1** 579	**48.9** 43	*52.8* *622*
	2: NO	**46.9** 511	**51.1** 45	*47.2* *556*
	COL TOTAL	*100.0* *1,090*	*100.0* *88*	*100.0* *1,178*
Means		1.47	1.51	1.47
Std Devs		.50	.50	.50

Color coding:	<-2.0	<-1.0	<0.0	>0.0	>1.0	>2.0	Z
N in each cell:	Smaller than expected			Larger than expected			

Summary Statistics for fund = 2(Other Religous Groups)

Eta* =	.02	Gamma =	.08	Chisq(P) =	.59	(p= 0.44)
R =	.02	Tau-b =	.02	Chisq(LR) =	.59	(p= 0.44)
Somers' d* =	.04	Tau-c =	.01	df =	1	

*Row variable treated as the dependent variable.

TABLE 6.3

association is supported. Let us examine some additional data showing how control variables deepen our understanding of causal associations and the interactions between other potential causal elements.

With the 1994 GSS database, we will explore the crosstabulation between marital status and people's feelings of personal happiness—whether they describe themselves as very happy, somewhat happy or not happy at all. Table 6.4 shows the presently married to be more inclined to report feelings of happiness than all other subgroups. Correspondingly, those now separated also report higher levels of unhappiness than all others with diverging marital statuses. We will now examine this same hypothesis among men (Table 6.5) and women (Table 6.6) separately, to see if it yields any additional insights.

For women alone, the pattern appears to be much the same as for both genders combined, with the married being the happiest subgroup, and the separated the least happy. However, something divergent is noted for males, in that widowed men seem to be the most unhappy of

Frequency Distribution						
	marital					
Cells contain: -Column percent -N of cases	1 MARRIED	2 WIDOWED	3 DIVORCED	4 SEPARATED	5 NEVER MARRIED	*ROW TOTAL*
happy 1: VERY HAPPY	38.1 585	18.1 52	18.0 80	13.7 14	20.7 126	*28.8* *857*
2: PRETTY HAPPY	54.4 835	62.4 179	64.2 285	58.8 60	65.2 397	*59.0* *1,756*
3: NOT TOO HAPPY	7.5 115	19.5 56	17.8 79	27.5 28	14.1 86	*12.2* *364*
COL TOTAL	*100.0* *1,535*	*100.0* *287*	*100.0* *444*	*100.0* *102*	*100.0* *609*	*100.0* *2,977*
Means	1.69	2.01	2.00	2.14	1.93	1.83
Std Devs	.60	.61	.60	.63	.59	.62

Color coding:	<-2.0	<-1.0	<0.0	>0.0	>1.0	>2.0	Z
N in each cell:	Smaller than expected			Larger than expected			

Summary Statistics				
Eta* =	.24	Gamma = .31	Chisq(P) =	182.52 (p= 0.00)
R =	.18	Tau-b = .19	Chisq(LR) =	182.17 (p= 0.00)
Somers' d* =	.17	Tau-c = .17	df =	8

*Row variable treated as the dependent variable.

TABLE 6.4

Statistics for sex = 1(MALE)						
	marital					
Cells contain: -Column percent -N of cases	1 MARRIED	2 WIDOWED	3 DIVORCED	4 SEPARATED	5 NEVER MARRIED	*ROW TOTAL*
happy 1: VERY HAPPY	**38.7** 281	**10.2** 5	**15.2** 25	**17.6** 6	**21.4** 66	*29.9* *383*
2: PRETTY HAPPY	**53.9** 391	**53.1** 26	**69.5** 114	**52.9** 18	**66.3** 205	*58.8* *754*
3: NOT TOO HAPPY	**7.4** 54	**36.7** 18	**15.2** 25	**29.4** 10	**12.3** 38	*11.3* *145*
COL TOTAL	*100.0* 726	*100.0* 49	*100.0* 164	*100.0* 34	*100.0* 309	*100.0* *1,282*
Means	1.69	2.27	2.00	2.12	1.91	1.81
Std Devs	.60	.64	.55	.69	.57	.61

Color coding:	<-2.0	<-1.0	<0.0	>0.0	>1.0	>2.0	Z
N in each cell:	Smaller than expected			Larger than expected			

Summary Statistics for sex = 1(MALE)				
Eta* =	.26	Gamma = .31	Chisq(P) =	105.91 (p= 0.00)
R =	.17	Tau-b = .18	Chisq(LR) =	97.56 (p= 0.00)
Somers' d* =	.18	Tau-c = .16	df =	8

TABLE 6.5

all subgroups. In sharp contrast, when we examine women's responses separately, we observe that widowed women are not much more likely to report themselves as being unhappy than divorced and never married females. For men it is quite different: widowers stand out from all the rest in being the most prone to feeling unhappy.

We may wonder why widowed men and women differ so greatly in their reports of unhappiness. For one thing, women live longer than men in our society. Consequently, it is probably a lot easier for women to find friends and companionship in advanced age than it may be for men to do so. Studies of aging and mental health problems show suicide to be far more common among elderly males than for elderly females. Owing to higher male death rates, the loss of one's peers probably troubles men more than it does women.

In addition, women ordinarily play pivotal roles in family life and in maintaining family relationship ties. As women grow older, they usually have more roles available—to babysit for grandchildren, to help care for infirm family members, to assist with other domestic activities, such as

Statistics for sex = 2(FEMALE)						
Cells contain: -Column percent -N of cases	marital					
	1 MARRIED	2 WIDOWED	3 DIVORCED	4 SEPARATED	5 NEVER MARRIED	*ROW TOTAL*

happy		1 MARRIED	2 WIDOWED	3 DIVORCED	4 SEPARATED	5 NEVER MARRIED	*ROW TOTAL*
	1: VERY HAPPY	**37.6** 304	**19.7** 47	**19.6** 55	**11.8** 8	**20.0** 60	*28.0* *474*
	2: PRETTY HAPPY	**54.9** 444	**64.3** 153	**61.1** 171	**61.8** 42	**64.0** 192	*59.1* *1,002*
	3: NOT TOO HAPPY	**7.5** 61	**16.0** 38	**19.3** 54	**26.5** 18	**16.0** 48	*12.9* *219*
	COL TOTAL	*100.0* *809*	*100.0* *238*	*100.0* *280*	*100.0* *68*	*100.0* *300*	*100.0* *1,695*
Means		1.70	1.96	2.00	2.15	1.96	1.85
Std Devs		.60	.60	.63	.61	.60	.62

Color coding:	<-2.0	<-1.0	<0.0	>0.0	>1.0	>2.0	Z
N in each cell:	Smaller than expected			Larger than expected			

Summary Statistics for sex = 2(FEMALE)					
Eta* =	.24	Gamma = .30	Chisq(P) =	98.08	(p= 0.00)
R =	.19	Tau-b = .19	Chisq(LR) =	98.99	(p= 0.00)
Somers' d* =	.17	Tau-c = .18	df =	8	

*Row variable treated as the dependent variable.

TABLE 6.6

homecare and meal preparation. Women usually assume dominant positions in arranging family get togethers at holiday time and they disseminate the family news about who got married, who is sick, etc. Widowed women usually find solace in their multifold family attachments upon the loss of their husbands.

For men, growing older usually represents a situation of loss. Widowers losing their wives may also feel a diminished connection to family with that loss. With advanced age, men also give up their jobs and earning power, and the respect and prestige that may have accompanied it. Thus, widowers apparently experience more marginality than widows. The GSS94 data suggests such gender-related differences with advancing age.

Therefore, the subdivision of data by applying a control variable—in this case, gender—yielded some valuable insights about the original hypothesis, and about how gender, age and marital status interact together. It revealed some very interesting differences between men and women in their feelings of personal happiness, depending upon their marital status and age. In this case the application of the control variable enabled us to understand something that would have otherwise been obscured.

Another important question that can be investigated in compound crosstabular analyses comes in assessing the strength of associations between related phenomena. We may wonder whether one or another association is stronger in its relationship with a dependent variable. We can do this by calculating what are known as delta values. Chi-Square probabilities do not themselves provide reliable information on the magnitude of associations. They simply indicate whether an association is likely (or unlikely) to occur by chance, given its marginal values. In order to gain some insight into the strength of associations, one must look elsewhere for answers—by comparing *delta values.* A delta is the amount of variation in the dependent variable that the independent variable causes or brings. We can calculate delta as the sum of the percentage differences in the dependent variable, as it ranges from its lowest to its highest value across the independent variable differences (column categories).

We will illustrate by calculating deltas in an investigation of several correlates to ever getting divorced to see which correlate is the most pow-

Frequency Distribution			
		family16	
Cells contain: -Column percent -N of cases	1 Lived with both parents	2 Not always lived with both parents	*ROW TOTAL*
divorce — 1: YES	**21.9** 295	**26.2** 116	*23.0* *411*
divorce — 2: NO	**78.1** 1,051	**73.8** 326	*77.0* *1,377*
COL TOTAL	*100.0* *1,346*	*100.0* *442*	*100.0* *1,788*
Means	1.78	1.74	1.77
Std Devs	.41	.44	.42

Color coding:	<-2.0	<-1.0	<0.0	>0.0	>1.0	>2.0	Z
N in each cell:	Smaller than expected			Larger than expected			

Summary Statistics					
Eta* =	.04	Gamma =	-.12	Chisq(P) =	3.52 (p= 0.06)
R =	-.04	Tau-b =	-.04	Chisq(LR) =	3.45 (p= 0.06)
Somers' d* =	-.04	Tau-c =	-.03	df =	1

*Row variable treated as the dependent variable.

TABLE 6.7

erful. In 1994, 23 percent of GSS respondents reported having been divorced during their lifetimes, among all people reporting having married. Let us entertain several possible correlates to getting divorced: parents' successful or failed marriage, one's education, their social class position, and whether one got married earlier or later in life. You may have already formed some thoughts about which of the above correlates is the most and least powerful one related to getting divorced. Table 6.7 shows the relationship between parents' marriage success or failure and their children's chances of getting divorced.

It is hardly necessary to compute the delta for this association since the relationship failed to meet the .05 test criteria. Even if we had a larger sample, which would bolster the significance level slightly to clear the .05 criteria, we wouldn't see a significant variability in the dependent variable across the column variable. In this case; it is 26 percent minus 22 percent, or 4 percent.

Table 6.8 shows the relationship between one's chance of getting divorced and completing different levels of education. The table shows significant differences with well-educated people having a lower likelihood of divorce than the less well educated. Delta in this case would be 26 percent minus 14 percent, suggesting a 12 percent gain in predicting the dependent variable from knowing the independent one.

Table 6.9 shows the relationship between getting divorced by social class. Again, this variable shows significant differences with lower and

Frequency Distribution					
Cells contain: -Column percent -N of cases		**educ**			
		1 1-12	2 13-15	3 16-20	*ROW* *TOTAL*
divorce	1: YES	**26.1** 247	**26.7** 109	**14.0** 65	*23.2* *421*
	2: NO	**73.9** 698	**73.3** 299	**86.0** 398	*76.8* *1,395*
	COL TOTAL	*100.0* *945*	*100.0* *408*	*100.0* *463*	*100.0* *1,816*
Means		1.74	1.73	1.86	1.77
Std Devs		.44	.44	.35	.42

Color coding:	<-2.0	<-1.0	<0.0	>0.0	>1.0	>2.0	Z
N in each cell:	Smaller than expected			Larger than expected			

Summary Statistics						
Eta* =	.13	Gamma =	.21	Chisq(P) =	29.23	(p= 0.00)
R =	.11	Tau-b =	.10	Chisq(LR) =	31.59	(p= 0.00)
Somers' d* =	.07	Tau-c =	.09	df =	2	
Row variable treated as the dependent variable.						

TABLE 6.8

Frequency Distribution

Cells contain:
- Column percent
- N of cases

		class				
		1 LOWER CLASS	2 WORKING CLASS	3 MIDDLE CLASS	4 UPPER CLASS	ROW TOTAL
divorce	1: YES	27.1 / 16	27.0 / 200	20.1 / 189	19.1 / 13	23.1 / 418
	2: NO	72.9 / 43	73.0 / 541	79.9 / 753	80.9 / 55	76.9 / 1,392
	COL TOTAL	100.0 / 59	100.0 / 741	100.0 / 942	100.0 / 68	100.0 / 1,810
	Means	1.73	1.73	1.80	1.81	1.77
	Std Devs	.45	.44	.40	.40	.42

Color coding:	<-2.0	<-1.0	<0.0	>0.0	>1.0	>2.0	Z
N in each cell:	Smaller than expected			Larger than expected			

Summary Statistics

Eta* =	.08	Gamma =	.17	Chisq(P) =	12.35 (p= 0.01)
R =	.08	Tau-b =	.08	Chisq(LR) =	12.29 (p= 0.01)
Somers' d* =	.06	Tau-c =	.07	df =	3

*Row variable treated as the dependent variable.

EVER BEEN DIVORCED OR SEPARATED BY SUBJECTIVE CLASS IDENTIFICATION

TABLE 6.9

working class members being more divorce-prone than middle and upper class members. The delta computation shows an 8 percent differential (19 from 27 percent). Here, we appear to be dealing with a less powerful correlate (by an ever so slight margin) than education.

Table 6.10 displays the last table in this analysis, the likelihood of getting divorced by the age when people married (for the first time). We are comparing three groups: those who were married by the age of 20; those marrying between 21 and 25; and last, those marrying after 25.

Here, there appears to be a larger differential than with any of the other independent variables. The differential is 32 minus 11, a 21 percent difference. Knowing that it accounted for a 21 percent improved prediction in the dependent variable, our final conclusion would therefore be that one's age at marriage is the most powerful of all the correlates examined here in accounting for divorce variability.

Yet, before we can be totally convinced that we have found the strongest causal link to divorce, we should run several control variable analyses to see if any of these other significant correlates are confounded together. We may be dealing with an influential force from any one of these other variables that could be at least as much or more influential (than marriage age) and may dissolve the relationship between marriage age and divorce. It is altogether possible that class differences or educational differences could be the main reasons why people marry earlier or later and that the age-at-first-marriage/divorce relationship could be a spurious one.

Examining Tables 6.11 and 6.12 together suggests that age-at-first-marriage still remains significantly related to divorce when we separate the

Frequency Distribution				
Cells contain: -Column percent -N of cases	agewed			
	1 12-20	2 21-25	3 26-58	*ROW TOTAL*
divorce 1: YES	**31.6** 104	**18.3** 71	**10.5** 21	*21.4* *196*
2: NO	**68.4** 225	**81.7** 318	**89.5** 179	*78.6* *722*
COL TOTAL	*100.0* *329*	*100.0* *389*	*100.0* *200*	*100.0* *918*
Means	1.68	1.82	1.90	1.79
Std Devs	.47	.39	.31	.41

Color coding:	<-2.0	<-1.0	<0.0	>0.0	>1.0	>2.0	Z
N in each cell:	Smaller than expected			Larger than expected			

Summary Statistics				
Eta* =	.20	Gamma = .40	Chisq(P) =	36.87 (p= 0.00)
R =	.20	Tau-b = .19	Chisq(LR) =	37.49 (p= 0.00)
Somers' d* = .14		Tau-c = .18	df =	2

*Row variable treated as the dependent variable.

TABLE 6.10

sample into working and lower class members and middle and upper class ones.

Again, examining Tables 6.13, 6.14, and 6.15 suggests that age-at-first-marriage is a powerful correlate in its own right. Even when class and education differences are considered, it still remains a powerful correlate to marriage success or failure.

An additional benefit available from a compound analysis like this would be to offer assistance in developing models of causal influences. This will only work when the temporal sequence of events is very clear. In many research situations, however, it is especially difficult to develop causal models because many causative agents may occur nearly simultaneously with one another and it becomes difficult to judge which event preceded another. In these cases, all we can say is that the factors are highly correlated. But in the present situation, we are advantaged in making a causal analysis model because of the clear temporal sequencing of events. Invariably, people must get married before they can get divorced; thus age-at-first wedding always precedes getting divorced. And obtaining one's education usually (but not always) precedes getting married, as well.

There are three logically possible causal models that could explain the relationship between divorce, age-at-first wedding and education, where age-at-first-wedding = A; divorce = B, and level of education = C. The models are presented on pages 100–101.

Statistics for class = 1(Lower and working class)				
Cells contain: -Column percent -N of cases	**Agewed**			
	1 12-20	2 21-25	3 26-58	*ROW TOTAL*
divorce 1: YES	**29.4** 50	**19.5** 29	**17.4** 12	*23.5* *91*
2: NO	**70.6** 120	**80.5** 120	**82.6** 57	*76.5* *297*
COL TOTAL	*100.0* *170*	*100.0* *149*	*100.0* *69*	*100.0* *388*
Means	1.71	1.81	1.83	1.77
Std Devs	.46	.40	.38	.42

Color coding:	<-2.0	<-1.0	<0.0	>0.0	>1.0	>2.0	Z
N in each cell:	Smaller than expected			Larger than expected			

Summary Statistics for class = 1(Lower and working class)

Eta* =	.13	Gamma =	.25	Chisq(P) =	6.10	(p= 0.05)
R =	.12	Tau-b =	.12	Chisq(LR) =	6.08	(p= 0.05)
Somers' d* =	.09	Tau-c =	.11	df =	2	

*Row variable treated as the dependent variable.

TABLE 6.11

Statistics for class = 2(Middle and upper class)				
Cells contain: -Column percent -N of cases	**Agewed**			
	1 12-20	2 21-25	3 26-58	*ROW TOTAL*
divorce 1: YES	**34.0** 53	**16.9** 40	**6.9** 9	*19.5* *102*
2: NO	**66.0** 103	**83.1** 196	**93.1** 122	*80.5* *421*
COL TOTAL	*100.0* *156*	*100.0* *236*	*100.0* *131*	*100.0* *523*
Means	1.66	1.83	1.93	1.80
Std Devs	.48	.38	.25	.40

Color coding:	<-2.0	<-1.0	<0.0	>0.0	>1.0	>2.0	Z
N in each cell:	Smaller than expected			Larger than expected			

Summary Statistics for class = 2(Middle and upper class)

Eta* =	.26	Gamma =	.52	Chisq(P) =	35.11	(p= 0.00)
R =	.26	Tau-b =	.24	Chisq(LR) =	35.81	(p= 0.00)
Somers' d* =	.17	Tau-c =	.22	df =	2	

*Row variable treated as the dependent variable.

TABLE 6.12

Statistics for educ = 1(1-12)				
Cells contain: -Column percent -N of cases	agewed			
	1 12-20	2 21-25	3 26-58	ROW TOTAL
divorce 1: YES	**30.2** 68	**18.3** 31	**17.9** 14	*23.9* *113*
divorce 2: NO	**69.8** 157	**81.7** 138	**82.1** 64	*76.1* *359*
COL TOTAL	*100.0* *225*	*100.0* *169*	*100.0* *78*	*100.0* *472*
Means	1.70	1.82	1.82	1.76
Std Devs	.46	.39	.39	.43

Color coding:	<-2.0	<-1.0	<0.0	>0.0	>1.0	>2.0	Z
N in each cell:	Smaller than expected			Larger than expected			

Summary Statistics for educ = 1(1-12)						
Eta* =	.14	Gamma =	.27	Chisq(P) =	9.32	(p= 0.01)
R =	.13	Tau-b =	.13	Chisq(LR) =	9.35	(p= 0.01)
Somers' d* =	.10	Tau-c =	.12	df =	2	

*Row variable treated as the dependent variable.

TABLE 6.13

Statistics for educ = 2(13-15)				
Cells contain: -Column percent -N of cases	Agewed			
	1 12-20	2 21-25	3 26-58	ROW TOTAL
divorce 1: YES	**36.6** 26	**19.8** 20	**4.9** 2	*22.5* *48*
divorce 2: NO	**63.4** 45	**80.2** 81	**95.1** 39	*77.5* *165*
COL TOTAL	*100.0* *71*	*100.0* *101*	*100.0* *41*	*100.0* *213*
Means	1.63	1.80	1.95	1.77
Std Devs	.49	.40	.22	.42

Color coding:	<-2.0	<-1.0	<0.0	>0.0	>1.0	>2.0	Z
N in each cell:	Smaller than expected			Larger than expected			

Summary Statistics for educ = 2(13-15)						
Eta* =	.27	Gamma =	.54	Chisq(P) =	15.82	(p= 0.00)
R =	.27	Tau-b =	.26	Chisq(LR) =	17.53	(p= 0.00)
Somers' d* =	.19	Tau-c =	.24	df =	2	

*Row variable treated as the dependent variable.

TABLE 6.14

Statistics for educ = 3(16-20)				
Cells contain: -Column percent -N of cases	Agewed			
	1 12-20	2 21-25	3 26-58	*ROW TOTAL*
divorce 1: YES	**31.2** 10	**16.8** 20	**6.2** 5	*15.2* *35*
divorce 2: NO	**68.8** 22	**83.2** 99	**93.8** 75	*84.8* *196*
COL TOTAL	*100.0* *32*	*100.0* *119*	*100.0* *80*	*100.0* *231*
Means	1.69	1.83	1.94	1.85
Std Devs	.47	.38	.24	.36

Color coding:	<-2.0	<-1.0	<0.0	>0.0	>1.0	>2.0	Z
N in each cell:	Smaller than expected			Larger than expected			

Summary Statistics for educ = 3(16-20)					
Eta* =	.22	Gamma =	.51	Chisq(P) =	11.64 (p= 0.00)
R =	.22	Tau-b =	.21	Chisq(LR) =	11.58 (p= 0.00)
Somers' d* =	.14	Tau-c =	.16	df =	2

*Row variable treated as the dependent variable.

TABLE 6.15

Model I

A is significantly associated with B; C, too, is significantly associated with B; and each possesses an independent influence on B.

A ——————> B

C ——————> B

Model II

A affects C, which in turn affects B.

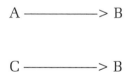

A ——————> C ——————> B

Model III

C affects A, which in turn affects B.

C ——————> A ——————> B

If we think about the empirical likelihood of Model II, of people getting married, then going on to complete their educations and finally getting divorced, this sequence of events would probably not occur frequently in our society. Thus, the real choice is between whether Model I or Model III is the most appropriate one to explain the particular chain of causal events between these three variables. If Model III was the most appropriate one, we would have witnessed the relationship between age-at-first-wedding dissolving when the education control was applied. But age-at-first-wedding still remained significant when we examined the data subgrouped by each educational category. Thus, the most appropriate causal model appears to be Model I with both education and age-at-first marriage having separate influences on the likelihood of divorce. Again, students should keep in mind that in social science the best that can be done will very often be to establish that several or fewer variables are highly interrelated with one another.

SUMMARY

In this chapter, we have delineated several additional questions that can be investigated with crosstabular analyses. Three-way crosstabulations can be used to identify spurious associations—relationships, though valid in experience, that have little causal or theoretical importance. These more complex analyses of crosstabulation can also illuminate relationships that may not be observable in examinations of bivariate associations. An example was investigated showing how personal happiness and marital status differed for men and women of advanced age. This compound analysis can also show the unique conditions when a bivariate relationship may prevail and the conditions where the relationship may be dissolved.

The pattern of three-way crosstabulations also can provide valuable guidance on the direction of causal influences. The size of delta values differences is also important for determining the strength of relationships. Thus, compound crosstabulations can clarify many matters of social scientific interest.

CHAPTER 7

Socialization

For most lay people, "socialization" may mean something along the lines of partying or interaction. For the sociologist, a different meaning applies: It is the process by which an individual learns how to become a functioning member of his or her society; it refers to internalizing the appropriate behavior patterns, values, and attitudes, as well as the acquisition of necessary skills and information. Socialization involves implanting culture within the individual, enabling the person to survive effectively in his or her social world. It is a lifelong process; individuals alter their adaptations unceasingly as they respond to the changing conditions of their physical and social environment.

There are many influences that adapt people to society. These agencies of socialization, as they are called, include family, peers, schools, the media, the workplace, religious institutions, and many others. In the United States, as in most other societies, the family is the most important socializing agent.

Religious attendance and convictions are as good an example as any of a U.S. behavior pattern that is acquired through socialization. The GSS regularly collects data on people's religious involvement, which enables us to evaluate how families and other social institutions shape a person's religious commitment. In the 1989 GSS, the subject of religiosity was more exhaustively investigated. Our first question investigates the impact of a mother's church attendance on children's level of church attendance.

1. Go to the SDA website at http://sda.berkeley.edu.
2. Click **SDA Archive**, and then select the **GSS Cumulative Datafile 1972–2002**. Select "Frequencies or crosstabulation" and click **Start**. You will see the layout shown in Figure 7.1.
3. Put the **DEPENDENT** variable in the "Row" box and the **INDEPENDENT** variable in the Column box.
4. Since we are working from the 1989 GSS file, be sure to type year(1989) in the "Selection Filter(s)" Box.
5. Select the "Statistics" and "Question text" option from the "Table Options" box.
6. *Don't forget to apply the correct recode language for each question.*

Tabulate **ATTEND**, the frequency of a respondent's attendance at religious services (as the dependent variable) by **MAATTEND**, mother's religious participation when the respondent was growing up, to investigate whether a mother's religious activity has any bearing on one's participation. Do not use the above two variables directly: Be sure to use the recodes provided at the end of this chapter. You can also access the recodes electronically at: www.ncc.edu/users/feigelb/sda.htm or www.ablongman.com/feigelman3e.

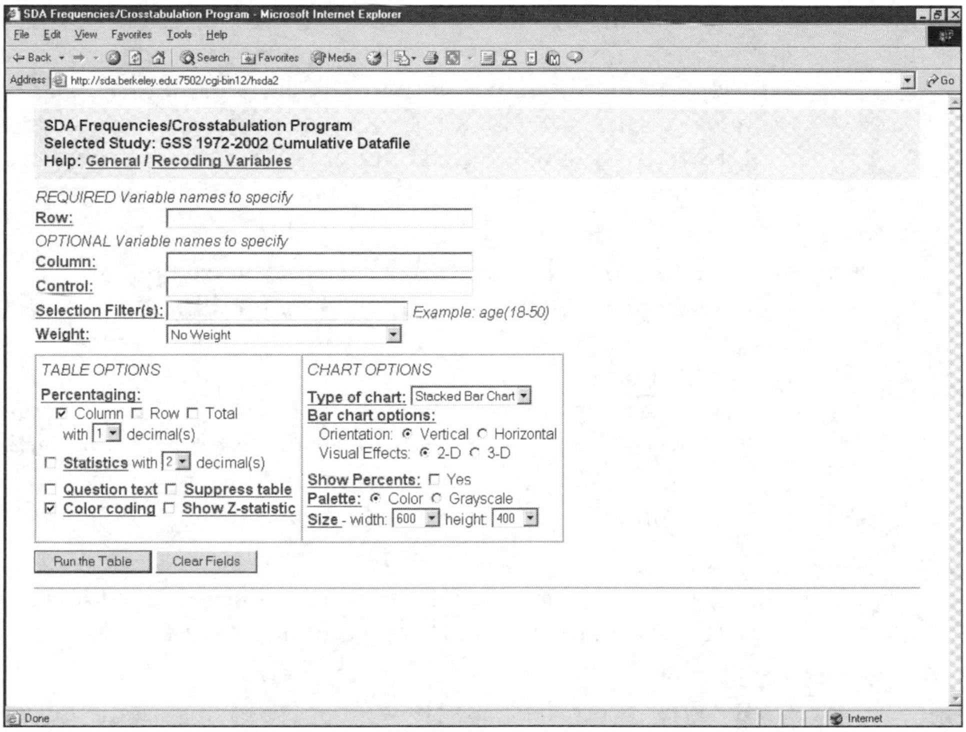

FIGURE 7.1

Now, answer the following questions.

1. Does a mother's level of religious participation show an association with the respondent's level of participation?
   a. Yes
   b. No
   c. Unclear
   d. Only for very active participating mothers
2. The association between **ATTEND** and **MAATTEND** is:
   a. Statistically significant.
   b. Statistically insignificant.
   c. Unclear and/or of borderline significance.
   d. There are too few cases to make any firm conclusions.

The next question will explore whether mother's church attendance influences sons and daughters differently. To answer the question, we need to do a three-way crosstabulation with **ATTEND** as the dependent variable, **MAATTEND** as the independent variable, and **SEX** as the control variable. Remember to enter **year(1989)** into the "Selection Filter(s)" Box.

3. Does a mother's participation affect men and women's participation differently?
   a. It seems associated with her daughter's level of involvement, but not with her son's participation.
   b. It seems associated with her son's level of involvement, but not with her daughter's participation.
   c. It appears to be significantly associated with both son's and daughter's level of religious participation.
   d. It appears to be associated with neither son's nor daughter's level of religious participation.

Now, run **ATTEND** as the dependent variable with **PAATTEND**, the father's religious attendance while the respondent was growing up, as the independent variable. Compare the delta values (percentage points differences) for the fathers' attendance at religious services at different levels of participation among respondents who never attend religious services with mothers' levels of religious participation.

4. Which parent's religious participation seems to exert the bigger influence on respondents who never attend religious services?
   a. Mother's.
   b. Father's.
   c. There are no differences whatsoever between fathers and mothers in influencing their children's lack of religious participation.
   d. Neither parent's religious participation shows much of an association to the child's participation.

Now, compare mothers and fathers at differing levels of religious activity, among respondents who attend services weekly or more often.

5. What does the data show about which parent influences children's religious activity the most at the highest level of participation?
   a. Mothers appear more influential.
   b. Fathers appear more influential.
   c. No differences whatsoever in influence are shown.
   d. Neither parent shows any apparent influence here.

Now, run years spent attending a church or parochial school (**CHURHSCH**) against religious participation (**ATTEND**), with **ATTEND** as the dependent variable.

6. Tabulating religious participation by parochial school experience, what does the data show?
   a. The results seem inconclusive; the data shows a weak association of possibly borderline significance between the two.
   b. Parochial school attendance is definitely associated with religious attendance.
   c. Parochial school attendance is definitely not associated with religious attendance.
   d. Only at the lowest level of religious school participation is there any association between the two.

Let us now consider belief in an afterlife (**POSTLIFE**) as an important dimension of a person's religious commitment. The question we will now seek to probe is whether parental exposure or religious academic experiences are more important in supporting a belief in an afterlife.

With **PAATTEND**, **MAATTEND**, and **CHURHSCH** as independent variables and with **POSTLIFE** as the dependent variable, perform three separate cross-tabulations and answer the following question. (Hint: Compare Chi-Square significance test results as a guide to answering this question.)

7. Which seems to be a more potent influence on sustaining one's belief in an afterlife: parental religious participation or parochial school experience?
   a. Parental religious participation.
   b. Parochial school experience.
   c. Both are equally influential.
   d. Neither appears to have much of an influence.

So far we have explored various hypotheses about socialization that underscore it as a learning process. People are socialized by the conscious efforts of parents, peers, teachers, and many others: Their intentional efforts and examples produce changes within the socialized person.

Socialization analysts also note that the structure of a social situation has an impact upon the socialization process. Some research has delved into the importance of one's place within the family—whether one is a first-born child, a latter-born child, or an only child—and the influence it has as a factor that affects socialization outcomes. It has, for example, been claimed that first-born and elder children are more likely to be successful in life—to complete more schooling and to make more money—than latter-born children.

Let us investigate this hypothesis with the GSS data. Enter **year(1990)** in the "Selection Filter(s)" Box for questions 8 through 13. Tabulate educational attainment (**EDUC**) by sibling position (**SIBORDER**) and answer the following question:

8. Which of the following statements best summarizes the findings on the presumed association between **EDUC** and **SIBORDER**?
   a. Only and eldest children are significantly less likely to be highly educated than younger children.
   b. Only and eldest children are somewhat more likely to be highly educated than younger children, although the differences fall slightly short of achieving statistical significance.
   c. Sibling order position has no apparent association with education.
   d. Sibling order position may have a slight association with education, but considerably below the level of achieving statistical significance.

Now tabulate personal income (**RINCOME**) by sibling ordinal position (**SIBORDER**).

9. Which statement below best summarizes the findings on the presumed association between **RINCOME** and **SIBORDER**?
   a. Only and eldest children are significantly less likely to have higher incomes than younger children.
   b. Only and eldest children are significantly more likely to have higher incomes than younger children.
   c. Sibling order position has no apparent association with personal income.
   d. Sibling order position has a slight association with income, but below the level of statistical significance.

An important element that can influence the course of socialization is the family's social class position. In the following questions we cannot be certain if a person's social class membership rather than his or her sibling ordinal position might account for some of the observed variations in incomes and education.

Do two separate three-way crosstabulations, one with **EDUC** as the dependent variable and another with **RINCOME** as the dependent variable; in both crosstabulations use **SIBORDER** as the independent variable, and **PRESTIGE** as the control variable. (Please note, **PRESTIGE** has two values, low and high status, based upon the Hodge, Siegel, Rossi occupational prestige rating scores, ranging from 0 to 100. Forty-one and under were considered low prestige occupations, those above, high.)

10. How would you describe the results of **EDUC** by **SIBORDER**, controlled by **PRESTIGE** looking at high status respondents?
    a. Education and sibling position now appear unrelated, suggesting that social class best explains educational differences among high status respondents.
    b. Education and sibling position are related, suggesting that sibling position, rather than class, carried more weight.
    c. No changes were noted between these results and the bivariate association between **EDUC** and **SIBORDER**.
    d. None of the above.

11. How would you describe the results of **EDUC** by **SIBORDER**, controlled by **PRESTIGE**, looking at low status respondents?
    a. Education and sibling position now seem to run in the opposite direction, with latter born children more likely to go to college than only or elder children.
    b. Education and sibling position may be related, suggesting that sibling position, rather than class, carried more weight among low status respondents.
    c. No changes were noted between these results and the bivariate association between **EDUC** and **SIBORDER**.
    d. None of the above.

12. How would you describe the results of **RINCOME** by **SIBORDER**, controlled by **PRESTIGE** among high status respondents?
    a. Income and sibling position now appear unrelated, suggesting that social class best explains income differences among high status respondents.
    b. Income and sibling position are related, suggesting that sibling position, rather than class, carried more weight.
    c. No appreciable changes were noted between these results and the bivariate association between **RINCOME** and **SIBORDER**.
    d. None of the above.

13. How would you describe the results of RINCOME by SIBORDER, controlled by PRESTIGE, among low status respondents?
    a. Income and sibling position now seem to run in the opposite direction with latter born children more likely to go to college than only or elder children.
    b. Income and sibling position may be related as before, suggesting that sibling position, rather than class, carried more weight among low status Rs.
    c. No substantial changes were noted between these results and the earlier bivariate association between RINCOME and SIBORDER.
    d. None of the above.

Another important part of the socialization process includes the development of a person's gender role. From early infancy and afterwards, men and women are socialized differently to assume contrasting gender roles. Today, such sexual differentiation continues, even though in most postindustrial societies like our own, sex roles are in an unprecedented state of flux. Nowadays, the difference in expectations for men and women are rapidly changing, especially with respect to women's roles.

During earlier generations of industrial society men were groomed for the full variety of roles in the production process, while women were obliged to function more narrowly as household caretakers, wives, and mothers. Today, women can look forward to a much broader range of occupational choices, besides traditional female roles.

In many GSS survey years, respondents are asked various questions about their acceptance (and rejection) of contemporary female role possibilities. An index of sex role traditionalism will be prepared from the following survey questions:

"Do you agree or disagree with this statement: Women should take care of running their homes and leave running the country up to men?" (FEHOME)

"Do you approve or disapprove of a married woman earning money in business or industry if she has a husband capable of supporting her?" (FEWORK)

"Tell me whether you agree or disagree with this statement: Most men are better suited emotionally for politics than most women?" (FEPOL)

Creating an index on SDA is not hard. You will simply need to use the following instructions.

Step 1: Create a new variable (FEWORK1)

1. Go to: http://sda.berkeley.edu/cgi-bin12/hsda?harcsda+gss02.
2. Select "Compute a new variable".

3. Click **Start**.
4. Type: if (fework eq 1) fework1 = 2 else if (fework eq 2) fework1=1 into the box labeled "EXPRESSION TO DEFINE THE NEW VARIABLE".
5. Select 'Yes' for the option "Replace that variable, if it already exists?"
6. Click Start Computing.

Step 2: Create a new variable (TRADSEXR)

1. Go to: http://sda.berkeley.edu/cgi-bin12/hsda?harcsda+gss02 (you can also click the **Back** button twice within your browser).
2. Select "Compute a new variable".
3. Click **Start**.
4. Type: tradsexr=fehome+fepol+fework1 into the box labeled "EXPRESSION TO DEFINE THE NEW VARIABLE".
5. Select 'Yes' for the option "Replace that variable, if it already exists?"
6. Click Start Computing.

The newly created sex role traditionalism scale (**TRADSEXR**) has a few categories. Those respondents who showed support for modern women's roles on all three questions will have a score of 6. If you run a table for **TRADSEXR** for 1998 data, you will find that this response was predominate, with 63 percent of all respondents answering this way. A semi-traditional response was shown when a respondent gave a traditional response to only one question (23 percent answered this way). The remaining respondents showed high traditionalism (about 14%), shown when a respondent answered two or three questions displaying expectations for women to behave in a traditionalistic way. Be sure to enter **year(1998)** in the "Selection Filter(s)" Box when answering the next set of questions.

Since the rejection of traditional sex roles is a newer ideology, we might suspect it to be related to a respondent's age. Run **TRADSEXR** by **AGE** and answer the following question:

14. What does the data show about age and sex role attitudes?
    a. Surprisingly, elder respondents tend to be more accepting of modern female gender roles.
    b. As expected, younger respondents tend to be more accepting of newer gender roles for women.
    c. Age doesn't make much of a difference to peoples' acceptance of modern female roles.
    d. Though statistically significant, age subgroup variations are negligible in percentage differences.

It is possible that whatever contrasting patterns might have been noted in the preceding question, educational variability, rather than age, may account for these differences. Now, run the same crosstabulation, but this time run education (**EDUC**) as a control variable. (Remember that to do a three-way crosstabulation, you need to type the control variable, in this case **educ**, in the "Control" box.)

15. What is the most plausible conclusion that one can now draw?
    a. Younger respondents still tend to be more accepting of newer female roles in each of the educational subgroups.
    b. Older respondents still tend to be more accepting of newer female roles in each of the educational subgroups.
    c. The differences that were noted in the two-way crosstabs are now no longer true.
    d. Age appears to make more of a difference now.
    e. None of the above.

Several social learning hypotheses are suggested to explain why some respondents may be more accepting of modern female gender roles than others:

- One grew up in a home where one's mother worked (MAWRKGRW).
- One's mother was more highly educated (MAEDUC), as more highly educated mothers may impart greater support for modern female role conceptions among their children.
- One may have grown up in a disrupted family (FAMILY16).

Evaluate each of these hypotheses, and then answer the following questions.

16. What does the data show about the relationship between maternal employment and sex role attitudes?
    a. Those who grew up in homes where mothers worked are more accepting of modern sex roles.
    b. Those who had working mothers tend to hold more traditional concepts of female roles.
    c. Having had a working mother makes for little differentiation in one's attitudes towards female sex roles.
    d. None of the above.
17. What does the data show about the relationship between a mother's educational attainments and a respondent's sex role attitudes?
    a. Those with more highly educated mothers are more accepting of modern sex roles.
    b. Those with more highly educated mothers hold more traditional concepts of female roles.
    c. Having had a more highly educated mother makes for little differentiation in one's attitudes towards female sex roles.
    d. None of the above.
18. What does the data show about the relationship between parental family disruption and sex role attitudes?
    a. Those whose parents split are significantly more accepting of modern sex roles.
    b. Those with parents who divorced while they were still living at home hold more traditional female role concepts.
    c. Those whose parents split appear to hold largely similar attitudes on female sex roles compared to those whose parents stayed together. Differences fall short of statistical significance.
    d. None of the above.

19. Comparing the delta values (percentage points differences) for the three above associations, which appears to be strongest? (Hint: Select the category of low traditional response as your criteria for evaluating percentage points differences.)
    a. TRADSEXR by MAWRKGRW
    b. TRADSEXR by MAEDUC
    c. TRADSEXR by FAMILY16
    d. All three associations seem to be of equal strength
    e. Answers a and b seem to be of equal strength

Some socialization analysts claim that families in diverging social classes endorse contrasting values that guide the rearing of their children. The precepts that parents hold for themselves and their children make it easier for their children to remain at the parents' social level and facilitate the fulfillment of the specific occupational expectations that children will eventually confront. Melvin Kohn (the most well known researcher on this subject) and others have been investigating this issue since 1959.

The GSS regularly asks respondents various questions about values that parents deemed important for living. Respondents were asked to assign an order of importance to several values to be imparted to children. The questions covered the following behaviors: obeying, being popular, showing independent thought, working hard, and helping others.

Let us now investigate whether the parents in different social classes show variability in their endorsement of these basic values as Kohn and others maintain. Run each of the following crosstabulations with **OBEY, POPULAR, THNKSELF, HELPOTH,** and **WORKHARD** as dependent variables and **PRESTG80** as the independent variable. Note: For Questions 20 through 24, make sure to type **year(2002)** in the "Selection Filter(s)" field.

20. The crosstabulation between **OBEY** and **PRESTG80** shows:
    a. Emphasis on obedience is significantly linked to higher class membership.
    b. Emphasis on obedience is significantly linked to lower class membership.
    c. There is no significant association between these variables.
    d. There might be a trend between the variables.
    e. No apparent association between the variables can be noted.
21. The crosstabulation between **POPULAR** and **PRESTG80** shows:
    a. Emphasis on popularity is significantly linked to higher class membership.
    b. Emphasis on popularity is significantly linked to lower class membership.
    c. There might be a trend between the variables.
    d. No apparent association between the variables can be noted.

22. The crosstabulation between THNKSLF and PRESTG80 shows:
    a. Emphasis on independent thinking is significantly linked to higher class membership.
    b. Emphasis on independent thinking is significantly linked to lower class membership.
    c. There is no significant association between these variables.
    d. There might be a trend between the variables.
    e. No apparent association between the variables can be noted.
23. The crosstabulation between HELPOTH and PRESTG80 shows:
    a. Emphasis on helping others is significantly linked to higher class membership.
    b. Emphasis on helping others is significantly linked to lower class membership.
    c. There is a significant association between the variables, though it is not altogether clear which class favors helping others the most.
    d. There might be a trend between the variables.
    e. No apparent association between the variables can be noted.
24. The crosstabulation between WORKHARD and PRESTG80 shows:
    a. Emphasis on industriousness is significantly linked to higher class membership.
    b. Emphasis on industriousness is significantly linked to lower class membership.
    c. There might be a trend between the variables.
    d. No apparent association between the variables can be noted.

We will next examine the 1995 National Survey of Adolescents in the United States to explore other issues related to socialization. There are two major issues to be examined. First, we will study the impact of family structure on the deviant behavior of adolescents. Specifically, we will look at the behavioral patterns of those adolescents who have always lived with both parents and those who have not. Do adolescents not living with both biological parents show a greater likelihood to be deviant? Secondly, we will examine whether exposure to deviant behavior significantly increases the likelihood of adolescents committing deviant acts.

1. Go to the SDA website at www.icpsr.umich.edu/cgi/SDA/hsda?nacjd+nsa.
2. Select "Run frequency or crosstabulation" and click **Start**. You will see the layout shown in Figure 7.2.

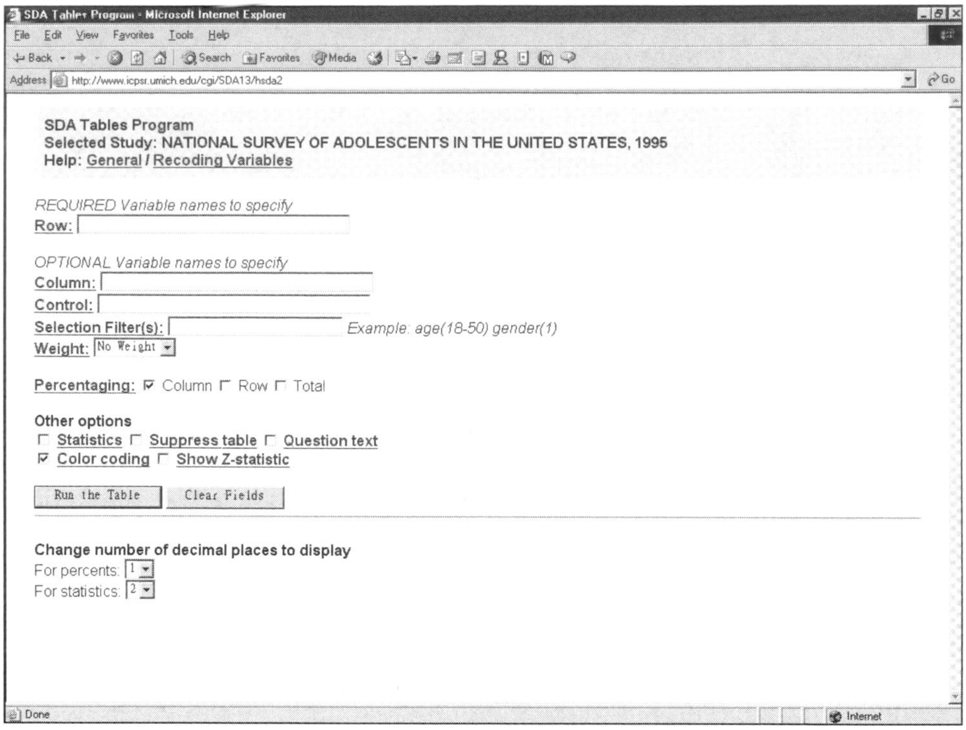

FIGURE 7.2

3. Put the **DEPENDENT** variable in the "Row" box and the **INDEPENDENT** variable in the Column box.
4. Select the "Statistics" and "Question text" options from the "Other Options" section.

   You are now ready to answer the following questions:

25. What percentage of adolescents have always lived with their biological parents? (Hint: Use **Q38A** as your row variable.)
    a. 94%
    b. 84%
    c. 74%
    d. 64%
    e. 36%

26. Run **Q27A** (ever tried smoking) by **Q38A** (always lived with both biological parents). Which of the following statements is most accurate?
    a. Adolescents who have always lived with both parents are significantly less likely to smoke than their counterparts.
    b. Adolescents who have always lived with both parents are significantly more likely to smoke than their counterparts.
    c. The result from the table is unclear.
    d. There is no significant difference between the two groups with respect to ever having tried smoking.

27. Run **Q28A** (ever drank alcohol) by **Q38A** (always lived with both biological parents). Which of the following statements is most accurate?
    a. Adolescents who have always lived with both parents are significantly less likely to have ever drunk alcohol than their counterparts.
    b. Adolescents who have always lived with both parents are significantly more likely to have ever drunk alcohol than their counterparts.
    c. The result from the table is unclear.
    d. There is no significant difference between the two groups with respect to ever having drunk alcohol.

28. Run **DELL** (ever committed delinquent offense) by **Q38A** (always lived with both biological parents). Which of the following statements is most accurate?
    a. Adolescents who have always lived with both parents are significantly less likely to have committed a delinquent offense than their counterparts.
    b. Adolescents who have always lived with both parents are significantly more likely to have committed a delinquent offense than their counterparts.
    c. The result from the table is unclear.
    d. There is no significant difference between the two groups with respect to having ever committed a delinquent offense.

29. Run **SA** (ever been sexually assaulted) by **Q38A** (always lived with both biological parents). Which of the following statements is most accurate?
    a. Adolescents who have always lived with both parents are significantly less likely to have ever been sexually assaulted than their counterparts.
    b. Adolescents who have always lived with both parents are significantly more likely to have ever been sexually assaulted than their counterparts.
    c. The result from the table is unclear.
    d. There is no significant difference between the two groups with respect to ever having been sexually assaulted.

We will now examine the impact of exposures to delinquent behavior on an adolescent's own delinquent acts.

30. Run **Q28A** by **Q48AE**. Are adolescents with friends who ever drank alcohol more likely to drink alcohol themselves than those adolescents with friends who never drank?
    a. The data suggest that teenagers with friends who drink alcohol significantly increase their own chances of drinking.
    b. The data suggest that teenagers with friends who drink alcohol significantly decrease their chances of drinking.
    c. The result from the table is unclear.
    d. No significant statistical relationship between the two variables is found.

31. Run **Q49AA** (ever stole more than $100) by **Q48AH** (friends ever stole more than $50). Which of the following statements is most accurate?
    a. Adolescents with friends who ever stole are less likely to steal themselves.
    b. Adolescents with friends who ever stole are more likely to steal themselves.
    c. The result from the table is unclear.
    d. No significant statistical relationship between the two variables is found.

32. Run **Q49AD** (ever involved in gang fights) by **Q48AD** (friends ever hit/threatened to hit someone). Which of the following statements is most accurate?
    a. Adolescents with friends who ever hit or threatened to hit someone are less likely to be involved in gang fights.
    b. Adolescents with friends who ever hit or threatened to hit someone are more likely to be involved in gang fights.
    c. The result from the table is unclear.
    d. No significant statistical relationship between the two variables is found.

33. Run **DELL** (ever committed delinquent offense) by **Q48AI** (friends suggested you do something against law). Which of the following statements is most accurate?
    a. Adolescents with friends who suggested to them that they break the law are less likely to commit a delinquent offense.
    b. Adolescents with friends who suggested to them that they break the law are more likely to commit a delinquent offense.
    c. The result from the table is unclear.
    d. No significant statistical relationship between the two variables is found.

The final question in this chapter examines the impact of school programs on alcohol/drug abuse.

34. Run **Q28A** (ever drank alcohol) by **P12A** (whether one's school has a program on alcohol/drug abuse). Which of the following statements is most accurate?
    a. Adolescents who attended schools with alcohol/drug abuse programs are less likely to drink alcohol.
    b. Adolescents who attended schools with alcohol/drug abuse programs are more likely to drink alcohol.
    c. The result from the table is unclear.
    d. No significant statistical relationship between the two variables is found.

ESSAY QUESTIONS

7–A   From the GSS database, create your own hypothesis of a potential determinant of acceptance of modern female sex roles. Test it, and summarize the results; relate your findings to previous research on the topic.

7–B   Develop an explanation or theory for the pattern of relationships between sibling ordinal position and lifetime achievements, such as educational attainments and personal earnings. Explain how having a specific sibling order position could influence the socialization process and its outcomes. Delve into previous research literature on this topic as well. Compare and contrast your analysis of these findings with the conclusions of previous research.

7–C   Develop an explanation or theory for the pattern of relationships in questions 10 through 13. Why would there be contrasting patterns of association among the differing class subgroups? Delve into previous research literature on this topic as well. Compare and contrast your explanations for these results with those of prior research.

7–D   Consult some of the published research of Melvin Kohn and others on social class and parental values of child rearing. Compare and contrast your findings with those established by earlier studies. Explain as well as possible why there would be divergences between the classes on certain value dimensions; explain why there would also be class convergence.

7–E   Sociologists frequently state that sociology often possesses a debunking motif—its findings may take sharp exception to the commonsense views of social relationships held by many members of society. Referring to any of the data trends presented in this chapter, discuss how this notion could be true in this particular case. What are the commonsense understandings about the trend or relationship? How do these GSS findings take exception to it? What are the theoretical dimensions to the issue that many lay people may be overlooking? Discuss.

CHAPTER PROJECT

In this chapter, you investigated how maternal and paternal religious participation, and attendance at a parochial school may be associated with a respondent's belief in an afterlife and their own attendance at religious services. Now, re-examine these hypotheses, within each of the two major American religious subgroups: Catholics and Protestants (variable **RELIG**) to compare and contrast how each of the three groups differ in inspiring religiosity among their members. Are there differences among each in their beliefs in an afterlife (**POSTLIFE**), the strength of their faith (**RELITEN**), and in their religious attendance (**ATTEND**)? How does each group differ in socializing their members in terms of the above theoretical model? Investigate how religious socialization responses differ (and remain alike) among Catholics and Protestants (**RELIG**). If you can figure out a way to compare Jews to the other two groups on these criteria, given their smaller numbers in the sample, bring this group into the comparison, as well. Be sure to type **year(1989)** in the "Selection Filter(s)" field.

SYNTAX GUIDE

RECODES

Please note that all recodes can also be copied and pasted from either www.ncc.edu/users/feigelb/sda.htm or www.ablongman.com/feigelman3e. If you type the recode syntax in, make sure that you type *exactly* what is shown below.

age(r:*-39 "18-39"; 40-64 "40-64"; 65-95 "65 years or older")

attend(r: 0 "Never"; 1-3 "Several times a year"; 4 "Once a month"; 5-6 "2 to 3 times a month"; 7-8 "Once a week or more")

churhsch(r: 0 "Never went or less than half a year"; 1-5 "1 to 5 years"; 5-* "More than 5 years")

educ(r: *-11 "Less than high school"; 12 "High School"; 13-* "Some College or higher")

family16(r: 0, 2-8 "not living with both parents"; 1 "living with both parents")

helpoth(r: 1 "Most important"; 2-3 "2nd/3rd"; 4-5 "4th/5th")

maattend(r: 0 "Never"; 1-3 "Several times a year"; 4 "Once a month"; 5-6 "2 to 3 times a month"; 7-8 "Once a week or more")

maeduc(r: *-11 "Less than high school"; 12 "High School"; 13-* "Some College or higher")

obey(r: 1 "Most important"; 2-3 "2nd/3rd"; 4-5 "4th/5th")

p12a(1,2)

paattend(r: 0 "Never"; 1-3 "Several times a year"; 4 "Once a month"; 5-6 "2 to 3 times a month"; 7-8 "Once a week or more")

popular(r: 1 "Most important"; 2-3 "2nd/3rd"; 4-5 "4th/5th")

prestg80(r:*-41 "Low prestige"; 42-* "High prestige")

prestige(r:*-41 "Low prestige"; 42-* "High prestige")

q27a(1,2)

q28a(1,2)

q28a(1,2)

q38a(1,2)

q48ad(1,2)

q48ae(1,2)

q48ah(1,2)

q48ai(1,2)

q49aa(1,2)

q49ad(1,2)

relig(1,2,3)

rincome(r:*-11 "Less than $25,000"; 12 "$25,000 or more")

siborder(r: 0 "First born"; 1-16 "Later born"; 95 "Only child")

thnkself(r: 1 "Most important"; 2-3 "2nd/3rd"; 4-5 "4th/5th")

tradsexr(r: 3-4 "High traditional value"; 5 "Moderate traditional value"; 6 "Low traditional value")
   Note: You need to create this variable.

workhard(r: 1 "Most important"; 2-3 "2nd/3rd"; 4-5 "4th/5th")

No recode needed: DELL; MAWRKGRW; POSTLIFE; RELITEN; SA; SEX

CHAPTER 8

Social Stratification and Social Mobility

In this chapter we will examine some aspects of the system of social ranking in American society. Every society has some degree of social stratification, and the United States is no exception, despite the emphasis among many of its citizens upon social equality, democracy, and the principle of meritocracy.

SOCIAL CLASS AND STRATIFICATION

Americans as a group possess a limited recognition of social class and stratification. If you examine the GSS 2002 dataset and tabulate the variable **CLASS** you will note that only about 10 percent of Americans recognize themselves at the top or the bottom of U.S. society. Most (approximately 90 percent, to be exact) see themselves in the middle, as either middle or working class.

You can also note a correspondence between people's awareness of their class rank and their differences in income. Wealthier people tend to see themselves as upper or middle class, while the poor more often picture themselves as lower or working class. See for yourself when you cross-tabulate **CLASS** by **INCOME98**.

Americans are by no means clear about where they stand in the class structure. You will observe that about a third of the individuals with less than $15,000 annual incomes saw themselves as middle class or higher; whilst about 27 percent of those making over $60,000 yearly, identified themselves as members of the working class or lower status. Such data attests to the vagueness and uncertainty about social class itself and to the imprecise understanding about one's rank within the American class structure.

Yet, social class is a very real experience—with dire consequences for the many Americans who are on the low end of the status hierarchy. Most Americans conceptualize social class around income differences. As our first task, let us examine income differences between families.

1. Go to the University of California's SDA site at **http://sda.berkeley .edu**.
2. Click on **SDA Archive** on the upper left corner of the page.
3. Under the subtitle "National Omnibus Surveys" click on **GSS Cumulative Datafile 1972–2002**.
4. Select "**Frequencies or crosstabulation**".
5. Click the **Start** button.

For all questions, be sure to use the recoded variables (which can be found at the end of this chapter). Also remember to put the dependent variable in the Row Box and the independent variable in the Column Box. Always select **Statistics** and **Question Text** from "Other Options" before clicking **Run the Table**. For this chapter, unless otherwise stated, we'll use GSS 2002 data to answer all questions. To use the GSS 2002 data, simply enter **year(2002)** in the Selection Filter(s) Box.

Let's first tabulate **INCOME98** to get the frequency distribution of total family incomes for 2002. With this output, answer the following questions:

1. What percentage of U.S. families in 2002 had incomes below $15,000? (Hint: type **income98** in the Row Box and **year(2002)** in the "Selection Filter(s)" Box.)
   a. 18 percent
   b. 28 percent
   c. 40 percent
2. What percentage of U.S. families had incomes below $30,000?
   a. 21 percent
   b. 38 percent
   c. 60 percent
3. Based upon the tabulation of the perception of one's family income as above or below average (**FINRELA**) indicate the percentage of respondents who identified their households as having below-average incomes.
   a. 18 percent
   b. 31 percent
   c. 40 percent

Now do a crosstabulation of **INCOME98** (total family income) as the dependent variable by **FINRELA** and answer the following questions.

4. Identify the income level at which most people feel that their family's income is below average. (Hint: At what level do most members of the subgroup feel that their income is that way?)
   a. Under 15K
   b. Under 30K
   c. Under 35K
5. With the same table identify the income level at which most people feel that their family's income is above average.
   a. Between 15–29.9K
   b. Between 30–59.9K
   c. Over 60K

INCOME

Let us now investigate why families may be rich or poor. Previous research has established a number of correlates for family income (**INCOME98**) differences including: variations in marital status (**MARITAL**), occupational prestige (PRESTG80), education (EDUC), urban-rural differences (SRCBELT), and regional (REGION) and ethnic variations (ETHNIC). Making the cross-tabulations with INCOME98 as the dependent variable, investigate each of these associations and then answer the following questions.

6. Which statement below is true?
   a. Married couples have higher incomes than the divorced.
   b. The divorced have higher incomes than the never married.
   c. The association between marital status and family income is statistically insignificant.
   d. The widowed have the highest incomes of all subgroups.
   e. All of the above.

7. Is there a statistically significant association between family income (INCOME98) and occupational prestige differences (PRESTG80)?
   a. Yes
   b. No
   c. Unclear or mixed results

8. Which statement below is true?
   a. It is generally supported that the higher the level of education, the higher the level of family income.
   b. The evidence shows little family income differences between today's high school graduates and dropouts.
   c. There is a statistically significant association between family income and education.
   d. a and c only.
   e. All of the above.

9. Which statement below is true?
   a. More wealthier families appear to be located in the suburbs.
   b. Wealthier families appear to be located in the large cities.
   c. The highest percentage of the poorest families are found in the largest cities.
   d. Only a and c of the above.
   e. None of the above.

10. Which statement below is true?
   a. All regions show similar levels of family income.
   b. The South appears to be behind most other regions in family income levels.
   c. There is a statistically significant association between family income and region.
   d. only b and c.
   e. all of the above.

11. Which statement below is true?
   a. All ethnic groups show similar distributions of family income.
   b. Italian Americans have the highest percentages of low income families.
   c. There is a statistically significant association between family income and ethnicity.
   d. Asian Americans report the lowest percentages of high income families.
   e. All of the above.

A frequently made claim, which most students have heard, is that "it pays to go to school." Evaluate this notion with the GSS data by crosstabulating personal income (RINCOM98) by education (EDUC).

12. Is there a statistically significant association between personal income and education?
    a. Yes
    b. No
    c. Unclear or mixed results

It has also been asserted that having a rich father may be just as good as, or better than, going to school if one wants to become rich. First, evaluate the two-variable hypothesis of RINCOM98 (personal income) by father's occupational prestige (PAPRES80). Then try running RINCOM98 by INCOM16 (family income status at age 16). Finally, do a three-way crosstabulation running personal income (RINCOM98) as the dependent variable by EDUC as the independent variable, with family income at 16 as the control variable. As you perform these analyses, answer the following questions.

13. Is there a statistically significant association between personal income differences (RINCOM98) and father's prestige (PAPRES80)?
    a. Yes
    b. No
    c. Unclear results
14. Is there a statistically significant association between personal income differences (RINCOM98) and family income at 16 (INCOM16)?
    a. Yes
    b. No
    c. Unclear or mixed results
15. Looking at the delta values (percentage points difference) across those earning $60K and over annually, which of the three factors produces the biggest variations in personal income differences, apparently producing the biggest influence on making high incomes?
    a. Education
    b. Father's occupational prestige
    c. Family income differences at age 16
    d. All three factors present virtually identical delta values
16. Does applying the control variable of family income at age 16 alter the association between education (EDUC) and personal income (RINCOM98)? To do this, type rincom98 in the Row Box, educ in the Column Box, incom16 in the Control Box, and year(2002) in the "Selection Filter(s)" Box.
    a. Yes, in every subgroup relationship; the bivariate relationship is now no longer observable.
    b. Yes, but only in families with above-average incomes at age 16; in lower income families education is still related to personal income.
    c. No; in all subgroups education is still related to income differences.
    d. Mixed or unclear results.

17. How would you best describe this control variable analysis and what differences are noted in the relationship of education and personal income when people grow up in rich, average, or poor homes (at age 16)?
    a. In poor and average income homes education still correlates highly with personal income differences.
    b. The proportion of respondents with college education making $60,000 or more are more likely to be found in rich families.
    c. In all subgroups the incomes of the most well educated exceeds those receiving less education.
    d. All of the above.
    e. a and c only.

It is well known that women generally have lower earnings than men. Explaining economic sexism is a complex matter, to some extent a product of the different educational attainments of men and women, differences in work roles, occupational prestige differences, and differences in the monetary rewards received by male and female workers.

Looking at the GSS 2002 data, try running personal income (RINCOM98) by gender (SEX) to see if the gender earnings gap still persists. Then, answer the following questions.

18. Comparing the sexes in their annual personal incomes shows:
    a. Men still earn slightly more than women, although women exceed men in earnings at the intermediate incomes levels ($30K to $60K yearly).
    b. Men outearn women at the higher income levels and women are more likely to be overrepresented at the lowest income levels.
    c. Differences between the sexes in personal earnings are statistically significant.
    d. a and c.
    e. b and c.

19. Crosstabulate personal income differences (RINCOM98) by education (EDUC) controlling for gender (SEX). What seems to be the most appropriate interpretation of the two tables? (Hint: put rincom98 in the Row Box, educ in the Column Box, sex in the Control Box, and year(2002) in the Selection Filter(s) Box.)
    a. Men clearly make more money as they complete more education but the same cannot be said for women.
    b. Women clearly make more money as they complete more education but the same cannot be said for men.
    c. Both men and women seem to be advantaged economically by completing more education.
    d. The economic benefits of completing high school appear to be greater for men than for women, though women gain similarly as men do by completing some college or more education.

20. Do a two-way crosstabulation between RINCOM98 and occupational differences (OCC80). What does it show?
    a. Professionals and managerial workers are the most likely of all types of worker to be well paid.
    b. Service workers and operatives are least likely to be well paid.
    c. Skilled manual workers appear to make more than those employed in service occupations.
    d. All of the above.
    e. a and b only.

21. Tabulating occupational differences (OCC80) by gender (SEX) shows which of the following patterns:
    a. More men seem to be concentrated in relatively higher paying occupations like doing skilled manual work.
    b. More women seem to be concentrated in relatively lower paying jobs like administrative and technical support occupations.
    c. The relationship between OCC80 and SEX is statistically significant.
    d. All of the above.
    e. a and b only.

22. Now, do a three-way crosstabulation between RINCOM98 and occupational differences (OCC80) controlled by gender (SEX). What does it show? (Hint: put rincom98 in the Row Box, occ80 in the Column Box, sex in the Control Box, and year(2002) in the Selection Filter(s) Box.)
    a. A higher percentage of male professional employees earn over $60K annually than women.
    b. Women show a higher percentage making between $15–30K annually than men.
    c. Women show a higher percentage making $15K or less annually in every occupational category.
    d. All of the above.
    e. Only a and b.

OCCUPATIONAL PRESTIGE

Although both occupational prestige and income are used in different sociological studies, most sociologists prefer to use *occupational prestige* as the single best indicator of a person's rank. Conceptually, occupation comes closest to reflecting the multidimensional components of status, such as the differences between people in power, skills, specialized training, patterns of intimate association, and life style. Riches alone do not immediately confer status, especially when we consider the low esteem generally accorded to successful racketeers, prostitutes, and other practitioners of immoral deeds—who often possess considerable wealth. On the other hand, consider the high regard society usually pays to ministers, military officers, and teachers, despite their usually modest, and in many cases near-poverty level, incomes.

Research on stratification has found occupational prestige to be an extremely stable indicator of rank. Studies done at different times have found considerable agreement among respondents on the relative standings of various occupational categories. Cross-national comparisons, including data from some underdeveloped countries, also show little variation in the prestige rankings of occupations. Such findings suggest there is a relatively fixed hierarchy of prestige associated with the positions and institutions of industrial society.

We will now shift our focus from income differences between groups to occupational prestige. We will follow the Hodge, Siegel, and Rossi occupational prestige rating scheme employed in the GSS surveys, where occupations were rated on a scale of 1 to 100 (Hodge, Siegel and Rossi, 1964). In the following exercises, prestige is broken down into four groups: lowest (prestige ratings below 30) low (prestige ratings between 31 and 40), medium (ratings between 41 and 50), and high (ratings above 51)—PRESTG80.

It has often been said that social class rank is the single most important factor influencing the course of a person's life, affecting everything that happens from one's birth to death. It affects life expectancy, schooling, friendship patterns, where and how people live, what they do in their leisure time, the foods they eat—in short, everything they do, from the sublime to the mundane. There are a number of possible correlates of social rank that can be evaluated (use PRESTG80 as your independent variable):

- hours worked (HRS1)
- cigarette smoking (SMOKE)
- whether a respondent voted in 2000 (VOTE00)
- political views (POLVIEWS)
- owning or renting housing (DWELOWN)
- marital stability (DIVORCE)
- number of children (CHILDS)
- hours of TV viewing (TVHOURS).

As you run each crosstabulation, answer the following questions. Be sure to enter year(2000) in the "Selection(s) Filter" box for questions 23 and 25–30.

23. Which of the following statements is true?
    a. Lower class respondents tend to work longer hours than upper status ones.
    b. Working class (or low prestige) respondents tend to work longer hours than all other status groups.
    c. Medium and high status respondents work the longest of all prestige subgroups.
    d. There are no significant differences in hours usually worked among the different prestige subgroups.
24. Which of the following statements is true? (Use GSS 1994 data for this question.)
    a. Lower class respondents are more likely to smoke than medium and high status ones.
    b. Upper class respondents are more likely to smoke than lower status ones.
    c. There are no significant differences in smoking among the different prestige subcategories.
    d. There are some class differences in smoking, falling short of statistical significance.

25. Which statement below is true?
    a. There are practically no differences in voting between middle status respondents and upper status ones.
    b. Most lower class respondents tend to vote in a presidential election, although their frequency of voter participation is lower than that of upper status ones.
    c. There are no significant differences in voting among the different prestige subcategories.
    d. Voting differences among different prestige subcategories, although noticeable, fall short of statistical significance.

26. Based on the evidence from the GSS data, which of the following statements is true?
    a. Upper class respondents tend to be more politically conservative, while lower class respondents tend to be more liberal.
    b. There are no statistically significant differences in political ideologies between the different prestige subcategories.
    c. Upper class respondents tend to be more conservative, while lower status respondents are more moderate in their political positions.
    d. All of the above.

27. Based on the evidence from the GSS data, which of the following statements is true?
    a. Although nearly statistically significant, the differences in home ownership levels between the different prestige subcategories are not very substantial.
    b. Differences in home ownership levels between the different prestige subcategories are substantial and significant.
    c. More than half of low prestige respondents own their residences.
    d. a and c.
    e. b and c.

28. Based on the evidence from the GSS data, which of the following statements is true?
    a. Probably owing to their greater monetary resources and ability to afford a divorce, upper status respondents are more likely to have been divorced than lower status respondents.
    b. In comparison to the upper status groups, divorce rates could be higher among the lower classes, although differences fell short of statistical significance.
    c. Divorce rates don't differ much by class.
    d. A regrouping of medium and low prestige respondents, compared to high prestige respondents, might show statistically significant differences between the classes.
    e. b, c and d may all be correct.

29. Based on the evidence from the GSS data, which of the following statements is true?
    a. The upper classes tend to have somewhat more children than the lower classes.
    b. Status doesn't appear to have much of an influence on child bearing.
    c. Lower class members appear to have more children compared to medium and high status groups, and differences are statistically significant.
    d. Only a and b.
30. Based on the evidence from the GSS data, which of the following statements is true?
    a. The upper classes watch TV about as much as the lower classes.
    b. Status doesn't appear to have much of a relationship to time spent watching TV.
    c. Members of the lower class usually spend substantially more time watching TV than upper status respondents.
    d. Only a and b.

SOCIAL CLASS AND LIFESTYLES

Social mobility is another important subject in the study of social stratification. Sociologists usually talk about several different kinds of mobility. One important way of subdividing mobility is to distinguish between horizontal and vertical mobility. In *horizontal mobility* one moves from one position to another of approximately equal rank. If a carpenter gave up carpentry for plumbing we would probably call this a case of horizontal mobility. In *vertical mobility*, one moves up or down in status. An assembler who became a foreman is an example of upward mobility, while a dress shop owner who became a sewing machine operator is an instance of downward mobility.

Sociologists also differentiate between career mobility and intergenerational mobility. In *career mobility*, one changes positions during the course of one's own work history. In *intergenerational mobility*, changes take place over one or more generations. Although it may seem sexist, sociologists usually assess people's upward or downward movements in relation to their father's position. In most U.S. homes, the husband/father's occupation becomes the baseline for assessing the family's status in the community.

In the United States, of course, the great dream and hope of most is to experience upward social mobility—the so-called "American Dream." With the GSS we have focused on inter-generational mobility between fathers and respondents. In assessing the amount of mobility going on— whether downward, upward or remaining stable—we have excluded the respondent population aged between 18 and 29. Enough of these people are going to school or still launching their careers that their inclusion might overstate the amount of downward mobility. Prestige scores ranging from 1 to 100 according to the Hodge, Siegel and Rossi scale were collected from respondents and about their fathers. These ratings were collapsed into a four-point scale, 1–30 = 1; 31–40 = 2; 41–50 = 3; and 51 and above = 4. Respondents who remained at the level of their father's status were defined as non-mobile; those moving relationally up or down in comparison to their father's prestige score were regarded as upwardly and downwardly mobile respectively.

Creating a new variable social mobility (**SOCMOBIL**) requires you to do the following:

1. Go to http://sda.berkeley.edu/cgi-bin12/hsda?harcsda+gss02.
2. Click **Compute a new variable** and then click **Start**.
3. You will see the layout shown in Figure 8.1.

FIGURE 8.1

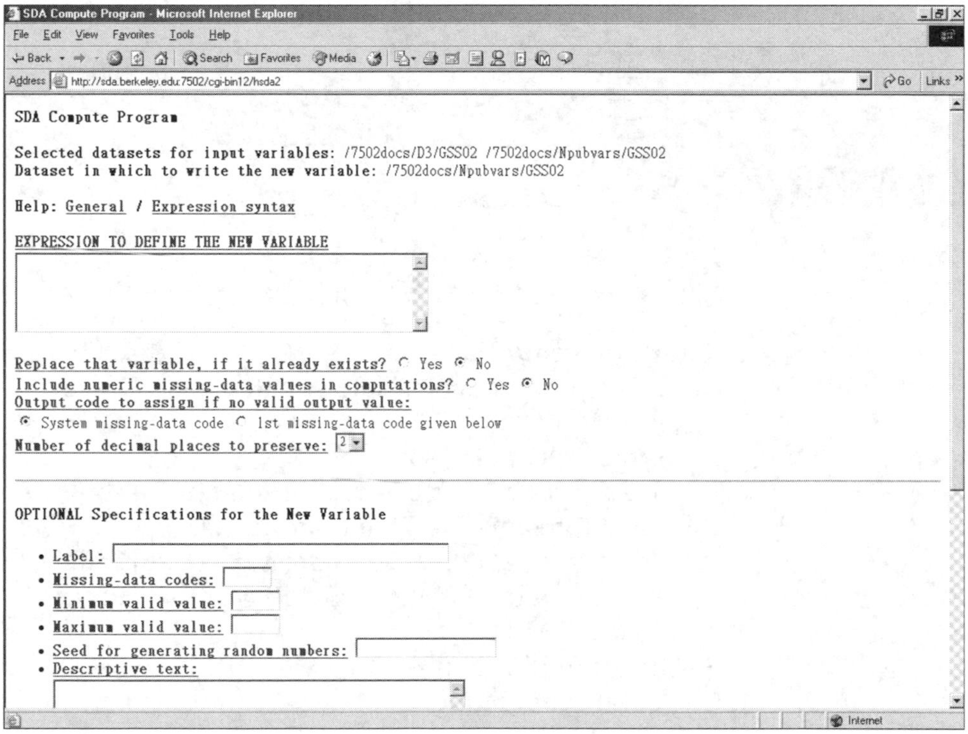

4. Type:
   > if (papres80 LE 30) palevel = 1
   > else if (papres80 GE 31 and papres80 LE 40) palevel = 2
   > else if (papres80 GE 41 and papres80 LE 50) palevel = 3
   > else if (papres80 GE 51 and papres80 LE 86) palevel = 4
   > into the box labeled "EXPRESSION TO DEFINE THE NEW VARIABLE"
5. Select **Yes** in the "Replace that variable, if it already exists?" option.
6. Click **Start Computing**. To make sure you understand the procedure, check the layout shown in Figure 8.2.

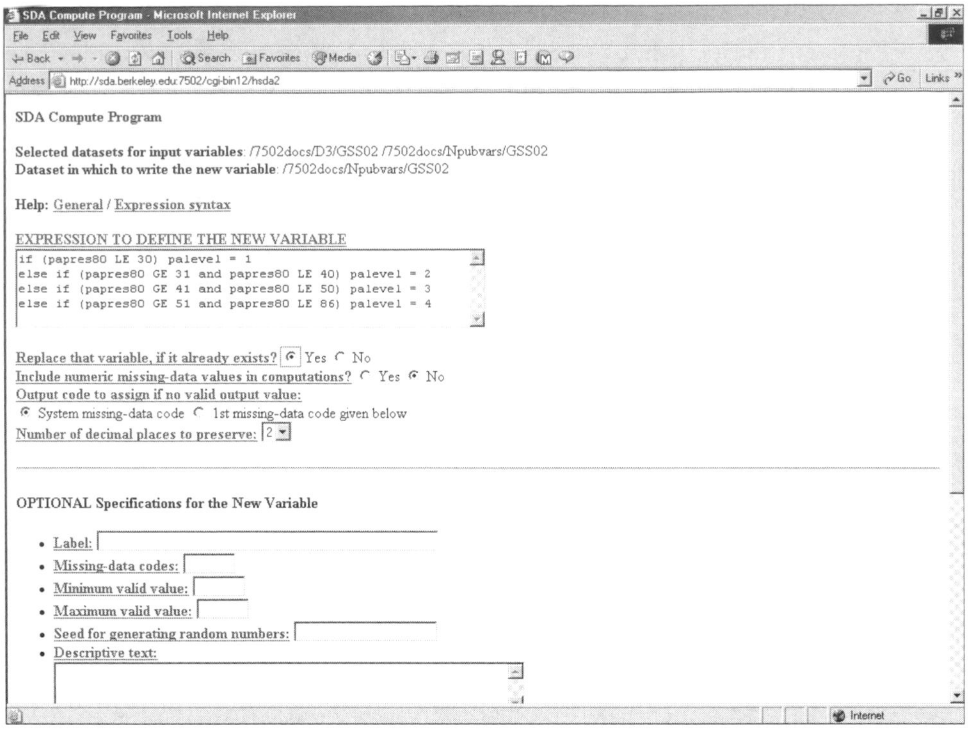

FIGURE 8.2

We will now create a variable for the son's prestige level.

7. Return to http://sda.berkeley.edu/cgi-bin12/hsda?harcsda+gss02.
8. Click **Compute a new variable** and then click **Start**.
9. Type:
   > if (prestg80 LE 30) sonlevel = 1
   > else if (prestg80 GE 31 and prestg80 LE 40) sonlevel = 2
   > else if (prestg80 GE 41 and prestg80 LE 50) sonlevel = 3
   > else if (prestg80 GE 51 and prestg80 LE 86) sonlevel = 4
   > into the box labeled "EXPRESSION TO DEFINE THE NEW VARIABLE"
10. Select **Yes** in the "Replace that variable, if it already exists?" option.
11. Click **Start Computing**.

Finally, we will create the SOCMOBIL variable

12. Again, return to http://sda.berkeley.edu/cgi-bin12/hsda?harcsda+gss02, select **Compute a new variable** and then click **Start**.
13. Type
    > if (sonlevel EQ palevel) socmobil=3
    > else if (sonlevel GT palevel) socmobil=2
    > else if (sonlevel LT palevel) socmobil=1
    > into the box labeled "EXPRESSION TO DEFINE THE NEW VARIABLE".
14. Select **Yes** in the "Replace that variable, if it already exists?" option.
15. Do not include numeric missing-data values in computations.

You are now ready to tabulate social mobility (SOCMOBIL) and answer the following question. (Remember to use the recoded variable SOCMOBIL found at the end of this chapter.)

31. Based on the evidence in the 2002 GSS data, which of the following statements is true? (Hint: be sure to enter **age(30-99) year(2002)** in the Selection Filter(s) box.)
    a. The largest group of people do not undergo upward or downward social mobility.
    b. Upward mobility seems to exceed downward mobility.
    c. Downward mobility is not an especially uncommon event.
    d. All of the above.
    e. Only b and c.

Our final concern here will be to investigate the correlates of social mobility. At least four variables come to mind that might be related to upward or downward movement: occupations (OCC80); education (EDUC); the number of their organizational memberships (MEMNUM); and the age at which a person first married (AGEWED). Try them out and see if there are any correlations.

Answer the last group of questions. (Make sure to run each of the four above variables as independent variables with social mobility as the dependent variable.)

32. Based on the evidence in the GSS data, which of the following statements is true? (Hint: be sure to enter **year(2002)** in the Selection Filter(s) box.)
    a. Most of those undergoing upward social movement were in professional and managerial occupations.
    b. Most of those experiencing downward movement were employed as operatives and as personal service workers.
    c. The relationship between SOCMOBIL and OCC80 is statistically significant.
    d. All of the above.
    e. None of the above.
33. Based on the evidence from the GSS data, which of the following statements is true?
    a. The data showed that the most highly educated were more likely to experience upward mobility.
    b. High school graduates didn't appear to obtain any substantial upward mobility gains over those dropping out of high school.
    c. Not graduating from high school significantly increases one's likelihood of moving downward in status.
    d. All of the above.
    e. None of the above.

34. Based on the evidence from the 1994 GSS data, which of the following statements is true? (Hint: be sure to enter **year(1994)** in the "Selection Filter(s)" box).
   a. The data suggested that people who did not belong to an organization generally remained at the same social level.
   b. There may be some association between mobility and joining organizations, but the relationship was not a directly linear one.
   c. The association between mobility and joining voluntary organizations fell short of statistical significance.
   d. All of the above.
   e. None of the above.

35. Based on the evidence from the 1994 GSS data, which of the following statements is true? (Hint: be sure to enter **year(1994)** in the "Selection Filter(s)" box).
   a. There appears to be a trend showing downward movement associated with early marriage.
   b. The evidence suggests upward movement could be linked to getting married for the first time between the ages of 21 and 25.
   c. Getting married after age 25 could be associated with remaining stationary in social status.
   d. All of the above.
   e. None of the above.

ESSAY QUESTIONS

8–A   Taking any one, or several, of the hypothesized correlates of family income differences (such as differences in marital status, occupational prestige, education, urban–rural residence, region, or ethnicity) explain why there is an association between that variable and family income differences. Consult some of the previous research literature on this selected hypothesis and compare and contrast past findings with the GSS 2002 findings.

8–B   Run personal income differences (**RINCOM98**) by gender (**SEX**) while controlling for differences in education. Examine your results and answer whether there are levels of educational accomplishment where the gender gap in incomes is minimal? If so, at what level is it most profound? Explain these variations. Consult the previous research literature that bears upon the question of explaining variations in earnings between similarly educated men and women.

8–C   Compare and contrast differences between men and women in occupational activities and prestige. Evaluate these differences upon gender earnings differentials. Refer also to the data on gender differences in educational attainments. Taking into account differences in the kinds of work done by men and women, differences in their occupational prestige, and whatever else you wish to consider, how do you explain why men may still make more than women? Wherever it may be appropriate to do so, your answer should refer to the 2002 GSS data findings.

8–D   Develop two of your own hypotheses from the database of 2002 GSS variables and run the crosstabulations with PRESTG80 as the independent variable. Interpret your results.

8–E   Develop a theory or overview explaining how or why differences in social class produce differences in attitudes and behavior patterns.

8–F   Run the crosstabulations for the same group of dependent variables (HRS1, SMOKE, VOTE92, POLVIEWS, DWELOWN, EVERDIV, CHILDS, TVHOURS), but this time run RINCOM91 as the independent variable (instead of PRESTG80). Compare and contrast the outcomes with what resulted when PRESTG80 was the independent variable. Now, run subjective class awareness CLASS as the independent variable against the eight dependent variables. Give an interpretation for any differences obtained by these different ways of measuring status.

CHAPTER PROJECT

Write a short essay detailing how and why the timing of one's first marriage and the joining of voluntary associations may be linked to upward or downward movement in social status. Use previous social science research evidence in formulating your answer. Using the instructions provided in Chapter 8, generate a new variable displaying memberships as a two value category. Your new variable should have two values: those not belonging to any organizations, and those belonging to one or more. Re-run your new variable against social mobility and compare the results with those previously obtained from running MEMNUM. Interpret your findings and relate them to what you found in your review of this research literature.

REFERENCES

Davis, James A., & Smith, Tom W. 1987. *General Social Surveys, 1972–1987: Cumulative Codebook.* Chicago: National Opinion Research Center.

Hodge, R. W., Siegel, P. M., & Rossi, P. H. 1964. Occupational Prestige in the United States, 1925–1963. *American Journal of Sociology, 70,* 286–302.

Smith, Tom W., Bradley, J. Arnold, & Wesely, Jennifer K. 1995. *Annotated Bibliography of Papers Using the General Social Surveys.* 10th edition. Ann Arbor, MI: Inter-university Consortium for Social and Political Research.

SYNTAX GUIDE

GENERAL SOCIAL SURVEY
Go to: http://sda.berkeley.edu/cgi-bin12/hsda?harcsda+gss02
Select "Frequencies or crosstabulation"
Click Start

General Social Survey Recodes

Please note that all recodes can also be copied and pasted from either www.ncc.edu/users/feigelb/sda.htm or www.ablongman.com/feigelman3e. If you type the recode syntax in, make sure that you type *exactly* what is shown below.

agewed(r: *-20 "20 or younger"; 21-25 "21-25"; 26-* "26 or older")

childs(r: 0 "0"; 1 "1"; 2 "2"; 3 "3"; 4-* "4 or more")

dwelown(r: 1 "Own or is buying"; 2 "Rent")

educ(r: *-11 "Less than high school"; 12 "High School"; 13-* "Some College or higher")

ethnic(r:1,39 "Af";4,8,24 "En";14 "Iri";15 "Ita";2,6,13,21,23,33-35 "EEu";11 "Ger";7,9,19,26 "Sca";17,22,25,28,38 "His";3,10,18,27,36 "WEu";5,16,20,31,37,40 "As"; 97 "US"; 30 "AIn";12,29,32,41 "Otr")

finrela(r: 1-2 "Below average"; 3 "Average"; 4-5 "Above average")

hrs1(r: *-20 "20 or less"; 21-34 "21-34"; 35-45 "35-45"; 46-* "46 or more")

incom16(r: 1-2 "Below average"; 3 "Average"; 4-5 "Above average")

income98(r: 1-10 "Less than $15,000"; 11-15 "$15,000-$29,999";16-19 "$30,000-$59,999"; 20-23 "$60,000 or more")

memnum(r: 0 "None"; 1 "One"; 2 "Two"; 3-* "Three or more")

occ80(r:3-199 "Professional/managerial"; 200-389 "Technicians/sales/ admin. support"; 400-469 "Service"; 473-699 "Farmers/fisherman/ skilled manual workers"; 703-889 "Operatives")

papres80(r:*-30 "Lowest"; 31-40 "Low"; 41-50 "Medium"; 51-* "High")

polviews(r: 1-3 "Liberal"; 4 "Moderate"; 5-7 "Conservative")

prestg80(r:*-30 "Lowest"; 31-40 "Low"; 41-50 "Medium"; 51-* "High")

region(r: 1-2 "Northeast"; 3-4 "Central"; 5-7 "South"; 8-9 "West")

rincom91(r: 1-10 "Less than $15,000"; 11-15 "$15,000-$29,999";16-19 "$30,000-$59,999"; 20-21 "$60,000 or more")

rincom98(r: 1-10 "Less than $15,000"; 11-15 "$15,000-$29,999";16-19 "$30,000-$59,999"; 20-23 "$60,000 or more")

socmobil(r: 1 "Downward mobility"; 2 "Upward mobility"; 3 "No mobility")

srcbelt(r: 1-2 "Large city"; 3-4 "Suburbanite"; 5 "Small city"; 6 "Rural and farm")

tvhours(r: 0-1 "0-1 hour"; 2 "2 hours"; 3 "3 hours"; 4-* "4 or more hours")

vote00(r: 1 "Voted"; 2 "Did not vote")

No recode needed: **CLASS; DIVORCE; MARITAL; SEX; SMOKE**

QUESTION #31

Three steps are required to create the new variable SOCMOBIL

Step 1: Create a new variable, PALEVEL

1. Go to: http://sda.berkeley.edu/cgi-bin12/hsda?harcsda+gss02
2. Select "Compute a new variable"
3. Click **Start**
4. Type:
   if (papres80 LE 30) palevel = 1
   else if (papres80 GE 31 and papres80 LE 40) palevel = 2
   else if (papres80 GE 41 and papres80 LE 50) palevel = 3
   else if (papres80 GE 51 and papres80 LE 86) palevel = 4
   into the box labeled "EXPRESSION TO DEFINE THE NEW VARIABLE"
5. Click **Start Computing**

Step 2: Create a new variable, SONLEVEL

1. From your brower, click **Back**. Or go to http://sda.berkeley.edu/cgi-bin12/hsda?harcsda+gss02
2. Select "Compute a new variable"
3. Click **Start**
4. Type:
   if (prestg80 LE 30) sonlevel = 1
   else if (prestg80 GE 31 and prestg80 LE 40) sonlevel = 2
   else if (prestg80 GE 41 and prestg80 LE 50) sonlevel = 3
   else if (prestg80 GE 51 and prestg80 LE 86) sonlevel = 4
   into the box labeled "EXPRESSION TO DEFINE THE NEW VARIABLE"
5. Click **Start Computing**

Step 3: Create the variable SOCMOBIL

1. From your brower, click Back. Or go to http://sda.berkeley.edu/cgi-bin12/hsda?harcsda+gss02
2. Select "Compute a new variable"
3. Click **Start**
4. Type
   if (sonlevel EQ palevel) socmobil=3
   else if (sonlevel GT palevel) socmobil=2
   else if (sonlevel LT palevel) socmobil=1
   into the box labeled "EXPRESSION TO DEFINE THE NEW VARIABLE"
5. Click **Start Computing**

CHAPTER 9

Minority/Majority Relations

Looking back to our nation's beginnings, we can observe that the United States has had an unenviable record for intergroup relations. With its extermination of Native Americans and the enslavement of African Americans, this country has long suppressed its minorities, subjecting them to an almost unending progression of mistreatment. Now, as we consider those grim early years, we can recognize some gains in recent times toward reducing the persecution of minorities and improving intergroup relations.

When we think back to the mid-1960s—when our newspapers reported near daily rioting and interracial urban strife—we can now see indications of a more accepting and pluralistic society. However, we would be gravely mistaken to conclude racial and cultural equality now prevail, or that the present represents a state of tolerant and harmonious intergroup relations. Occasional incidents of anti-minority vandalism, of unprovoked violence against racial and ethnic minority members by our law enforcement personnel, and similar occurrences continually confront us in our national news media. These events remind us that the state of interracial relations still falls despairingly short of being harmonious.

Sociologists have had a longstanding interest in studying intergroup relations, and in carefully gauging how intergroup relations have improved (or worsened) and opportunities for minority advancement have changed. In the 1920s the American sociologist Emory Borgardus developed a social distance scale to systematically measure how members of society accept one another. Borgardus saw social intimacy ranging from minimal acceptance—allowing a group into one's country, to maximal acceptance—allowing group members to be fully intimate, to be potential kin by marriage.

In the 1990 General Social Survey a variety of questions were asked measuring potential social intimacy, following this long established line of research. To answer the first three short answer questions, you need to tabulate separately each of the following six variables: LIVEJEWS, LIVEBLKS, LIVEASNS, LIVEHSPN, LIVENO, and LIVESO and take note of the results. These variables refer to people's willingness to have a specific group member—a Jew, Black, Asian, Hispanic, Northern White and Southern White—as a neighbor. To get started:

1. Go to http://sda.berkeley.edu/cgi-bin12/hsda?harcsda+gss02.
2. Select "Frequencies or crosstabulation" and click **Start**.
3. Type **livejews** in the Row box. Remember to use the recoded variables (see the list at the end of this chapter).

4. Click **Run the Table**.
5. You will need to repeat this for the other five variables.

Now answer the following questions.

1. Which ethnic subgroup is the most opposed as a neighbor?
   a. African Americans
   b. Hispanics
   c. Asians
   d. Jews
   e. Northern whites
2. Which ethnic subgroup is the most accepted as a neighbor?
   a. African Americans
   b. Hispanics
   c. Asians
   d. Jews
   e. Northern whites
3. Is there a complete correspondence in the ratings given to accepted and opposed groups (i.e., are the groups that are opposed, also those least likely to be accepted; and correspondingly, are the groups that are least opposed, most accepted)?
   a. Yes, completely congruent and complementary
   b. Not completely complementary, although similar
   c. An unclear pattern prevails

Tabulate the six variables **MARJEW**, **MARBLK**, **MARASIAN**, **MARHISP**, **MARNO**, and **MARSO** to investigate people's willingness to have relatives marry people from these groups: Jews, Blacks, Asians, Hispanics, Northern Whites and Southern Whites. After taking note of the results for each separate tabulation, answer questions 4–6. Remember to use the recoded variables.

4. Members of which ethnic subgroup are the least acceptable as potential marriage partners?
   a. African Americans
   b. Hispanics
   c. Asians
   d. Jews
   e. Northern whites
5. Members of which ethnic subgroup are the most acceptable as potential marriage partners?
   a. African Americans
   b. Hispanics
   c. Asians
   d. Jews
   e. Northern Whites

6. Compare and contrast the results found in the above questions. Are there any discrepancies between how much members of a group are opposed as neighbors and how acceptable they are for marriage?
   a. Yes
   b. Opposition to both neighboring and marriage are perfectly matched
   c. Favored groups for neighboring and marriage, although not matched perfectly, correspond closely
   d. All of the above
   e. Only a and c

The above analysis demonstrates that minority members are still found as less acceptable in WASP (White Anglo Saxon and Protestant) America.

Now let's examine more recent data. The 2002 GSS survey has a topical module on race relations. We'll use some questions from that module to explore interracial relationships:

1. Go to: http://sda.berkeley.edu/cgi-bin12/hsda?harcsda+gss02.
2. Select "Frequencies or crosstabulation" and click **Start**.
3. Enter **feelblks** in your Row box (reminder: be sure to use the recoded variable **FEELBLKS**).

Now answer the following questions:

7. What percentage of respondents feel warmly towards African Americans?
   a. 7%
   b. 41%
   c. 52%
   d. 70%
   e. None of the above
8. What percentage of respondents feel warmly towards Asian Americans (**FEELASNS**)?
   a. 7%
   b. 47%
   c. 57%
   d. 70%
   e. None of the above
9. What percentage of respondents feel warmly towards Hispanics (**FEELHSPS**)?
   a. 30%
   b. 40%
   c. 50%
   d. 70%
   e. None of the above

10. What percentage of respondents feel warmly towards whites (FEELWHTS)?
    a. 36%
    b. 46%
    c. 56%
    d. 66%
    e. None of the above

In the following set of questions, we'll explore some bivariate relationships about the acceptance of cultural pluralism. Pluralism is the idea that people accept each others' cultural differences. In GSS 2002 respondents were asked if they believed that each ethnic group has the right to maintain its own unique traditions (ETHTRADS). Most Americans, over 80 percent, believed that members of ethnic minorities have a right to maintain their traditions while living in the United States. When people agree with this idea less often or when they disagree with it, they are likely to be expressing their racial or ethnic animosities. In this set of questions we will try to explore why some Americans are less likely to accept pluralism.

1. Go to http://sda.berkeley.edu/cgi-bin12/hsda?harcsda+gss02
2. Select "Frequencies or crosstabulation" and click **Start**
3. Put the dependent variable ETHTRADS in the Row Box (with the appropriate recode language) and put each requested independent variable(s) in the Column Box for each problem
4. In the "Selection Filter(s)" box, enter **year(2002)**
5. From Table Options, select "Statistics" and "Question text"

You are now ready to answer the following set of questions.

11. Is opposition to pluralism (ETHTRADS) related to urbanicity (SRCBELT)?
    a. Yes, suburbanites show the greatest acceptance of pluralism, rural residents the least.
    b. No, there are no statistically significant differences in pluralistic views across the differences in urbanicity.
    c. Big city residents show substantially more acceptance of pluralism than all the other subgroups.
    d. It can not be determined.
12. Is opposition to pluralism (ETHTRADS) related to race (RACECEN1) and ethnic differences (ETHNIC)?
    a. It is not related to race but related to ethnic differences.
    b. It is related to race but not related to ethnic differences.
    c. It is not related to either race or ethnic differences.
    d. It is related to both race and ethnic difference.
    e. It can not be determined.
13. Is opposition to pluralism related to being born in the US or being foreign born (BORN)?
    a. Yes
    b. No
    c. It can not be determined

14. Is opposition to pluralism related to religious differences (RELIG) and to differences in religious participation (ATTEND)?
   a. It is not related to religious differences, but is related to differences in religious participation with more active churchgoers showing greater acceptance of pluralism.
   b. It is clearly related to religious differences and clearly not related to differences in religious participation.
   c. There appears to be a borderline relationship with religion, with Protestants showing lower acceptances than Jews, but there is no relationship to religious participation.
   d. It is clearly related to both religious differences and to differences in religious participation.
   e. It can not be determined.

15. Is opposition to pluralism related to economic and/or social class differences? (CLASS; RINCOM98)
   a. More high status and upper income people accept pluralism more than those who are less advantaged.
   b. More self-identified working and middle class people accept pluralism than the lower and upper classes and more lower income people appear to be on fence about pluralism than higher income recipients.
   c. It is not related to either class or income differences.
   d. It is related to both class and income differences with the lower classes showing greater acceptance of pluralism than the more advantaged in society.
   e. It can not be determined.

16. Is opposition to pluralism related to differences in educational attainments (EDUC)?
   a. Yes, there is a clear statistically significant difference showing the more highly educated accepting pluralism more than the less well educated.
   b. Yes, there is a clear statistically significant difference showing the less well educated accepting pluralism more than more highly educated members of society.
   c. No, although there is a statistically significant difference, percentage differences are small and show no consistent trends.
   d. It can not be determined.

17. Is opposition to pluralism related to perceived economic disappointments or frustrations (FINRELA)?
   a. Yes, those who see their incomes as falling far below average are less accepting of pluralism than all other groups.
   b. Clearly not, since those who see their incomes as above average are less accepting of pluralism.
   c. Not at all.
   d. It can not be determined.

18. Is opposition to pluralism related to age differences (AGE)?
   a. Yes, younger people appear to accept pluralism more than older folks.
   b. Yes, older people accept pluralism more than younger folks.
   c. There is no variability in acceptances of pluralism across the age spectrum.
   d. It can not be determined.

19. Is opposition to pluralism related to gender differences (SEX)?
    a. There are clearly considerable differences between men and women on this point showing women more against pluralism than men.
    b. Yes, there was a statistically significant difference showing men less accepting of pluralism than women though the difference was not a very substantial one.
    c. No, men appear more accepting of pluralism but the differences were not statistically significant.
    d. There were no statistically significant differences between men and women on acceptance of pluralism.
    e. It can not be determined.

Another very important aspect of studying intergroup relations is to evaluate how prejudice and discrimination affect minority members themselves. How does dominant group prejudice and discrimination diminish and constrain the life chances of minority group members? And with the passage of many newer civil rights laws and the establishment of affirmative action policies, do minority members now find it easier to overcome prejudice and discrimination, than past generations did?

Such questions can be approached with the data from the GSS. Knowing as we all do how important education is for promoting people's success aspirations, let us begin by first comparing the educational attainments of all racial groups from one another. First, tabulate educational attainment (EDUC) by race (RACECEN1) to establish which groups have achieved the most and least education. Be sure to enter year(2002) in the Selection Filter Box for the following questions.

20. Tabulating (EDUC) by (RACECEN1), which of the following groups has gained the most education?
    a. Whites
    b. African Americans
    c. Native Americans
    d. Asians
    e. The racial subgroups do not show statistically significant differences in education
21. Tabulating (EDUC) by (RACECEN1), which group has gained the least education:
    a. Whites
    b. African Americans
    c. Native Americans
    d. Asians
    e. The racial subgroups do not show statistically significant differences in education

Alternatively, we can compute the mean years of education completed for each subgroup from the SDA website. To do this:

1. Go to http://sda.berkeley.edu/cgi-bin12/hsda?harcsda+gss02.
2. Select "Comparison of means" and click **Start**.
3. Type **educ** into the Dependent box and **racecen1** into the Row box.
4. In the Selection Filter(s) box, enter year(2002).

5. For this comparison of means tests, do not apply the recode language for **EDUC** (educational attainments); simply use **EDUC**.
6. Select "Question text" and "ANOVA stats" from Table Options.
7. Click **Run the Table**

Now answer the following question:

22. Try to get the means of educational attainments for each race/ethnic subgroup. (Remember, your dependent variable is **EDUC** and the row variable is **RACECEN1**.) What do these results show?
    a. Complete convergence with the previous method
    b. Partial convergence
    c. No convergence at all

Let's extend our analysis to ethnic differences and their linkages to differences in educational attainments. Repeat what you did for the previous question. This time, however, use the variable **ETHNIC** instead of **RACECEN1** (make sure you use the recoded variable). Now answer the following question. Remember to select the comparison of means option.

23. Of the following ethnic groups which has the highest mean years of education?
    a. Eastern Europeans
    b. Irish
    c. Italians
    d. Germans
    e. Scandinavians

We're sure you've heard many times over education should pay off in better jobs, higher pay, less unemployment, better chances to own a home, and to amass more savings. The question many racial minority members may ask is: Will it produce the same gains for members of ethnic minorities as it does for whites?

In the following set of questions you will be asked to evaluate whether each racial minority group has the same opportunities as whites when their educational attainments are matched (i.e. when they have completed college or have greater educational attainments). Are minorities able to extract the same life experience benefits as whites? We will specifically evaluate four things: having a professional occupation; avoiding unemployment; having high earnings; and being able to become a homeowner. For each of these criteria you will be asked to compare the percentages across each table to see if they project the same or a different pattern of association for African Americans, Asians and Hispanics as compared to whites.

However, before we proceed any further we will have to examine whether these different racial group members share similarities in their high levels of educational attainments. If whites generally possess higher educational attainments than their highly educated minority counterparts, that factor alone could explain the other differences that we are interested in comparing.

24. When high educational attainments are compared among African Americans, whites, Asians and Hispanics which of the following options does the data show? (For this analysis you will apply the following recoded language for education: educ(r: 16;17-20). With this definition we are able to compare college graduates and those with higher educational attainments. Omit the category 3 group "Native Americans"—there were too few numbers in this group for making any meaningful comparisons.
    a. Whites are significantly more likely to get more years of schooling beyond college graduate level than other racial groups.
    b. African Americans are significantly more likely to get more years of schooling beyond college graduate level than other racial groups.
    c. Asians are significantly more likely to get more years of schooling beyond college graduate level than other racial groups.
    d. Hispanics are significantly less likely to get more years of schooling beyond college graduate level than other racial groups.
    e. There are no statistically significant differences between the groups.

From your knowledge of stratification issues you can anticipate that educational attainments will be related to a number of other factors including: differences in being a professional worker (OCC80), avoiding unemployment (WRKSTAT), income differences (RINCOM98), and owning a home (DWELOWN). The question is, do they work in the same way for African Americans and other minorities, as they do for whites? After running each of the specified crosstabs below, examine the results and choose the best answer for each of the next five questions.

1. First, tabulate occupational status (OCC80) by RACECEN1. Note that we will have to omit Native Americans with only five cases.
2. For questions 25 through 28 only, use racecen1 (r: 1 "Whites"; 2 "Blacks"; 4-14 "Asians"; 16 "Hispanics") as your recoded variable.
3. Put year(2002) as your selection filter so that we can focus on 2002 GSS.
4. To see if completed education helps the races differently put educ (r:16-20) in the Control Box. This will limit the comparison to those with college degrees and more education.

You are now ready to answer questions 25–28.

25. Which of the following statements best describes the results from this analysis?
    a. The percentage of African Americans employed as professionals and managers is higher than for Asians and whites
    b. The percentage of whites employed as professionals and managers is higher than for Asians and African Americans
    c. The percentage of Hispanics employed as professionals and managers is higher than for Asians
    d. Whites, African Americans and Asians appear to be significantly more likely to be employed as professionals than Hispanics and more highly educated Blacks are working in service occupations
    e. None of the above, once education is controlled in this way, the relationship between OCC80 and RACECEN1 disappears

26. Next, tabulate work status (WRKSTAT) by RACECEN1, again comparing only those that have completed college or had higher educational attainments (use educ (r:16-20) as your control variable). In this manner you will be able to examine the variability in unemployment experiences among these four race subgroups. What do you find?
    a. The percentage of unemployed whites exceeded that for all other minorities.
    b. Compared to whites, the three racial subgroups experienced significantly greater unemployment.
    c. Asians were the least likely of all groups to experience unemployment.
    d. There were no significant differences in unemployment among the four subgroups.
    e. None of the above.

27. Now, tabulate income (RINCOM98) by race/ethnic group differences (RACECEN1), again comparing only those that have completed college or had higher educational attainments (use educ (r:16-20) as your control variable). What do you find?
    a. More whites and Asians earned incomes exceeding $60,000 than African Americans and Hispanics.
    b. There were no significant differences between the four subgroups in earning $60,000 or more yearly.
    c. More Asian respondents earned incomes exceeding $60,000 than any of the other groups.
    d. College educated Blacks exceeded all other groups in being higher earners.
    e. None of the above.

28. Now, tabulate owning a home (DWELOWN) by race (RACECEN1), again comparing only those that have completed college or had higher educational attainments (use educ (r:16-20) as your control variable). What do you find?
    a. The racial gap in home ownership doesn't amount to much among well educated respondents.
    b. The racial gap in homeownership is very substantial among well educated respondents.
    c. Fewer than half of African Americans and Hispanics with college degrees were homeowners, while about 70% of white college graduates owned homes.
    d. All of the above.
    e. b and c only.

Past research has found that marital status (MARITAL) is positively related to homeownership. We also know that African Americans are less likely to be married than other race/ethnic groups (you can verify this yourself by tabulating MARITAL by RACECEN1). A low marriage rate among African Americans may account for their lower rate of home ownership. If this is true, the gap in homeownership between race/ethnic groups may be reduced once marital status is controlled. We will now evaluate whether controlling for marital status will reduce or eliminate the effect of race on homeownership among this segment of well-educated respondents.

29. Tabulate owning a home (**DWELOWN**) by race (**RACECEN1**), again comparing only those that have completed college or had higher educational attainments (use **educ(r:16-20)** as your control variable). This time put **marital(1)** in the selection filter box (this will narrow the comparison to include only currently married persons). What do you find?

   a. The racial gap in home ownership doesn't exist among well educated and currently married respondents.

   b. The racial gap in home ownership diminishes but does not disappear completely among well educated and currently married respondents.

   c. The racial gap in home ownership persists when the comparison is made among well educated and currently married respondents.

   d. Among currently married respondents, African Americans and Asians are three times more likely to be renters than whites.

   e. c and d only.

30. Overall, the analysis of highly educated whites and other minority members in questions 25–29 has shown that:

   a. There is a minimal racial gap in opportunities to be home owners, earn high pay, avoid unemployment, and to get professional work.

   b. There is a consistent and sometimes substantial racial gap in opportunities to own homes, earn high pay, and to get professional work.

   c. Aside from a gap in minority homeowning, there were minimal differences between the races in earning higher pay, avoiding unemployment, and in getting professional work.

   d. None of the above.

ESSAY QUESTIONS

9–A   The answer to multiple choice question no. 20 on the racial/ethnic differences in educational achievement has been the subject of much recent research (see for example, L. Steinberg, *Beyond the Classroom*, NY: Simon & Schuster, 1996). Review the past research literature on the patterns of ethnic and race differences in high school achievement. Explain why, sociologically, some groups do better than others. Wherever it is possible to test hypotheses based upon your outside reading with the available GSS data, make the tests and discuss the similarities and differences between your and others' findings on the subject.

9–B   Reviewing the findings from multiple-choice questions 11–19, develop a theory for the acceptance or rejection of cultural pluralism. Explain why the various factors you investigated were related to the acceptance or rejection of pluralism. Review previous studies on this subject and discuss how your findings did or did not converge with past studies. It would especially be helpful to consult Gordon Allport's classic study, *The Nature of Prejudice*, in answering this question.

9–C   Devise your own theory of anti-African American prejudice. Examine any potentially confounding or spurious factors that could have produced any causally inappropriate bivariate associations. Run the three-way crosstabulations and investigate whether or not the relationships hold up when the appropriate control variables are introduced.

9–D   If your college is a member of ICPSR, you will be able to use the *Multi-Cities Study of Urban Inequality study* from your campus computers to examine the racial differences in homeownership (ATENURE), and family income (EFAMINC). Visit http://www.icpsr. umich.edu/cgi/SDA-ID/hsda?icpsr+02535-0001 to go to this data file. Do the findings differ from the patterns shown with the GSS data?

9–E   Take any of the hypotheses that have appeared in this chapter that are of interest to you and attempt to validate it with either an additional or different data source. Write a short essay stating your hypothesis, presenting the data, discussing the results, and drawing your conclusions accordingly.

9–F   Using GSS, compare and contrast the economic opportunities available for African American men and African American women from white men and women. Do African American women have an easier or more difficult time (compared to African American men) in getting educated, getting professional employments, being well paid, owning homes, getting savings, or any thing else available for analysis. Compare and contrast gender inequality cross-racially among African Americans and whites. Select only a limited number of economic opportunities to investigate.

9–G   Choose any subject (or variable) of interest to you in the GSS databases related to race and ethnic relations. Then, develop a hypothesis about this variable or variables in relation to other variables in the data base. (If there is a control variable involved, make sure to include that, too.) Interpret your findings on the association between these two or more variables. Review the previous research literature on your hypothesis. Compare and contrast your results, and attempt to reconcile any inconsistencies with those obtained by previous studies.

CHAPTER PROJECT

In this project, you will examine the relative progress in education (EDUC), income (RINCOME), occupation (OCC80), and homeownership (DWELOWN) between African Americans and whites during the past few decades. You need to demonstrate whether the gap in the above four variables has narrowed, widened or remained unchanged from the 1970s to the present. To answer this question, use GSS data and be sure to enter **year** in the control Box and **race** in the column Box.

SYNTAX GUIDE

Go to: http://sda.berkeley.edu/cgi-bin12/hsda?harcsda+gss02
Select "Frequencies or crosstabulation"
Click **Start**

RECODES

Please note that all recodes can also be copied and pasted from either **www.ncc.edu/users/feigelb/sda.htm** or **www.ablongman.com/feigelman3e**. If you type the recode syntax in, make sure that you type *exactly* what is shown below.

age(r:18-35;36-50;51-64;65-90)

attend(r:0 "Never";1-2 "Yearly"; 3 "Several X yearly";4 "Monthly";5-8 "2-3 X monthly or more")

dwelown(r: 1 "Own or is buying"; 2 "Rent")

educ(r:1-12 "high school or less"; 13-15 "some coll"; 16 "college grad"; 17-20 "grad sch or higher")

ethnic(r:1,39 "Af";4,8,24 "En";14 "Iri";15 "Ita";2,6,13,21,23,33-35 "EEu";11 "Ger";7,9,19,26 "Sca";17,22,25,28,38 "His";3,10,18,27,36 "WEu";5,16,20,31,37,40 "As"; 97 "US"; 30 "AIn";12,29,32,41 "Otr")

ethtrads(r: 1-2 "Agree"; 3 "Neither Agree nor Disagree"; 4-5 "Disagree")

feelasns(r: 1-3 "Warm"; 4-6 "Neutral"; 7-9 "Not Warm")

feelblks(r: 1-3 "Warm"; 4-6 "Neutral"; 7-9 "Not Warm")

feelhsps(r: 1-3 "Warm"; 4-6 "Neutral"; 7-9 "Not Warm")

feelwhts(r: 1-3 "Warm"; 4-6 "Neutral"; 7-9 "Not Warm")

liveasns(r: 1-2 "Favor"; 3 "Neutral"; 4-5 "Opposed")

liveblks(r: 1-2 "Favor"; 3 "Neutral"; 4-5 "Opposed")

livehsps(r: 1-2 "Favor"; 3 "Neutral"; 4-5 "Opposed")

livejews(r: 1-2 "Favor"; 3 "Neutral"; 4-5 "Opposed")

liveno(r: 1-2 "Favor"; 3 "Neutral"; 4-5 "Opposed")

liveso(r: 1-2 "Favor"; 3 "Neutral"; 4-5 "Opposed")

marasian(r: 1-2 "Favor"; 3 "Neutral"; 4-5 "Opposed")

marblk(r: 1-2 "Favor"; 3 "Neutral"; 4-5 "Opposed")

marhisp(r: 1-2 "Favor"; 3 "Neutral"; 4-5 "Opposed")

marital(r: 1 "Married"; 2-5 "Not married")

marjew(r: 1-2 "Favor"; 3 "Neutral"; 4-5 "Opposed")

marno(r: 1-2 "Favor"; 3 "Neutral"; 4-5 "Opposed")

marso(r: 1-2 "Favor"; 3 "Neutral"; 4-5 "Opposed")

occ80(r:3-199 "Professional/managerial"; 200-389 "Technicians/sales/admin. support"; 400-469 "Service"; 473-699 "Farmers/fisherman/skilled manual workers"; 703-889 "Operatives")

racecen1(r: 1 "Whites"; 2 "Blacks"; 3 "Native Americans"; 4-14 "Asians"; 16 "Hispanics")

relig(r:1 "Protestant"; 2 "Catholic"; 3 "Jewish"; 4 "None"; 5-8 "Other")

rincom98(r: 1-19 "$59,999 or less"; 20-23 "$60,000 or more")

rincome(r: 1-9 "Less than $15,000"; 10-11 "$15,000-$25,000";12 "$25,000 and higher")

srcbelt(r:1-2 "Urban"; 3-4 "Suburban"; 5 "Small city"; 6 "Rural")

wrkstat(r: 1-3, 5-8"working/student/housewife/other"; 4 "unemployed")

year(r: 1972-1974 "1972-74"; 1975-1979 "1975-1979"; 1980-1984 "1980-84"; 1985-1989 "1985-89"; 1990-1994 "1990-94"; 1995-2000 "1995-2002")

No recode needed: CLASS; FINRELA

MULTICITY STUDY RECODES

Please note that all recodes can also be copied and pasted from either www.ncc.edu/users/feigelb/sda.htm or www.ablongman.com/feigelman3e. If you type the recode syntax in, make sure that you type *exactly* what is shown below.

atenure(1,2)

crace(1,2,3,4)

efaminc(r: 1-3 "Less than $15,000"; 4-6 "$15,000-$30,000"; 7-9 "$30K-$45K"; 10-12 "45K-60K"; 13-17 "60K-100K"; 18-* "$100K or higher")

No recode needed: CITY

CHAPTER 10

Marriage and Family in the United States

The family is an indispensable social institution. Without it, society is not likely to last for very long. The United States is no exception in relying upon its families. Today, however, many commentators have remarked that American families are falling by the wayside in unprecedented numbers. With soaring divorce rates, many claim that marriage is becoming more like a crapshoot, with a fifty/fifty chance of succeeding. As a prelude to our investigation of family life, we will examine patterns and attitudes on marriages. Divorce will be another important focus of the chapter. This analysis will begin by drawing upon the data found from the General Social Surveys.

1. Go to the SDA website at http://sda.berkeley.edu.
2. Click **SDA Archive**, and then select the **GSS Cumulative Datafile 1972–2002**. Select "Frequencies or crosstabulation" and click **Start**.
3. Put the **DEPENDENT** variable in the "Row" box and the **INDEPENDENT** variable in the "Column" box. *Don't forget to apply the correct recode language for each question.*
5. Select the "Statistics" and "Question text" option from the "Table Options" box.
6. Press **Run the Table**.

We will begin by answering the following questions:

1. Looking at a representative slice of the American adult population, identify what percentage are currently married (enter **marital** in the "Row" field) in 2002. Be sure to type **year(2002)** in the "Selection Filter(s)" field.
   a. 32 percent
   b. 46 percent   45·9
   c. 52 percent
   d. 65 percent

Now let's examine the trend for the marital status. Use the variable **MARITAL** in the Row Box and **YEAR** (be sure to use the recoded variable) in the Control Box.

Put Year (1970 –2012) in column

2. Which of the following statements best describes the trend for marital status (MARITAL)?

    a. The percentage of married persons has been declining since the 1970s.

    b. The percentage of married persons has been increasing since the 1970s.

    c. There is no clear trend.

    d. None of the above.

3. Which of the following statements best describes the trend for those who have never married?

    a. The percentage of never married persons has declined from 1970s to 1990s.

    b. There have been no substantial changes in the percentage of people who never marry.

    c. The percentage of never married persons appears to have steadily increased.

    d. None of the above.

4. What percentage of 2002 GSS respondents considered it important for young people to get married (GETMAR)? (Hint: Enter getmar in the "Row" Box and year(2002) in the "Selection Filter(s)" Box).

    a. 24%   8.9

    b. 34%   14.1

    c. 44%   21.0

    d. 54%

    e. 64%

5. Is there a relationship between GETMAR and AGE? Hint: Enter getmar in the "Row" Box, age in the Column Box, and year(2002) in the "Selection Filter(s)" Box.

    a. There is no significant relationship between GETMAR and AGE.

    b. Younger people are more likely to consider it important for young people to get married.

    c. The elderly are more likely to consider it important for young people to get married.

    d. The middle age population (those aged 40 to 64) is most likely to consider it important for young people to get married.

    e. None of the above.

To answer the following question, simply enter getmar1 (age should get married) in the "Row" Box, and year(2002) in the "Selection Filter(s)" Box. Be sure to select "Statistics" and "Question Text" before clicking **Run the Table**. What is the mean ideal age for marriage (look for the statistic at the end of the table). Round off the age you find to the nearest whole number: .1 through .4 goes to the lower whole number; .5 through .9 rounds up to the next highest number.

6. According to the GSS 2002 data, what age is considered an ideal age to get married?

    a. 20

    b. 22

    c. 26   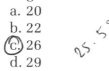 25.58

    d. 29

To answer Question 7, which considers gender differences in views of ideal age at marriage, you will need to visit the GSS analysis page, http://sda.berkeley.edu/cgi-bin/hsda?harcsda+gss02. Select the "Comparison of means" option and click **Start**. Now enter getmar1 in the "Row" Box, sex in the "Column" Box, and year(2002) in the "Selection Filter(s)" Box.

7. Which of the following statements is most accurate?
   a. Among male respondents, the ideal age at getting married is 29.
   b. Among female respondents, the ideal age at getting married is 27.
   c. The difference between male and female respondents in their view of ideal age at marriage is about 2 years.
   d. The difference between male and female respondents in their view of ideal age at marriage is very small.
   e. a, b, and c only.

8. Investigate whether there have been any shifts in age at first marriage by tabulating **AGEWED** by **YEAR** (Hint: Put **agewed** in the "Row" Box and **year** in the "Column" Box.) Which of the following statements best sums up your findings?
   a. The percentage of those who married young (under 21) has increased substantially from the 1970s to the 1990s.
   b. The percentage of those who married young (under 21) has decreased substantially from the 1970s to the 1990s.
   c. The percentage of those who married at age 26 or older has not changed from the 1970s to the 1990s.
   d. None of the above.

Do a three-way crosstabulation using **SEX** as a control variable and run the tendency to never marry (**MARITAL**) by age differences (**AGE**) to see whether there are any gender differences in remaining unmarried among younger respondents. (Hint: The dependent variable is **MARITAL** and the independent variable is **AGE**.)

9. What does this analysis show?
   a. Younger females are more likely to remain unmarried now than older generations of women.
   b. Younger males show similar trends to remain unmarried as older generations of men; men appear to be more inclined to remain unmarried compared to women.
   c. The data show no appreciable gender differences in the tendency to remain unmarried among younger respondents.
   d. None of the above.
   e. a and b.

Interracial marriage is an important sub-field in the study of marriage and family. In the next few questions, we will examine correlates of attitude toward interracial marriages. The GSS has been collecting data asking respondents whether they favor law against racial intermarriage (**RACMAR**) since 1972. First, let's look at the relationship between **RACMAR** and race (**RACECEN1**). Be sure to type racmar in the "Row" Box, racecen1 in the "Column" Box, and year(2002) in the "Selection Filter(s)" Box.

10. Based on the crosstabulation between **RACMAR** and **RACECEN1**, which of the following statements is true?
    a. African Americans are more approving of interracial marriage than whites.
    b. Whites are more approving of interracial marriage than African Americans.
    c. There is no significant racial difference in African American and white attitudes toward interracial marriage.
    d. None of the above.

Next, let's examine the relationship between **RACMAR** and age (**AGE**). Type **racmar** in the "Row" Box, **age** in the "Column" Box, and **year(2002)** in the "Selection Filter(s)" Box.

11. Based on the crosstabulation between **RACMAR** and **AGE**, which of the following statements is true?
    a. Those who are 65 years and older show the most approval for interracial marriage.
    b. Those younger than 30 years old show the most approval for interracial marriage.
    c. The relationship between **RACMAR** and **AGE** is not significant statistically.
    d. Those aged between 30 and 64 show the most approval for interracial marriage.
    e. None of the above.

Does one's religion have any impact on their attitude toward interracial marriage? Our next question will examine the relationship between **RACMAR** and religion (**RELIG**) using the GSS 2002 data.

12. Based on the crosstabulation between **RACMAR** and **RELIG**, which of the following statements is true?
    a. Protestants are less likely to support interracial marriage than other religious groups.
    b. Catholics are less likely to support interracial marriage than other religious groups.
    c. Jews are less likely to support interracial marriage than other religious groups.
    d. Those who have no religious affiliation are least likely to support interracial marriage.
    e. None of the above.

Another variable that may shed some light on one's attitude toward interracial marriage is one's socioeconomic status. To investigate this question, type **racmar** in the "Row" Box, **prestg80** in the "Column" Box, and **year(2002)** in the "Selection Filter(s)" Box.

13. Based on the crosstabulation between **RACMAR** and **PRESTG80**, which of the following statements is true?
    a. High prestige respondents are less likely to support interracial marriage than their lower prestige counterparts.
    b. Low prestige respondents are less likely to support interracial marriage than their high prestige counterparts.
    c. The results are unclear.
    d. The relationship between **RACMAR** and **PRESTG80** is not significant.
    e. None of the above.

Our next variable is education. Does one's level of education influence their attitudes toward interracial marriage? To investigate this question, type **racmar** in the "Row" Box, **degree** in the "Column" Box, and **year(2002)** in the "Selection Filter(s)" Box.

14. Based on the crosstabulation between **RACMAR** and **DEGREE**, which of the following statements is true?
    a. Those who have a low level of education (less than high school) are less likely to support interracial marriage.
    b. Those who completed high school are less likely to support interracial marriage.
    c. Those who have at least some college education are less likely to support interracial marriage.
    d. The results are unclear.
    e. The relationship between **RACMAR** and **DEGREE** is not significant.
15. How have people's attitude toward interracial marriage changed over the past few decades? Tabulate **RACMAR** (dependent variable) by **YEAR** (independent variable).
    a. People's attitudes have not changed during the past few decades.
    b. The data shows that respondents have become more conservative (favor laws against racial intermarriage) over the past few decades.
    c. The data suggests that respondents have become more accepting of racial intermarriage) during the past few decades.
    d. Although respondents have become more accepting over time, the relationship between **RACMAR** and **YEAR** fell short of statistical significance.
    e. a and d only.

One of the sociological findings in recent years regarding marriage is that African American women are finding it harder and harder to find a spouse. Presumably, the proportion of unmarried African American women will have increased in recent years. Let's explore this hypothesis. To do this, use **MARITAL** as the dependent variable, **RACE** as the independent variable, and **YEAR** as the control variable. In the "Selection Filter(s)" Box, enter **sex (2)**. This will limit our analysis to only female respondents. Now answer the following question.

16. According to the GSS data, which of the following is true?
    a. In the early 1970s, the proportion of African American women who were never married was comparable to those of whites.
    b. The data shows that the percentage of African American women who were never married has increased from 10% in the early 1970s to 38% during the period from 1995 to 2002.
    c. The data show that the percentage of white women who were never married has increased from 10% in the early 1970s to 17% during the period from 1995 to 2002.
    d. All of the above.
    e. Only a and c.

We will now shift our focus to divorce and investigate its correlates. For Questions 17 to 20, use the GSS 2002 data. (Hint: You can limit your analysis to the 2002 data by entering **year(2002)** in the "Selection Filter(s)" Box.)

17. Using the GSS 2002 data, tabulate the experience of getting divorced (**DIVORCE**), and answer the following question: What is the percentage of people who have divorced? (Hint: Put **divorce** in the "Row" Box and **year(2002)** in the "Selection Filter(s)" Box.)
    a. 24 percent   23.8
    b. 34 percent
    c. 44 percent
    d. 54 percent

18. Is there an association between having been divorced (**DIVORCE**) and living with both parents at the age of 16 (**FAMILY16**) for GSS 2002 data?
    a. Those who lived with both parents when they were growing up appear more divorce-prone than those who did not grow up with both parents.
    b. Those who lived with both parents when they were growing up appear less divorce-prone than those who did not grow up with both parents.
    c. There is definitely no association between being divorced and whether or not one lived with both parents when growing up.
    d. None of the above.

19. Past studies have found that working wives are more divorce prone than housewives. Is there an association between having been divorced (**DIVORCE**) and a wife's current work status (**WRKSTAT**)? Be sure to enter **year(1998-2002)** in the "Selection Filter(s)" Box.
    a. Career women are more divorce-prone than housewives.
    b. Housewives are more divorce-prone than career women.
    c. There is no clear association between being divorced and a woman's current work status.
    d. None of the above.

For Questions 20 and 21, use GSS 1994 data. (Hint: Enter year(1994) in the "Selection Filter(s)" Box.)

20. Is getting divorced (**DIVORCE**) significantly related to the timing of marriage (**AGEWED**)?
    a. Those marrying later in life are more divorce-prone.
    b. Those marrying at younger ages are more divorce-prone.
    c. There is no clear association between the timing of marriage and the likelihood of divorce.
    d. None of the above.
21. Tabulate ever being divorced (**DIVORCE**) with having cohabited before marriage (**COHABIT**). Does cohabitation before marriage reduce or increase the likelihood of divorce?
    a. Those cohabiting before marriage have greatly elevated chances of later divorcing.
    b. Those cohabiting before marriage have slightly greater chances of later divorce.
    c. No differences are noted between those with and without cohabitation experiences and divorce.
    d. Those cohabiting before marriage have a lower divorce risk.
    e. None of the above.

Let's now assess the impact of parental divorce on the lives of their children. First, we'll see if it has any impact upon an individual's likelihood of getting married. Before we proceed, we need to create a new variable for parental divorce. To do this, complete the following steps:

1. Go to http://sda.berkeley.edu/cgi-bin/hsda?harcsda+gss02.
2. Select "Compute a new variable" and click **Start**.
3. Type:
   ```
   if (family16 ne 1 and famdif16 eq 2) divor16 = 1
   else divor16 = 0
   ```
   into the "EXPRESSION TO DEFINE THE NEW VARIABLE" box.
4. Select "Yes" for the following two options: "Replace that variable, if it already exists?" and "Include numeric missing-data values in computations?".
5. Figure 10.1 shows a screen capture of this page with Steps 3 and 4 correctly entered.
6. Click **Start Computing**.

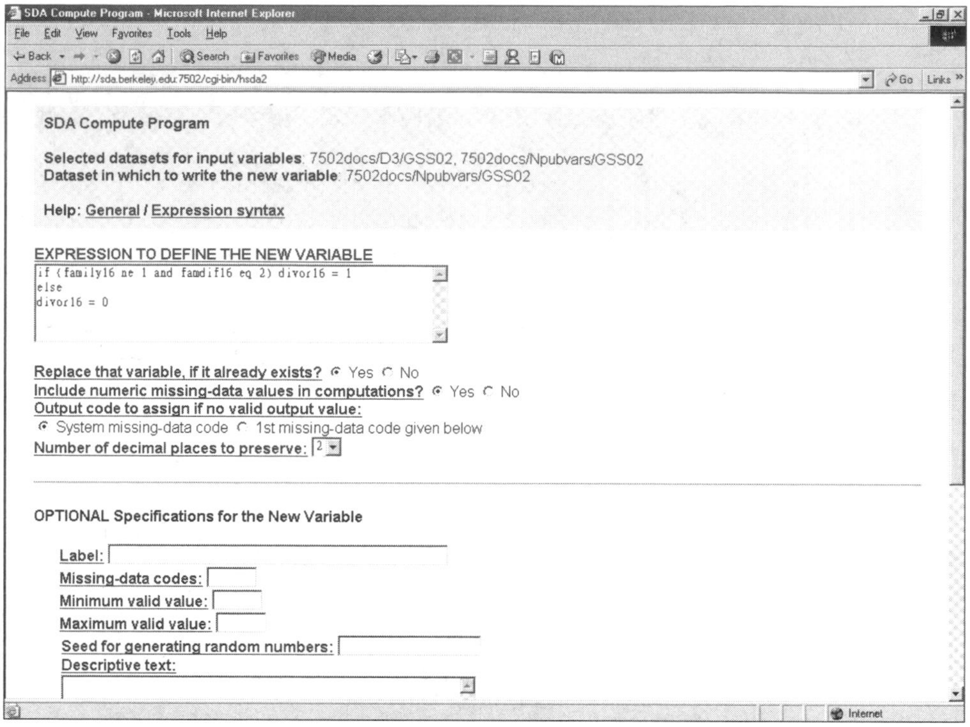

FIGURE 10.1

The new variable, DIVOR16, has now been created and you are now ready to answer the following questions.

22. Using the GSS 2002 data, tabulate an individual's likelihood of getting married (MARITAL) by the integrity of their parent's marriage (DIVOR16). What does the data show?
    a. People whose parents divorced are less likely to remain unmarried.
    b. People whose parents divorced are more likely to remain unmarried.
    c. There appears to be no statistically significant association between parental divorce and remaining unmarried.
    d. None of the above.

23. Now use the GSS 1994 data and tabulate an individual's likelihood of cohabiting before marriage (COHABIT) by the integrity of their parent's marriage (DIVOR16). What does the data show?
    a. People whose parents divorced are less likely to cohabit before marriage.
    b. People whose parents divorced are more likely to cohabit before marriage.
    c. There appears to be no statistically significant association between parental divorce and having cohabitation experiences.
    d. The differences approach but fail to achieve statistical significance.
    e. a and d only.

Does parental divorce increase the risk of having a child out-of-wedlock? To answer this question, we need to create another new variable, ILLEGIT.

1. Go to http://sda.berkeley.edu/cgi-bin/hsda?harcsda+gss02.
2. Select "Compute a new variable" and click **Start**.
3. Type:
   if (marital eq 5 and childs gt 0) illegit = 1
   else illegit = 0
   into the "EXPRESSION TO DEFINE THE NEW VARIABLE" box.
4. Select "Yes" for the following two options: "Replace that variable, if it already exists?" and "Include numeric missing-data values in computations?".
5. Click **Start Computing**.

The new variable, ILLEGIT, has now been created. Use the two recorded variables, ILLEGIT and DIVOR16, to answer the following questions (use the GSS 2002 data).

24. Tabulate an individual's likelihood of bearing a child out-of-wedlock (ILLEGIT) by the integrity of their parent's marriage (DIVOR16). What does the data show?
    a. People whose parents divorced are less likely to have children out-of-wedlock.
    b. People whose parents divorced are more likely to have children out-of-wedlock.
    c. There appears to be no statistically significant association between parental divorce and bearing illegitimate children.
    d. The differences approach, but fail to achieve, statistical significance.
    e. a and d only.
25. Does parental divorce (DIVOR16) impact upon their adult children's fertility (CHILDS); does it reduce/or increase the size of their children's families?
    a. People whose parents divorced are less likely to have large families when compared to those coming from intact parental homes.
    b. People whose parents divorced are more likely to have large families when compared to those coming from intact parental homes.
    c. There appears to be no statistically significant association between parental divorce and their children's fertility.
    d. The differences approach, but fail to achieve, statistical significance.
    e. c and d only.

26. Does parental divorce (**DIVOR16**) impact upon their adult children's educational and economic attainments; is it linked to the child's educational attainments (**DEGREE**) and personal incomes (**RINCOM98**)? (Hint: This problem will require doing two separate crosstabulations.)
    a. People whose parents divorced are less likely to have gone as far with their schooling and to make high earnings than those coming from intact parental homes.
    b. People whose parents divorced are more likely to have received more education and made higher earnings than those coming from intact parental homes.
    c. There appears to be no statistically significant association between parental divorce and their children's educational and economic attainments.
    d. The differences approach, but fail to achieve, statistical significance.
    e. c and d only.

Another important aspect of marriage is raising a family. As you have probably read elsewhere, during the last half of the twentieth century fertility declined drastically in the United States and in other urban-industrial societies. Diminished fertility is a result of many factors, including:

- changes in women's work roles
- urban and suburban living arrangements
- the increasing costs of raising children today (especially educational expenses)
- the timing of marriage and childbearing

Past research has established a very perplexing pattern in relating class rank to fertility: The classes who can least afford to have children have the greatest number of offspring; and the classes who can most afford them have the least.

27. To investigate whether this association still applies, crosstabulate the number of children ever born to a respondent (**CHILDS**) by their occupational prestige standing (**PRESTG80**). What do you find? (Hint: Pay particular attention to the percentages of respondents having four or more children).
    a. There is a trend falling short of statistical significance showing prestige rank inversely associated with the number of children.
    b. Prestige and the number of children are positively associated.
    c. There is an inverse association between prestige and number of children that is statistically significant.
    d. None of the above.

It is sometimes claimed that the lower classes actually want to have larger families than the more affluent classes.

28. Use the GSS 2002 data and run the number of children preferred (CHLDIDEL) by prestige rating (PRESTG80) and select the statement below that best describes your findings:
    a. The lower classes want more children than the rich, and the differences are statistically significant.
    b. Surprisingly, the upper classes want more children than the poor and the differences are statistically significant.
    c. There are no significant class differences in the numbers of children wanted between the three different prestige groups.
    d. None of the above.

The timing of marriage—as well as social rank—has been noted as an explanation for fertility differences. It is claimed that those marrying younger are more likely to have larger families.

29. Crosstabulate the number of children ever born to a respondent (CHILDS) by the timing of their marriage (AGEWED). What does the data show? (Hint: Use GSS 1994 data)
    a. Those marrying later appear to have fewer children.
    b. Those marrying later appear to have more children.
    c. There does not appear to be any association between the timing of one's marriage and the number of children they have.
    d. Those marrying later have somewhat fewer children, but subgroup differences fall short of statistical significance.

Researchers specializing in the study of fertility differences and change have identified numerous factors influencing decisions to have larger or smaller families. Three stand out in particular: religious differences (RELIG), differences in occupational prestige (PRESTG80) and educational attainments (DEGREE). By comparing and contrasting the delta values (percentage point differences) among those having four or more children, which of the three factors has the greatest impact upon child bearing (CHILDS)? (Hint: It will be necessary to do three separate cross-tabulations to answer this question.)

30. Using the GSS 2002 data, run the number of children born to a respondent (CHILDS) separately by religious (RELIG), prestige (PRESTG80) and educational differences (DEGREE). Which factor is the most powerful in the decision to have (or not to have) a large family?
    a. Religion
    b. Prestige
    c. Education
    d. Delta differences are extremely close; therefore no determination can be made

31. Run the same analysis again, but this time use child bearing preferences (CHLDIDEL) as the dependent variable. Which factor is the most powerful in the decision to have (or not to have) a large family?
    a. Religion
    b. Prestige
    c. Education
    d. Delta differences are extremely close; therefore no determination can be made

The next part of this chapter investigates personal happiness (HAPPY) and some of the many factors that may contribute to it, such as:

- satisfaction with one's work (SATJOB)
- marital happiness (HAPMAR)
- satisfaction with one's health (SATHEALT)
- satisfaction with one's financial situation (SATFIN)
- satisfaction with one's friendships (SATFRND)

32. Using the GSS 1994 data, run each of these five independent variables against personal happiness (HAPPY) and indicate which variable has the most influence on happiness scores among those who are very happy. (Hint: Indicate which relationship produces the highest delta value across all HAPPY respondents.)
    a. HAPPY by SATJOB
    b. HAPPY by HAPMAR
    c. HAPPY by SATHEALT
    d. HAPPY by SATFIN
    e. HAPPY by SATFRND

33. Using the GSS 2002 data, run SATJOB, HAPMAR, and SATFIN against personal happiness (HAPPY) and indicate which variable has the most influence on happiness scores among those who are very happy. (Hint: Indicate which relationship produces the highest delta value across all HAPPY respondents.)
    a. HAPPY by SATJOB
    b. HAPPY by HAPMAR
    c. HAPPY by SATFIN
    d. None of the above

34. Do you get the same result when you compare the same relationships among all the *least* happy respondents?
    a. Yes
    b. No
    c. It is too close to call

The final part of this chapter examines attitudes toward extramarital sex (XMARSEX). We will begin by examining the relationship between religion (RELIG) and XMARSEX. Does one's religion affect one's attitude toward extramarital sex (XMARSEX)? Tabulate XMARSEX (as the dependent variable) by RELIG (independent variable). Be sure to type year(2002) in the "Selection Filter(s)" Box.

35. According to the data, what is the relationship between religion and attitude toward extramarital sex?
    a. Protestants are more likely to believe that extramarital sex is always, or almost always, wrong than respondents from other religious groups.
    b. Catholics are less likely to believe that extramarital sex is always, or almost always, wrong than respondents from other religious groups.
    c. Jews are more likely to believe that extramarital sex is always, or almost always, wrong than respondents from other religious groups.
    d. Those without religious affiliation are less likely to believe that extramarital sex is always, or almost always, wrong than respondents who have a religious affiliation.
    e. a and d only.

Does one's level of education influence one's attitude toward extramarital sex? Type **xmarsex** in the "Row" Box and **degree** in the "Column" Box to answer this question. Again, you need to enter **year(2002)** in the "Selection Filter(s)" Box.

36. According to the crosstabulation between **XMARSEX** and **DEGREE**, which of the following statements is most accurate?
    a. Those who have a low level of education (less than high school) are most likely to support extramarital sex.
    b. Those who completed high school are most likely to support extramarital sex.
    c. Although the relationship between extramarital sex and education is statistically significant, those with some college education are slightly more accepting of extramarital sex than those with less education.
    d. The results are unclear.
    e. None of the above.

The next variable to be examined is age. Are older respondents more conservative than younger subjects in their attitude toward extramarital sex? Remember to use **XMARSEX** as the dependent variable and **AGE** as the independent variable. Again, use the GSS 2002 data to answer the following questions.

37. Based on the crosstabulation between **XMARSEX** and **AGE**, which of the following statements is most accurate?
    a. Those who are 65 years and older are most conservative in approving of extramarital sex.
    b. Those younger than 30 years old are most approving of extramarital sex.
    c. The relationship between **XMARSEX** and **AGE** is not statistically significant.
    d. Those aged between 30 and 64 are most approving of extramarital sex.
    e. None of the above.

38. How have people's attitudes toward extramarital sex changed over the past few decades? Hint: Tabulate **XMARSEX** (dependent variable) by **YEAR** (independent variable).
   a. People's attitudes have not changed over the past few decades.
   b. Compared to the early 1980s and earlier, attitudes towards extramarital sex appear to have shifted somewhat, with more people now believing that extramarital sex is always, or almost always, wrong.
   c. The data suggest that respondents have become more liberal in their attitude towards extramarital sex over the past few decades.
   d. Although respondents have become more liberal over time, the relationship between **XMARSEX** and **YEAR** fell short of statistical significance.
   e. a and d only.

ESSAY QUESTIONS

10–A   Using the GSS database, evaluate all the hypotheses that the data permit on the consequences of parental divorce on adult children. Present the appropriate tables and discuss the similarities and differences between the results.

10–B   Using the GSS database, identify any social factors (such as race, class, education or religion) that produces a discrepancy between the ideal numbers of children desired by the group and actual numbers of children born to it. Try to explain why this group has more children than members want, (or fewer as the case may be). Try to explain why your selected group falls short of or exceeds its desired number of children. Review past studies of this question.

10–C   Examine the relationship between **CHILDS**, **RELIG**, and **PRESTG80**. Describe how social status differences alter the association between fertility and religion. Review past studies on this subject. Write an essay on how class factors influence different Protestant adherents and Catholics to behave differently in terms of their fertility.

10–D   Choose any three variables that have not been covered in the multiple choice questions of this chapter and develop three hypotheses explaining how each factor may be associated with getting divorced (**DIVORCE**). Present the data and interpret the results indicating whether or not your hypotheses were supported.

10–E   Evaluate the results obtained from Questions 33 and 34 on the social factors related to personal happiness: Discuss what the implications and practical significance of these findings are.

10–F   How does having children affect marital happiness? Consult the family sociology literature and find out how children can help or hinder parents' marital happiness and see what the GSS shows on this issue. You can use GSS 2002 data and tabulate marital happiness (**HAPMAR**) by number of children (**CHILDS**). What do the results show? If your findings are not consistent with the literature, explain why.

10–G The General Social Surveys have found over the last 30 years that Americans have become much more accepting of gay behavior and less antagonistically disposed to homosexuals in general. Nevertheless, we may wonder whether there are differences in how people of different ages feel about homosexuality and whether they show any differences in support for gay rights. For this mini-essay go to the SDA GSS website and examine the following variables: **MARHOMO**, **SPKHOMO**, **COLHOMO**, **LIBHOMO**, **HOMOSEX**, **HOMOSEX1**. Crosstabulate each of these variables by age, using the following recode: age (r:18-35 "18-35"; 36-56 "36-56"; 57-90 "57-90"). Present all six tables and evaluate whether younger people are any more (or less) accepting of gays than middle-aged or older folks on these six different criteria. Remember to apply the .05 Chi-Square significance criteria and carefully compare percentage differences between these age subcategories. Pay close attention to which subtable differences are the most substantial. You should also pay attention to very large overall sample sizes. (With very large samples of 8,000 cases or more, a subcategory difference of a few percentage points could be a "statistically significant" one, but be sociologically meaningless.) Reports should include your tables and analysis.

CHAPTER PROJECT

Focusing on marital satisfaction (**HAPMAR**) as a dependent variable, and using GSS variables as a base, develop a theory of possible causes making for differences in marital satisfaction levels. Run the crosstabulations for each of your hypotheses to see if they are supported. Present your findings. Test your hypotheses among men and women separately to see if gender has any effect in leading men and women to perceive of marital satisfaction in different ways.

SYNTAX GUIDE

Go to: http://sda.berkeley.edu/cgi-bin12/hsda?harcsda+gss02
Select "Frequencies or crosstabulation"
Click **Start**

RECODES
Please note that all recodes can also be copied and pasted from either www.ncc.edu/users/feigelb/sda.htm or www.ablongman.com/feigelman3e. If you type the recode syntax in, make sure that you type *exactly* what is shown below.

age(r: 18-29 "18-29"; 30-39 "30-39"; 40-49 "40-49"; 50-64 "50-64"; 65-* "65 and older")

agewed(r:*-20 "Less than 21"; 21-25 "21-25"; 26-* "26 and older")

childs(r: 0 "None"; 1 "One"; 2 "Two"; 3 "Three"; 4-8 "Four or more")

chldidel (r: 0-1 "None or one"; 2 "Two"; 3 "Three"; 4-8 "Four or more")

degree(r:0"less than high school";1 "high school";2-4 "college or higher")

divor16(r: 0 "Not divorced"; 1 "Divorced")

everdiv(r: 0 "Never divorced" 1 "Ever divorced")

family16(r: 1 "Living with both parents at age 16"; 0, 2-8 "Not living with both parents at age 16")

getmar(r: 1-3 "Important"; 4-5 "Not Important")

illegit(r: 0 "No illegit birth"; 1 "Have out-of wedlock birth")

income91(r:1-10 "less than 15K";11-16"15K-35K";17-19"35-60K";20-21"60-90K";22-23 "90K and higher")

income98(r:1-10 "less than 15K";11-16"15K-35K";17-19"35-60K";20-21"60-90K";22-23 "90K and higher")

prestg80(r:*-41 "Low prestige"; 42-* "High prestige")

race(1,2)

racecen1(r: 1 "White"; 2 "Black"; 3-16 "Others")

region(r: 1-2 "Northeast"; 3-4 "Central"; 5-7 "South"; 8-9 "West")

relig(r:1 "Protestant"; 2 "Catholic"; 3 "Jewish";4"None";5-9"Other")

rincom98(r:1-10 "less than 15K";11-16"15K-35K";17-19"35-60K";20-21"60-90K";22-23 "90K and higher")

satfrnd(r: 1-2 "Very satisfied"; 3-4 "Somewhat satisfied"; 5-7 "Dissatisfied")

sathealt(r: 1-2 "Very satisfied"; 3-4 "Somewhat satisfied"; 5-7 "Dissatisfied")

satjob(r: 1 "Very satisfied"; 2 "Somewhat satisfied"; 3-4 "Dissatisfied")

wrkstat(r: 1-4 "Career women"; 7 "Housewives")

xmarsex(r : 1-2 "always or almost always wrong"; 3-4 "sometimes wrong or not wrong at all")

year(r: 1972-1974 "1972-74"; 1975-1979 "1975-1979"; 1980-1984 "1980-84"; 1985-1989 "1985-89"; 1990-1994 "1990-94"; 1995-2002 "1995-2002")

No recode needed: **COHABIT; DEGREE; DIVORCE; GETMAR1; HAPPY; HAPMAR; MARITAL; RACMAR; SATFIN; SEX**

Chapter 11

Aspects of U.S. Political Life

In this chapter, we will focus upon the presidential voting patterns that remain extremely important to an understanding of U.S. political life. Of course, many crucial factors affecting U.S. politics take place behind closed doors, in the interrelations between government officials and corporate leaders. The behind-the-scenes actions of the rich and powerful affect how political candidates get sponsored, and how nominees, once selected, are subsidized and supported. Many important political decisions never come before the electorate. Nevertheless, despite how these elements play out, the decisions of ordinary citizens to cast their electoral ballots remains very significant. Whether people vote or not, and whether they declare themselves as affiliates of the Republican or Democratic parties are crucial to understanding how elections are eventually decided.

There is a longstanding practice among political analysts to investigate how demographic factors are linked to vote choice. It is hoped that such an analysis will eventually lead to predicting electoral outcomes. For the present, only limited success has been made toward achieving this result. Demographic differences only account for a small percentage of the total variations of electoral differences. So far, the candidate and the immediate electoral issues still holds overshadowing importance to understanding who will win the fateful November contest. Eventually, however, political analysts may come to achieve a deeper understanding of the complex relationship between demographics and voting.

In the present analysis, we will explore some of the demographic correlates of vote choice, and how they are associated with different voting preferences. We will also look at voting to learn who votes and who is least likely to vote in recent U.S. presidential elections. Finally, we will also investigate whether there have been any shifts in the demographic correlates of voting preferences (and in voting itself) that may influence future elections. This analysis will begin by drawing upon General Social Surveys.

1. Go to the University of California's SDA site at http://sda.berkeley. edu.
2. Click on **SDA Archive** on the upper left corner of the page.
3. Under the subtitle "National Omnibus Surveys" click on **GSS Cumulative Datafile 1972–2002**.
4. Select "**Frequencies or crosstabulation**".
5. Click the **Start** button.

Remember to use the recoded variables (which can be found at the end of this chapter) for all analyses. Also remember to put the dependent variable in the Row Box and the independent variable in the Column Box. Always click **Statistics** and **Question Text** from "Other Options" before clicking **Run the Table**. To construct a new table, simply click the **Back** button in your browser. Be sure to enter **year(2000-2002)** in the "Selection Filter(s)" Box for questions 1, 3, 5, 7, 8, 9, 11 and 12.

1. Running political party preference (**PARTYID**) by race (**RACE**), which of the following statements best explains how African Americans and whites vote?
   a. Harkening back to the days of Lincoln, African Americans tend to give greater support to the Republican Party.
   b. Whites support the Democratic Party more than African Americans.
   c. The differences in voter choice by race are not statistically significant.
   d. All of the above.
   e. None of the above.

Now let's examine the trends for the relationship between political party preference (**PARTYID**) and **RACE**. Put **partyid** in the "Row" Box, **race** in the "Column" Box, and **year** in the Control "Box".

2. What is the trend for the relationship between political party preference and race?
   a. The relationship is not significant for the period 1972–1974.
   b. The proportion of whites identifying themselves as Democrats has been on the decline since the 1970s.
   c. The proportion of African Americans identifying themselves as Republicans has been on the rise since the 1970s.
   d. Both b and c.
   e. None of the above.
3. Running political party preference (**PARTYID**) by age (**AGE**), which of the following statements best explains how vote choice is associated with age differences?
   a. Younger voters tend to favor the Democratic Party, while there appears to be a preference for the Republican Party among voters in the over 65 age group.
   b. Younger voters are more likely to be aligned with third party candidates than older voters.
   c. According to the Chi-Square statistic, the differences in voter choice by age are only marginally significant.
   d. All of the above.
   e. None of the above.

The next question examines whether youth tendencies to prefer third party candidates have increased in latest elections periods. To answer this question, put **partyid** in the "Row" Box, **age** in the "Column" Box, and **year** in the "Control" Box.

4. What is the trend for youth tendencies to prefer third party candidates?
   a. There is a declining trend.
   b. There is a sharp increase of 10% points for youth to favor third party candidates from early the 1990s to the late 1990s and early 2000s.
   c. There is no clear trend.
   d. None of the tables showed a significant relationship between PARTYID and AGE.
   e. c and d only.

Now let's explore the relationship between party preference (PARTYID) and regional differences (REGION).

5. Which of the following statements is most accurate?
   a. The Northeast seems to have a higher percentage of Democrats than any other section of the country.
   b. The South seems to have a higher percentage of Republicans than any other section of the country.
   c. Support for third party candidates is higher in the West than in any other part of the country.
   d. a and b only.
   e. All of the above.

Now let's examine the trends for the relationship between political party preference (PARTYID) and REGION. Put partyid in the "Row" Box, region in the "Column" Box, and year in the "Control" Box.

6. What is the trend for the relationship between political party preference and region?
   a. The relationship is not significant for 1980–1984.
   b. The proportion of Northeastern respondents identifying themselves as Democrats has been on the decline since the 1970s.
   c. The proportion of Southern respondents identifying themselves as Democrats has been on the decline since the early 1980s.
   d. Both a and c.
   e. None of the above.
7. When we examine the crosstabulation of political party preference (PARTYID) by gender (SEX), we note:
   a. Female voters tend to favor the Republican Party, while male voters show greater preferences for the Democrats.
   b. Female voters tend to favor the Democrats, while male voters show greater preferences for the Republicans.
   c. Female voters appear to support third party candidates by a considerable margin, as compared to support for third party candidates by male voters.
   d. All of the above.
   e. Only a and b.

8. When we examine the crosstabulation of political party preference (PARTYID) by urban/rural residence (SRCBELT), we note:
   a. Suburban voters tend to favor the Republican Party.
   b. The second greatest level of support for the Republican Party is found in large cities.
   c. Small city residents show the least support of all subgroups for third party candidates.
   d. Residents of large cities show the greatest inclination of all subgroups to favor the Democratic Party.
   e. a and b only.

9. When we examine the crosstabulation of political party preference (PARTYID) by religious differences (RELIG), we note:
   a. Jewish voters are the most likely of all religious subgroups to favor the Democratic Party.
   b. Protestants are the most likely of all religious subgroups to favor the Republican Party.
   c. More Catholics favor the Democrats than any other political group.
   d. All of the above.
   e. None of the above.

Now let's examine the trends for the relationship between political party preference (PARTYID) and RELIG. Put partyid in the "Row" Box, relig in the "Column" Box, and year in the "Control" Box.

10. What is the trend for the relationship between political party preference and religion?
    a. The relationship is significant for all periods.
    b. The proportion of Catholic respondents identifying themselves to be Democrats has been on the decline since the 1970s.
    c. Except for the period between 1995 and 2002, the proportion of Jewish respondents identifying themselves to be Republicans has been on the rise since the 1970s.
    d. Only a and c.
    e. All of the above.

11. Running political party preference (PARTYID) by income differences (RINCOM98), which of the following statements best explains how vote choice is associated with income differences?
    a. Wealthier voters tend to favor the Democratic Party, while there appears to be a preference for the Republican Party among the poor.
    b. Wealthier voters tend to favor the Republican Party, while there appears to be a preference for the Democratic Party among the poor.
    c. The rich are more likely to be favor third party candidates than poorer voters.
    d. All of the above.
    e. None of the above.

12. Running political party preference (**PARTYID**) by educational differences (**EDUC**), which of the following statements best explains how vote choice is associated with educational differences?

    a. More well educated voters tend to favor the Democratic Party, while there appears to be a preference for the Republican Party amongst the less well educated.

    b. The preference for the Republican Party is higher among well educated voters than those with less than a high school education.

    c. The well educated are more likely to be favor third party candidates than less well educated voters.

    d. All of the above.

    e. None of the above.

13. Running political party preference (**PARTYID**) by prestige differences (**PRESTIGE**), which of the following statements best explains how vote choice is associated with prestige differences?

    a. More high prestige workers favor the Democratic Party, while there appears to be a preference for the Republican Party amongst lower prestige workers.

    b. More high prestige workers favor the Republican Party, while those with less prestige support the Democratic Party.

    c. High prestige workers seem to favor third party candidates more than lower prestige workers do.

    d. Only b and c.

    e. None of the above.

Another interesting election issue for us to better understand is the popularity of third party presidential candidates such as Ross Perot and Ralph Nader. Although he polled only 8 percent of the national vote in the 1996 election, Perot's popularity in 1992 extended to 19% of the electorate, when he gained nearly 20,000,000 votes. Not since 1912, when Theodore Roosevelt—running as a Progressive candidate—gained more votes than his Republican rival, William H. Taft, has a third party candidate polled as well as Perot did in 1992. Ralph Nader had an even bigger impact on the 2000 election. Even though his national popularity was less than 4 percent in the 2000 election, in the close races of New Mexico and Florida, Nader voters helped bring victory to George W. Bush, by pulling votes away from the Democratic candidate, Al Gore. Why did so many people flock to Perot's candidacy in 1992 and to Ralph Nader in the 2000 presidential election? What were the demographic characteristics of their supporters? Perhaps, by examining the bases of Perot supporters in 1992 and Nader affiliates in 2000, we may arrive at a deeper understanding of the supporters for third-party candidates. Let's try to answer these questions with the General Social Survey data.

14. Running support for Perot (**PRES92**) by age differences (**AGE**), which of the following statements best explains how support for Perot is associated with age?

    a. More older people favored Perot than leading party candidates.

    b. More younger voters favored Perot than leading party candidates.

    c. Perot's popularity was highest among the middle age set (45–64).

    d. Age was a nonsignificant factor regarding support for Perot.

    e. None of the above.

15. Running support for Perot (**PRES92**) by educational differences (**EDUC**), which of the following statements is most accurate?

    a. A larger proportion of the most well educated supported Perot than those who had only completed intermediate or lower levels of education.

    b. A larger proportion of high school dropouts favored Perot than more well educated voters.

    c. Perot's popularity was highest among high school graduates.

    d. Education was a nonsignificant factor related to support for Perot.

    e. None of the above.

16. Running support for Perot (**PRES92**) by racial differences (**RACE**), which of the following statements best explains how support for Perot is associated with race?

    a. A higher proportion of African Americans favored Perot than whites.

    b. A higher proportion of whites favored Perot than African Americans.

    c. Race was a nonsignificant factor related to support for Perot.

    d. Only a and c.

    e. None of the above.

17. Running support for Nader (**PRES00**) by race differences (**RACECEN1**), which of the following statements best explains how support for Nader is associated with race?

    a. A higher proportion of African Americans favored Nader than whites.

    b. A higher proportion of whites favored Nader than African Americans.

    c. Race was a nonsignificant factor related to support for Nader.

    d. Only a and c.

    e. None of the above.

18. Running support for Perot (**PRES92**) by political ideological differences (**POLVIEWS**), which of the following statements is most accurate?

    a. A higher proportion of political conservatives supported Perot than political moderates and liberals.

    b. A higher proportion of liberals favored Perot than political conservatives and moderates.

    c. Perot's popularity was highest among political moderates.

    d. Political ideological differences was a nonsignificant factor related to support for Perot.

    e. None of the above.

19. Running support for Perot (PRES92) by occupational differences (OCC80), which of the following statements best explains how support for Perot is associated with working at different occupations?
    a. Skilled manual workers favored Perot to a greater degree than other groups of workers.
    b. A higher proportion of professional and managerial workers favored Perot than other groups of workers.
    c. Perot's popularity was highest among unskilled manual workers (operatives).
    d. Occupational difference was a nonsignificant factor related to support for Perot.
    e. None of the above.

20. Running support for Perot (PRES92) by gender differences (SEX), which of the following statements is most accurate?
    a. A higher proportion of women favored Perot than men.
    b. A higher proportion of men supported Perot than women.
    c. Though statistically significant the gender differences in support for Perot were less than 2 percent.
    d. Gender was a nonsignificant factor related to support for Perot.
    e. None of the above.

21. Running support for Nader (PRES00) by gender differences (SEX), which the following statements is most accurate?
    a. A higher proportion of women favored Nader than men.
    b. A higher proportion of men supported Nader than women.
    c. Though statistically significant the gender differences in support for Nader were less than 2 percent.
    d. Gender was a nonsignificant factor related to support for Nader.
    e. None of the above.

22. Running support for Perot (PRES92) by political party differences (PARTYID), which of the following statements is most accurate?
    a. A higher proportion of political Independents favored Perot than Democrats or Republicans.
    b. A higher proportion of Republicans favored Perot than Democrats.
    c. Perot probably took more votes away from Bush (the Republican candidate) than he did from Clinton (the Democratic candidate).
    d. Only b and c.
    e. All of the above.

23. Running support for Nader (PRES00) by political party differences (PARTYID), which of the following statements is most accurate?
    a. A higher proportion of political Independents favored Nader than Democrats or Republicans.
    b. A higher proportion of Republicans favored Nader than Democrats.
    c. Nader probably took more votes away from Bush (the Republican candidate) than he did from Gore (the Democratic candidate).
    d. Only b and c.
    e. All of the above.

24. Running support for Perot (PRES92) by self-employment (WRKSLF), which of the following statements is most accurate?
   a. A higher proportion of the self-employed favored Perot than workers who worked for others.
   b. A higher proportion of workers who worked for others supported Perot than the self-employed.
   c. Although statistically significant, self-employment status differences in support for Perot were very small.
   d. Self-employment status was a nonsignificant factor related to support for Perot.
   e. None of the above.

Political sociologists have devoted much attention to voter participation. Obviously, if the political affiliates of one party are less likely to vote than their opponents, then, this too, can effect who wins an election. In this analysis we will rely upon data collected both in GSS surveys and in the National Election Studies. The NES conducts national surveys of the American electorate in presidential and mid-term election years. These studies began in 1948 and have continued to the present. The NES data file also includes demographic information that you will crosstabulate against voter participation.

For our first task we will assess whether there have been any long-term trends in voter participation. You can complete this analysis by going to the GSS datafile at the SDA website and doing separate frequency distributions for all presidential elections since 1968. Run frequency distributions for these variables: VOTE68, VOTE72, VOTE76, VOTE80, VOTE84, VOTE88, VOTE92, VOTE96, and VOTE00.

25. Which of the following statements best describes the pattern of voting in presidential elections since 1968?
   a. There has been no clear trend.
   b. There has been an almost steadily rising rate of voting since 1968.
   c. There has been an almost steadily falling rate of voting since 1968.
   d. There were participation peaks during the 1980, 1992 and 2000 elections.
   e. None of the above.

For our next task we'll try to assess why some people are more likely to vote and others are less inclined to do so. To complete this analysis:

1. Go to the University of California's SDA site at http://sda.berkeley.edu
2. Click on **SDA Archive** on the upper left corner of the page
3. Under the subtitle "National Omnibus Surveys" click on **NES Cumulative Datafile 1952–1992**
4. Select "**Frequencies or crosstabulation**"
5. Click the **Start** button

The format of the NES is exactly the same as the GSS. Again, you will need to use the recoded variables found at the end of this chapter to do the analyses. Remember to put the dependent variable in the "Row" Box and the independent variable in the "Column" Box. Always select **Statistics** and **Question Text** from "Other Options" before clicking **Run the Table**. This cumulative file enables us to pool together all the surveys from the 40-year period, under a single variable name. If you tabulate voter participation (**V702**) you will note that this sample—summing the results of 20 different bi-annual surveys from 1952 to 1992—includes some 36,500 respondents.

26. Running voter participation (**V702**) by age differences (**V102**), which of the following statements is most accurate?
    a. Voting participation is lowest among the youngest voters.
    b. Voting participation is highest among the middle aged and the "young-old" (45 to 74 years old).
    c. Infirm health could be a factor depressing the voter participation among the "old-old" (those over the age of 75).
    d. All of the above.
    e. None of the above.

Finally, we will study the trend for the relationship in the 1952 to 1992 dataset between voter participation and age. Put **v702** in the "Row" Box, **v102** in the "Column" Box, and **v4** (year of study) in the "Control" Box

27. Young voters (aged 17–24) were least likely to vote in what time period?
    a. The 1950s
    b. The 1960s
    c. The 1970s
    d. The 1980s
    e. 1990–1992
28. Running voter participation (**V702**) by race differences (**V105**), which of the following statements is the most accurate?
    a. Voter participation is lower among whites than African Americans.
    b. Voter participation is higher among whites than African Americans.
    c. The differences in voter participation by race do not appear to be very substantial, nor statistically significant.
    d. Only a and c.
    e. None of the above.
29. Running voter participation (**V702**) by party preference (**V303**), which of the following statements is the most accurate?
    a. Voter participation is lower among Democrats than Republicans.
    b. Voter participation is higher among Independents than major party affiliates.
    c. Republicans are most likely to participate in elections, Independents seem to be among the least.
    d. Only a and c.
    e. None of the above.

30. Running voter participation (V702) by liberal vs. conservative differences (V804), which of the following statements is the most accurate?
    a. Voter participation is lower among self-described moderates than among liberals or conservatives.
    b. Voter participation is higher among conservatives than among liberals.
    c. The differences in voter participation by political ideological differences do not appear to be very substantial, nor statistically significant.
    d. Only a and b.
    e. All of the above.

31. Running voter participation (V702) by religious preference (V128), which of the following statements is the most accurate?
    a. Voter participation is lower among Catholics than Protestants.
    b. Voter participation is highest among Jews than any other religious subgroup.
    c. Religious non-affiliates and those who profess faiths other than the three dominant religions are the groups most likely to abstain from voting.
    d. Only b and c.
    e. All of the above.

32. Running voter participation (V702) by educational differences (V110), which of the following statements is the most accurate?
    a. The relationship between voter participation and education is statistically significant.
    b. Voter participation is lowest among high school dropouts than among all other educational subgroups.
    c. Voter participation is highest among those who complete some college or receive higher level of education.
    d. Only b and c.
    e. All of the above.

33. Running voter participation (V702) by family income differences (V114), which of the following statements is the most accurate?
    a. The relationship between voter participation and family income is statistically significant.
    b. Voting rates increase directly with each level of advancement up the scale of receiving higher incomes.
    c. Approximately four-fifths of the highest income recipients participate in elections.
    d. All of the above.
    e. None of the above.

34. Running voter participation (V702) by occupational differences (V151), which of the following statements is the most accurate?
    a. Clerical workers and professional and managerial workers are more likely to vote than other occupational groups.
    b. Voting rates do not differ much by occupational differences.
    c. Laborers are more likely to vote than housewives.
    d. All of the above.
    e. None of the above.

35. Running voter participation (**V702**) by differences in urbanism (**V111**), which of the following statements is the most accurate?
    a. Big city residents are similarly inclined to vote as suburbanites .
    b. Voter participation rates for rural residents fall below those living in other types of communities.
    c. Suburbanites are substantially more inclined to vote than urbanites.
    d. Only a and b.
    e. None of the above.

ESSAY QUESTIONS

11–A   With the GSS data, select any five demographic attributes (such as sex, race, family income, etc.) and present the crosstabulation tables for these variables against political party affiliation (**PARTYID**). (If you have already answered the multiple-choice questions, you did this task when you answered the first twelve questions.) Now, let us compare and contrast these findings against the National Election Studies data. Running the same crosstabs with the NES dataset (use **V303** as the dependent variable), see whether the results are similar. For each of the five demographic variable hypotheses that you chose, present both sets of tables and discuss all similarities and differences between the findings.

11–B   Dating back to more than half a century ago, there is a long line of research into voter participation, starting with *The People's Choice* (Lazarsfeld, Berelson and Gaudet, NY: Duell, Sloan & Pearce, 1944). This study explored how the experience of "cross-pressures" can diminish a citizen's interest in politics and consequently their participation in elections. Review this theory and assess its relevance in explaining the voter turnout findings you obtained from the recent National Election Studies data. Is the theory still relevant? How may it be applied to this body of data? Are there any places now where the theory does not fit?

11–C   Evaluate the importance of social class, education and occupational prestige in affecting presidential vote participation. Using published research resources, evaluate whether those on the low end of these dimensions are more likely to vote differently to how they did 20 years ago.

11–D   The popularity of Ross Perot can be analyzed from a standpoint of considering it as a social movement. Generally, sociologists categorize social movements as one of several major types: revolutionary movements, reform movements, resistance movements, and expressive movements. Which one(s) seem(s) most appropriate for explaining the interest in Ross Perot? Explain at length why you have chosen this form of social movement. You should evaluate the data on the demographic characteristics of Perot supporters in your answer. If you can, consult the published literature on the

Perot movement as other political analysts have evaluated it; does the GSS data findings show convergence or divergence to what other analysts have concluded about this movement? Explain.

CHAPTER PROJECT

In this project, you will study the impact of religion (**RELIG**) on voting and political affiliations using the GSS data. Unlike the NES data, there are eight dependent variables to look at in examining voting trends: **VOTE68, VOTE72, VOTE76, VOTE80, VOTE84, VOTE88, VOTE92, VOTE96,** and **VOTE00.** The independent variable for this analysis is religion (**RELIG**). Run eight separate tables (i.e., **VOTE68** by **RELIG, VOTE72** by **RELIG,** etc). What patterns have you noticed? Which religious affiliations have changed in their levels of political participation? In the second part of this question, you will examine religious differences and political affiliations: **PRES68, PRES72, PRES76, PRES80, PRES84, PRES88, PRES92, PRES96** and **PRES00.** How have members of the major faiths changed over the last 30 years in their political affiliations? Be sure to use the recoded variables to run all the analyses. Review the sociological literature on religion and voting and vote choice. How do your findings converge with this material?

SYNTAX GUIDE

GSS DATASET
Go to: http://sda.berkeley.edu/cgi-bin12/hsda?harcsda+gss02
Select "Frequencies or crosstabulation"
Click **Start**

GSS Recodes

Please note that all recodes can also be copied and pasted from either www.ncc.edu/users/feigelb/sda.htm or www.ablongman.com/feigelman3e. If you type the recode syntax in, make sure that you type *exactly* what is shown below.

age(r:18-29 "18-29"; 30-44 "30-44"; 45-64 "45-64"; 65-89 "65 and over")

educ(r: *-11 "Less than high school"; 12 "High school"; 13-* "Some college or higher")

income98(r:1-10 "less than 15K";11-16"15K-35K";17-19"35-60K";20-21"60-90K";22-23 "90K and higher")

occ80(r:3-199 "Professional/managerial"; 200-389 "Technicians/sales/admin. support"; 400-469 "Service"; 473-699 "Farmers/fisherman/skilled manual workers"; 703-889 "Operatives")

partyid(r: 0-2 "Democrat"; 3, 7 "Independent"; 4-6 "Republican")

polviews(r: 1-3 "Liberal"; 4 "Moderate"; 5-7 "Conservative")

pres00(r: 3 "Voted for Nader"; 1-2 "Voted for Gore or Bush") pres92(r: 3 "Voted for Perot"; 1-2 "Voted for Clinton or Bush")

prestige(r:*-41 "Low prestige"; 42-* "High prestige")

racecen1(1,2)

region(r: 1-2 "Northeast"; 3-4 "Central"; 5-7 "South"; 8-9 "West")

relig(r:1 "Protestant"; 2 "Catholic"; 3 "Jewish"; 4 "None"; 5-9" Other")

rincom98(r: 1-10 "Less than $15,000"; 11-15 "$15,000-29,999"; 16-19 "$30,000-$59,999"; 20-23 "$60,000 or more")

srcbelt(r: 1-2 "Large city"; 3-4 "Suburbanite"; 5 "Small city"; 6 "Rural and farm")

vote00(1,2)

vote68(1,2)

vote72(1,2)

vote76(1,2)

vote80(1,2)

vote84(1,2)

vote88(1,2)

vote92(1,2)

vote96(1,2)

year(r: 1972-1974 "1972-74"; 1975-1979 "1975-1979"; 1980-1984 "1980-84"; 1985-1989 "1985-89"; 1990-1994 "1990-94"; 1995-2000 "1995-2002")

No recode needed: RACE; SEX; WRKSLF

NES DATASET
Go to: http://sda.berkeley.edu/cgi-bin12/hsda?harcsda+nes92c
Select "Frequencies or crosstabulation"
Click **Start**

NES Recodes

Please note that all recodes can also be copied and pasted from either www.ncc.edu/users/feigelb/sda.htm or www.ablongman.com/feigelman3e. If you type the recode syntax in, make sure that you type *exactly* what is shown below.

v4(r:1952-1959 "1950s"; 1960-1969 "1960s";1970-1979 "1970s";1980-1989 "1980s";1990-1992 "1990-92")

v306(1-3)

v307(1-3)

No recode needed: V102; V105; V110; V111; V112; V114; V128; V151; V303; V702; V804

Chapter 12

Crime and Violence: Serious U.S. Social Problems

If there are any leading social problems in the United States, crime and violence are at the top of the list. Fear of being criminally victimized now plagues most of our citizens. Indeed, more than half of our urban adult population is afraid to go out alone at night, for fear of becoming the victims of crime. When it comes to examining crime generally, we might say most of it is ordinary and unremarkable; and most of it is nonviolent. Occurences such as public drunkenness, smoking marijuana, shoplifting, breaking and entering into an unoccupied house, stealing a car for a joyride, vandalizing public property, taking business property from a workplace—these acts are the most common forms of crime in our society. Such acts overshadow less frequent, and more serious, crimes of violence such as assault, rape and murder. Of course, petty crimes can often lead to the most serious ones.

In this section of the chapter, we will focus our analysis on one of the most serious crimes: homicide. Murder is a crime that continues to deeply repel and, at the same time, fascinate us. Many of our citizens spend much of their free time watching television shows centered on homicide investigations or going to movies where they see films about homicidal violence. Nevertheless, many of our citizens fear being murdered, although the risk of being killed by someone else, is about as remote as drowning. Compared to all other acts of violence, murder is a unique crime. Murder rates do not fluctuate as drastically as most other crimes. Unlike most other crimes, which remain poorly recorded and unsolved, most murders are well known and reported to the police and are far more likely to be processed and adjudicated by the criminal-justice system.

This analysis of homicide behavior relies on a database of murder events, occurring between 1965 and 1994, tabulated from the city of Chicago. The investigators, Carolyn and Richard Block, coded original Chicago Police reports to examine how the crime of murder was changing in that city over time. The Blocks coded more than 20,000 killings that occurred in Chicago between 1964 and 1994. Chicago is typical of many large American cities; consequently, many features associated with its homicides will be comparable for the nation at large. Yet, in some respects Chicago homicide patterns are unique too, and must be carefully evaluated.

In this chapter you will be working with four different datasets: first, the Chicago Homicides Study (known as ICPSR # 6399); the Uniform Crime Reports Supplementary Homicides Reports, 1976–1999 (ICPSR # 3180); the 1995 National Survey of Adolescents (ICPSR #2833); and the Child Abuse and Victimization Study (ICPSR #3548). Each of these studies will be accessed from the Inter-University Consortium for Social and Political Research at the University of Michigan (ICPSR) website. To begin your analysis of problems with each of the above datasets, you will need to perform the following steps:

1. Go to the ICPSR home page at www.icpsr.umich.edu
2. You will see a box labeled "Web Site & Data Holdings". As you wish to proceed to the Chicago Homicides Study, type **6399** in the blank box and select "study number" from the drop down menu to its right. Press the **Search** button.
3. The first option in the resulting list should be labeled "6399 Homicides in Chicago, 1965-1995." Below this will be four links—select **online analysis**.
4. A new page will appear, giving you information about this study; at the bottom of the page click **Homicides in Chicago, 1965-1995**. This will open a familiar menu screen, much like the one at the SDA Berkeley website.

As you analyze each of the remaining datasets in this chapter, you will enter the appropriate study number and go through these same steps, taking you to the correct menu page for your analyses. Take particular care when selecting the correct data for the Uniform Crime Reports Supplementary Homicides Reports, 1976–1999. Make sure to select "Part 1, Victims" in this two part study. In each of the remaining cases, there will only be one choice available as you thread your way through the data selection process. You are now ready to proceed to the instructions for completing the questions on the Chicago Homicides Study.

1. We will begin this exercise at the menu page of the Chicago Homicides Study where you see the NACJD logo at the top with *Study: Homicides in Chicago 1965-1995* appearing below it.
2. Select "**Run frequencies or crosstabulation**".
3. Click the **Start** button.

For all questions, be sure to use the recoded variables (which can be found at the end of this chapter). Also remember to put the dependent variable in the Row Box and the independent variable in the Column Box. Always select **Statistics** and **Question Text** from "Other Options" before clicking **Run the Table**. To construct a new table, simply click the **Back** button on your browser. You are now ready to answer the following questions:

No R

1. Tabulate the month of occurrence (**INJMONTH**). Which month has the highest rate of murders?
   a. February
   b. June
   c. August
   d. September
   e. December

No R

2. Tabulate the day of occurrence (**INJDAY**). Which day of the week has the highest rate of murder?
   a. Wednesday
   b. Friday
   c. Tuesday
   d. Saturday
   e. Monday

3. Tabulate the time of occurrence (**INJTIME**). Which part of the day has the highest rate of murder?
   a. 12:01 am to 6:00 am
   b. 6:01 am to 12:00 noon
   c. 12:01 pm to 6:00 pm
   d. 6:01 pm to midnight

No R

4. Tabulate the place of occurrence (**PLACE**). Which location has the highest rate of murder?
   a. Street
   b. Home
   c. Vehicle
   d. Public transportation
   e. Outdoor, other

No R

5. Tabulate the number of victims in a homicide event (**NUMVIC**) Which of the following statements is most accurate?
   a. About 60 percent of murder events involve one killing and about 40 percent involve more than one victim.
   b. About 80 percent of murder events involve one killing and about 20 percent involve more than one victim.
   c. Over 90 percent of murder events involve one killing and less than 10 percent involve more than one victim.

No R

6. Tabulate the number of offenders involved in a homicide event (**NUMOFF**). Which of the following statements is most accurate?
   a. Usually one person commits a homicide alone.
   b. Usually more than one person is involved as murder offenders.
   c. It is about evenly divided between these two possibilities.

7. What percentage of murder cases involves one offender; and what percentage involves more than one?
   a. 80 percent involve one offender; and 20 percent involve more than one.
   b. 20 percent involve one offender; and 80 percent involve more than one.
   c. About 65 percent involve one offender, and the rest more than one.

No R

8. Do three separate tabulations of the sex (**VICSEX**), age (**VICAGE**) and race (**VICRACE**) of Chicago murder victims and then choose the best answer below:
   a. Most murder victims are Hispanic males, between 30 and 40 years of age.
   b. Murder victims are mostly males, of all ages, and whites are overrepresented among the victims.
   c. The overwhelming majority of murder victims are African American males, between 15 and 35 years of age.
   d. Most murder victims are African Americans, men slightly outpace women in being victims, and most victims are between 30 and 40 years of age.
   e. None of the above.

White non-latino 15.1
Black   "   71.1
Latino   12.9
Asian, other   .9

M → 81.6
F → 18.4

Less than 15 97.2
15-25   2.8

9. About what percentage of Chicago murder cases are cleared by arrest? (Hint: Tabulate **CLEARED** to answer this question.)

   a. 8 percent
   b. 16 percent
   c. 50 percent
   d. 73 percent
   e. 90 percent

   No R

10. Make three separate tabulations of the sex (**OFN1SEX**), age (**OFN1AGE**) and race (**OFN1R**) of those arrested for murder in Chicago. What are common characteristics of those who kill?

    a. Most of those arrested for murder are Hispanic males, between 30 and 40 years of age.
    b. Most of those arrested for murder are males, of all ages, and members of minorities are over-represented.
    c. The overwhelming majority of those arrested for murder are African American males, between 15 and 35 years of age.
    d. None of the above.

    No R   *Black 76.8*   *↗ R   M → 87.3   F → 12.7   less than 15   →80.9   15-25 → .5   46%older →18.6*

11. What percentage of Chicago murder cases are known to include the use of alcohol? (Hint: Tabulate **LIQUOR** to answer this question.)

    a. 8 percent
    b. 33 percent
    c. 50 percent
    d. 78 percent
    e. 90 percent

12. What percentage of Chicago murder cases are known to include the use of firearms? (Hint: Tabulate **WEAPON** to answer this question.)

    a. 8 percent
    b. 36 percent
    c. 50 percent
    d. 64 percent
    e. 90 percent

    R

13. What percentage of all Chicago murder cases are known to be gang-related acts of violence? (Hint: Tabulate **GANG** to answer this question.)

    a. 9 percent
    b. 28 percent
    c. 50 percent
    d. 78 percent
    e. 91 percent

    No R

14. Has gang-related violence increased as a percentage of all killings? (Hint: To identify whether gang killings have changed over time, you will need to tabulate gang killings (**GANG**) by incident year period (**INJYEAR**).)

    a. There have been some fluctuations in gang killings, but no significant changes in their occurrence over the study period.
    b. There has been near steady and continuous rises in the number of gang killings over the 30 year study period.
    c. There has been much up and down fluctuations, but no clear increasing occurrence of gang killings over the study period.
    d. a and c.
    e. None of the above.

15. Has gun-related violence increased as a percentage of all killings? (Hint: To identify whether guns are playing a larger (or smaller) role as murder weapons over time, you will need to tabulate the use of guns in homicides (**WEAPON**) by incident year period (**INJYEAR**).)
    a. Use of guns has fluctuated in killings, but no significant change has occurred over the 30-year study period.
    b. There has been a steady and continuous rise in the use of guns over the 30-year study period.
    c. There has been some up and down fluctuation of gun use and an apparent overall rise of gun use in homicides over the 30-year study period.
    d. Gun killings have declined in the 1990s when compared to their higher use in the 1980s.
    e. None of the above.

16. Has the number of killings increased over the 30-year study period? (Hint: Tabulate **INJYEAR** to answer this question.)
    a. Overall killings have fluctuated over the 30-year period, but no significant increase has occurred.
    b. There has been a steady and continuous rise in the number of killings over the 30-year period.
    c. There has been some up and down fluctuation in the number of killings, and an apparent overall rise during the latest period of the early 1990s.
    d. The number of killings has declined in the 1990s, compared to their highest incidence in the 1980s.
    e. None of the above.

17. Many whites are afraid they may be killed by an African American. What does the Chicago homicide facts say about the incidence of interracial homicide rates? (Hint: Tabulate the victim's race (**VICRACE**), by the race of the offender (**OFN1R**) to answer this question.)
    a. African Americans are the most likely of all subgroups to murder someone from within their race.
    b. Percentage-wise, more African Americans kill whites than whites kill African Americans, though differences in this respect are not very large.
    c. African Americans are the most likely of all subgroups to murder someone from outside their race.
    d. This data doesn't enable one to identify cross-racial killings.
    e. a and b.

We may wonder with the emancipation of women from traditional female roles whether they may be inclined to act more "male-like" in other respects too, such as acting violently.

18. Do a tabulation of a first offender's gender (**OFN1SEX**) by incident year period (**INJYEAR**), to identify whether women are playing a differing role as murderers over the course of the study period. Which of the following statements is most accurate?
    a. The data show a growing percentage of female killers, though differences fall short of statistical significance.
    b. The data show a rising percentage of female killers, and differences are statistically significant.
    c. There have been some fluctuations in killings by women with no apparent overall trend.
    d. The data show a falling percentage of female killers, that is statistically significant.
    e. None of the above.

We may also wonder whether, with women increasingly becoming involved in activities outside the home, murderers are increasingly targeting women.

19. Do a tabulation of the victim's gender (**VICSEX**) by incident year period (**INJYEAR**), to identify whether women have become increasingly targeted for murder over time. Which of the following statements is the most accurate?
    a. The data shows a growing percentage of female murder victims, though differences fall short of statistical significance.
    b. The data shows a rising percentage of female murder victims, and differences are statistically significant.
    c. There have been some fluctuations in females as murder victims, with no apparent overall trend.
    d. The data shows a falling percentage of female murder victims that is statistically significant.
    e. None of the above.

Let's compare these results, based on data from the city of Chicago, with national homicide data obtained from the United States Uniform Crime Reports, *Supplementary Homicide Reports, 1976–1999, Part 1: Victim Data*. Following the instructions given at the beginning of this chapter, go to ICPSR #3180 and thread your way to the menu page for *UCR Supplementary Homicide Reports, 1976–1999 Part I: Victim Data* and perform the following steps:

1. Select "**Run frequencies or crosstabulation**".
2. Click the **Start** button.
3. We will begin by tabulating the month of occurrence (**MONTH**) to identify which month has the highest rate of murders. To do this, simply type **month** in the "Row" box.
4. Select **Statistics** and **Question Text** from "Other Options".
5. Check that your input matches that shown in Figure 12.1 before clicking **Run the Table**.

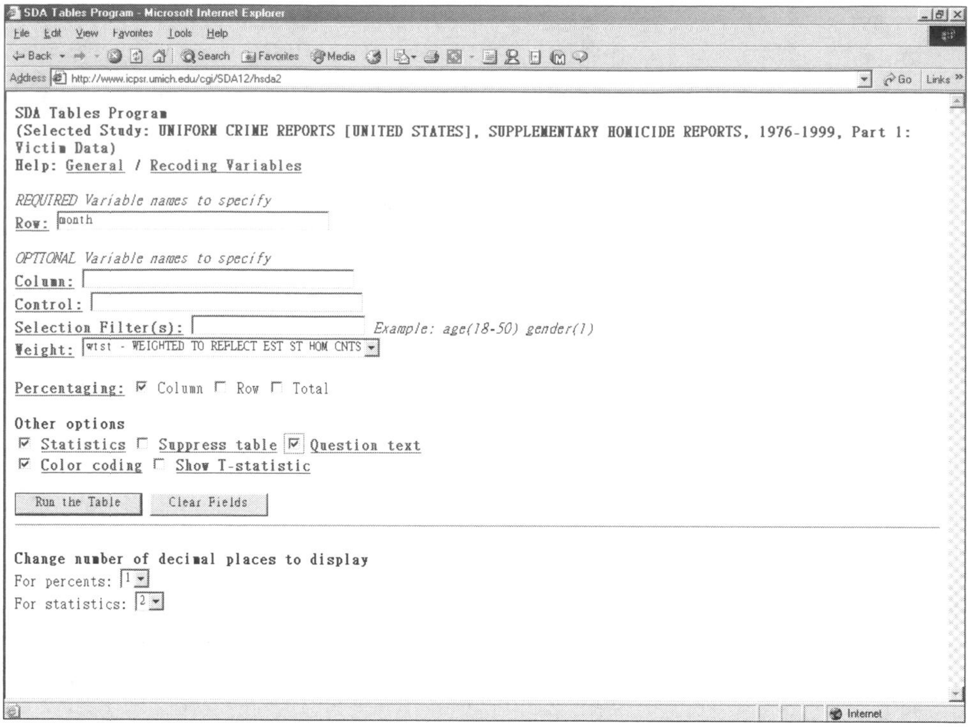

FIGURE 12.1

Remember to use the recoded variables found at the end of this chapter when answering the following questions.

20. Which month had the highest number of murder incidents?
    a. February   7.5
    b. June   8.3
    c. August   9.1
    d. September   8.5
    e. December   8.8

21. Do three separate tabulations of the sex (**VICSEX**), age (**VICAGE**) and race (**VICRACE**) of Uniform Crime Report murder victims. Which of the following statements is most accurate?
    a. Most murder victims are Hispanic males, between 30 and 40 years of age.
    b. Murder victims are mostly males, of all ages, and whites are over-represented among the victims.
    c. The overwhelming majority of murder victims are African American males, between 15 and 35 years of age.
    d. Most murder victims are African Americans; men slightly outpace women in being victims; and most victims are between 30 and 40 years of age.
    e. Most murder victims are males, between 15 and 35 years of age. About 47% of the victims are African Americans.

When working with this national data, which incorporates hundreds of thousands of actual murder cases, it is important to keep in mind that statistical significances often will not mean very much. When analyzing a large number of cases, the Chi-Square statistical significance test will yield statistically significant results even with small inter-category differences of one or two percentage points. Therefore, the thing to look for in making comparisons with very large case numbers is percentage differences: Do the subcategories in the comparison show differences of ten percent or greater from one another? In these cases, we could be looking at meaningful or theoretically important differences.

22. Do a tabulation of the first offender's gender (**OFFSEX**) by incident year period (**YEAR**) to identify whether women are playing a differing role as murderers over the course of the study period. Which of the following statements is most accurate?
    a. The data shows a growing percentage of female killers, though the differences are less than 5 percent.
    b. The data shows a sharply rising percentage of female killers, and differences are greater than 10 percent.
    c. There have been some fluctuations in killings by women with no apparent overall trend.
    d. The data shows a falling trend of female killers, of approximately 6 percent.
    e. Either a or c.

23. Do a tabulation of the victim's gender (**VICSEX**) by incident year period (**YEAR**), to identify whether women have become increasingly targeted by murderers over time. Which of the following statements is the most accurate?
    a. The data shows a growing percentage of female murder victims, though the differences are modest (between 5 and 10 percent).
    b. The data shows a rising percentage of female murder victims, and the differences are considerable (above 10 percent).
    c. There have been very small fluctuations in the number of female murder victims, showing differences between a fifth and a quarter of female murder victims with the comparison period.
    d. The data shows a considerable falling percentage of female murder victims of over 10 percent.
    e. None of the above.

24. Has gun-related violence increased as a percentage of all killings? (Hint: To answer this you will need to tabulate the use of guns in homicides (**WEAPON**) by incident year period (**YEAR**).)
    a. The use of guns has fluctuated greatly in killings. The highest level of gun use was in the 1980s.
    b. There has been steady and substantial rises in the use of guns killings over the 30 year study period.
    c. There has been some up and down fluctuation of gun use, with a range of fluctuation between 8 percent over the 30-year study period.
    d Gun killings have declined in the 1990s, compared to their higher use in the 1980s.
    e. a and d.

Black → 50.7

15 -25 → 42.6

26 -35 → 28.9

Male → 87.3

25. Make three separate tabulations of the sex (OFFSEX), age (OFFAGE) and race (OFFRACE) from the Uniform Crime Reports. What are common characteristics of those who kill?
    a. Most people arrested for murder are Hispanic males, between 30 and 40 years of age.
    b. Most people arrested for murder are males, of all ages, and members of minorities are over-represented.
    c. Most people arrested for murder are African American males, between 15 and 35 years of age.
    d. None of the above.

Youth is over-represented in crimes of violence and most ordinary crimes are committed by teenagers and young adults. Yet, one of the most remarkable things about youth crime is that as young people get older, they begin to pass up doing criminal activities and assume more conventional behavior patterns. Many studies document this.

When we try to measure crime as it occurs in the community we usually find police reports to be seriously flawed. Many citizens don't bother to report the everyday acts of property vandalism, burglary and robbery incidents. Citizens often feel it is not worth taking the time and trouble to report the incident, when, in the overwhelming majority of cases, no one will be apprehended for the misdeed. Other crimes like rape and assault may be underreported for different reasons, such as the fear of reprisal. Victimization surveys usually show that no more than half of the victims of most crimes call the police to report these incidents. Thus, community victimization surveys usually provide better indicators of the incidence of (and fluctuations in) ordinary and violent crime than police reports. The best measures of crime participation come from self-report surveys. In anonymous and confidential surveys, we are able to gauge how commonplace crime actually is, as well as who is most and least likely to commit offenses. Such surveys also help considerably in understanding the social dynamics of crime.

In the next section of this chapter, we will rely upon one such survey, the 1995 National Survey of Adolescents in the United States. This study included more than 4,000 respondents who were between the ages of 12 and 17 in 1995. In the survey, respondents were asked to provide information about their delinquent offenses during the past year. Following the instructions given at the beginning of this chapter, go to ICPSR #2833 and thread your way to the menu page for the *1995 National Survey of Adolescents*. At the menu page for this study select the "Run frequency or crosstabulation" option and click **Start**. You will see the layout shown in Figure 12.2.

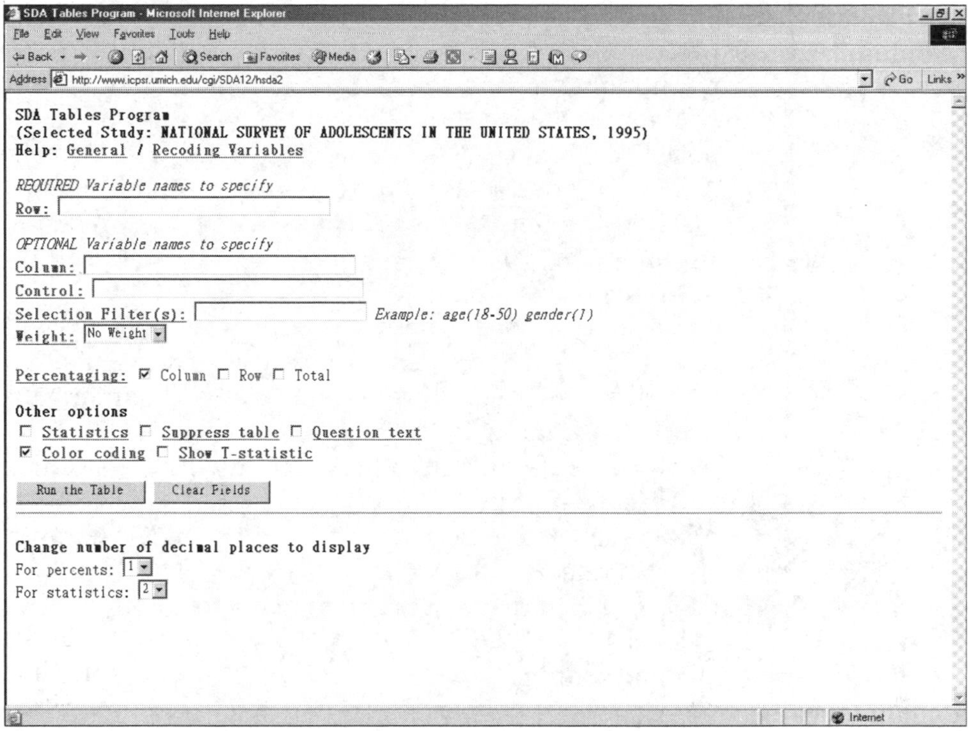

FIGURE 12.2

For the following questions, be sure to put the dependent variable in the "Row" box and independent variable in the "Column" box. Always select **Statistics** and **Question Text** from "Other Options" before clicking **Run the Table**.

26. What percentage of 12–17 year old respondents had committed delinquent offenses? (Hint: Tabulate **DELL** to answer this question.)
    a. 13 percent
    b. 23 percent
    c. 46 percent
    d. 54 percent
    e. 77 percent

27. Earlier research suggests that being a casualty of parental breakup or divorce may contribute to juvenile delinquency and crime. Crosstabulate juvenile delinquent offenses (**DELL**) with always lived with both biological parents (**Q38A**). Which of the following statements is most accurate?
    a. Adolescents who have always lived with both parents are significantly less likely to commit delinquent offenses than those who did not.
    b. Adolescents who have always lived with both parents are significantly more likely to committed delinquent offenses than those who did not.
    c. The result from the table is unclear.
    d. There is no significant difference between the two groups with respect to having ever committed a delinquent offense.

28. Crosstabulate juvenile delinquent offense (DELL) with family income (INCOME). Does delinquency vary with a family's income?
    a. Delinquents whose families had higher income were more likely to commit offenses than those with lower family incomes.
    b. Delinquents whose families had higher incomes were less likely to commit offenses than those with lower family incomes.
    c. Family income seems to be unrelated to differences in rates of youth delinquent offenses.
    d. None of the above.

29. Crosstabulate juvenile delinquent offense rates (DELL) with a respondent's race (RACE). Are there racial differences in delinquent offense rates?
    a. African Americans were more likely to commit youth delinquent offenses than whites.
    b. Whites were more likely to commit youth delinquent offenses than African Americans.
    c. Race seemed to be unrelated to differences in youth delinquent offense rates.
    d. Native Americans were more likely to commit youth delinquent offenses than others
    e. a and d only.

The final part of the chapter deals with the impact of child abuse victimization and later violent crime participation. The study is based on data obtained from a large urban county in the Northwest United States from 1980–1997. The central research question in the study examined how childhood victimization experiences were related to delinquency, adult criminality, and violent criminal behavior. We'll use their data to examine the relationship of child abuse and neglect victimization to adult criminality. Following the instructions given at the beginning of this chapter, go to ICPSR #3548 and thread your way to the menu page for the *Child Abuse and Victimization Study*. At the menu page for this study select "**Run frequencies or crosstabulation**" and click the **Start** button.

For all questions, be sure to use the recoded variables (which can be found at the end of this chapter). Also, remember to put the dependent variable in the Row Box and the independent variable in the Column Box. Always select **Statistics** and **Question Text** from "Other Options" before clicking **Run the Table**. To construct a new table, simply click the **Back** button on your browser. You are now ready to answer the following questions:

30. Is childhood victimization (SUB_CNLX) related to property crime activities (CR_PRP_A)? (Hint: SUB_CNLX is the independent variable.)
    a. There is no relationship between childhood victimization and property crime.
    b. Those children who were victimized showed lower chances of committing property crime than those who were not victimized, although the relationship is not significant.
    c. Victimized subjects showed higher chances of committing property crime than non-victimized subjects and the relationship is significant.
    d. Victimized subjects showed lower chances of committing property crime than non-victimized subjects and the relationship is significant.
    e. a and b only.

31. Is childhood victimization (SUB_CNLX) related to assault behavior (CH36V)? (Hint: CH36V is the dependent variable.)
    a. There is no relationship between childhood victimization and assault behavior.
    b. Those children who were victimized showed lower chances of assaulting others than those who were not victimized, although the relationship is not significant.
    c. Victimized subjects showed higher chances of assaulting others than non-victimized subjects and the relationship is significant.
    d. Victimized subjects showed lower chances of assaulting others than non-victimized subjects and the relationship is significant.
    e. a and b only.

32. What is the relationship between childhood victimization (SUB_CNLX) and the probability of committing adult violent crimes (VIOL_1_S)?
    a. The relationship is statistically insignificant.
    b. Those children who were victimized showed lower chances of committing adult violent crimes than those who were not victimized, although the relationship is not significant.
    c. Victimized subjects showed higher chances of committing adult violent crimes than non-victimized subjects.
    d. Victimized subjects showed lower chances of committing adult violent crimes than non-victimized subjects and the relationship is significant.
    e. a and b only.

ESSAY QUESTIONS

12–A   With the Chicago Homicides Study data, investigate the differences in killings by race. One of your key variables for this analysis will be OFN1R, the race of the first offender. Investigate whether there are any differences in the patterns of killings, such as weapons used, whether drugs or alcohol was present, whether it was a gang-related killing incident, or race of the killer. What do your findings show? How do the different races compare with each other in this respect? Investigate what has been found in the research literature on the race related correlates of murder. Compare your findings with what has been found in the existing research literature on this question.

12–B   Using any electronic bibliographic search resources available at your campus or at the National Criminal Justice Reference Service website (**www.ncjrs.org/statwww.html**), investigate why the experiences of child abuse and neglect would be correlated with later involvement in adult crime. Briefly explain why these relationships may be found. Then go to the data you have available in the ICPSR study number #3548 and do a crosstabular analysis of three critical hypotheses that would test the theory of relationships between childhood abuse and neglect victimization and later crime. Present the tables showing your results and summarize your findings.

12 C   Examine the codebook of survey questions asked in the 1995
National Survey of Adolescents and develop five different hypotheses that you think will explain differences in youth delinquency.
Use any electronic bibliographic search resources available at your
campus or the National Criminal Justice Reference Service website
(www.ncjrs.org/statwww.html) to investigate whether your hypotheses have been proven in any past research. Finally, run the crosstabulations for these hypotheses and interpret your findings and try
to explain any inconsistencies with the past research record.

CHAPTER PROJECT

Compare and contrast the Chicago homicide data trends with the national
(UCR) reports of killings. How are Chicago's homicide patterns similar and
different from the national trends and patterns of this crime? Discuss the
trends in one (or several) aspect(s) of interest to you, such as overall numbers of killings, stranger-related incidents, gang-related events, gun-related
killings, and/ or the demographic characteristics of victims and killers.

SYNTAX GUIDE

Please note that all recodes can also be copied and pasted from either
www.ncc.edu/users/feigelb/sda.htm or www.ablongman.com/feigelman3e.
If you type the recode syntax in, make sure that you type *exactly* what is
shown below.

CHICAGO HOMICIDES STUDY
Go to: www.icpsr.umich.edu/cgi/SDA/hsda?nacjd+homchi6595
Select "Run frequencies or crosstabulation"
Click **Start**

Chicago Homicides Study Recodes

injtime(r:1-600 "Midnight to 6:00 am"; 601-1200 "6:01 am to 12:00 noon";
    1201-1800 "12:01 pm to 6:00 pm"; 1801-2400 "6:01 pm to midnight")

injyear(r: 65-69 "65-69"; 70-74 "70-74"; 75-79 "75-79"; 80-84 "80-84"; 85-
    89 "85-89"; 90-95 "90-95")

liquor(r: 1 "Yes"; 2 "No")

ofn1age(r: 0-14 "Less than 15"; 15-25 "15-25"; 26-35 "26-35"; 36-45 "36-
    45"; 46-* "46 and older")

vicage(r: 0-14 "Less than 15"; 15-25 "15-25"; 26-35 "26-35"; 36-45 "36-45";
    46-* "46 and older")

weapon(r: 1-5 "Firearm"; 6-10 "Other weapons")

No recode needed: CLEARED; GANG; INJDAY; INJMONTH; NUMOFF; NUM-
    VIC; OFN1R; OFN1SEX; PLACE; VICRACE; VICSEX

UCR HOMICIDE SUPPLEMENTS
Go to: www.icpsr.umich.edu/cgi/SDA/hsda?nacjd+shr7699p1
Select "Run frequencies or crosstabulation"
Click **Start**

UCR Homicide Supplements Recodes

offage(r: 0-14 "Less than 15"; 15-25 "15-25"; 26-35 "26-35"; 36-45 "36-45"; 46-98 "46 and older")

offrace(r: 1 "White"; 2 "Black"; 3 "American Indian"; 4 "Asian and Pacific Islander"; 5 "Other")

offsex(r: 1 "Male"; 2 "Female")

vicage(r: 0-14 "Less than 15"; 15-25 "15-25"; 26-35 "26-35"; 36-45 "36-45"; 46-* "46 and older")

vicsex(r: 1 "Male"; 2 "Female")

weapon(r: 11-15 "Firearm"; 20-99 "Other weapons")

year(r: 76-79 "76-79"; 80-84 "80-84"; 85-89 "85-89"; 90-95 "90-95"; 96-99 "96-99")

No recode needed: MONTH; VICRACE

NATIONAL ADOLESCENT STUDY
Go to: www.icpsr.umich.edu/cgi/SDA/hsda?nacjd+nsa
Select "Run frequencies or crosstabulation"
Click **Start**

National Adolescent Study Recodes

income(r: 1-3 "20K or less"; 4-5 "20K-40K"; 6-9 "40K and higher")

q38a(1,2)

No recode needed: DELL; RACE

CHILDHOOD VICTIM AND ADULT CRIME STUDY
Go to: www.icpsr.umich.edu/cgi-bin/SDA/hsda?nacjd+03548-0001
Select "Run frequencies or crosstabulation"
Click **Start**

Childhood Victim and Adult Crime Study Recodes

sub_cnlx(r: 1 "Victimized subjects"; 2 "Non-victimized subjects")

viol_1_s(r: 0 "No"; 1-17 "Yes")

No recode needed: CR_PRP_A; CH36V

Chapter 13

Youth Problems

In this chapter, we will explore several datasets that have investigated various youth problems including heavy drinking, drug abuse, getting into fights, problem gambling, and other risk-taking behaviors. Actually, the analysis will extend beyond this realm into a variety of other problem subjects such as depression, suicide, and being a victim of certain crimes of violence. You will investigate these questions with several datasets collected among samples of youth, high school seniors, college age populations, with respondents like many of yourselves.

First, let's introduce some of the data we will be using. The two largest and longest running studies of Americans' drug use have been done annually since the early 1970s and are financed by the federal government. The National Household Survey of Drug Abuse (NHSDA) conducts its annual surveys by drawing on the non-institutionalized 12 and over population. Its 2002 survey drew on a nationally representative sample of over 54,000 respondents. The Monitoring the Future surveys (MTF) draw on national representations of U.S. high school seniors with annual samples of 12,000 or more. Their 2002 survey had over 13,000 respondents.

In this chapter you will be working with four different datasets: the 2002 Monitoring the Future Survey (known as ICPSR #3753); the 2002 National Household Survey of Drug Abuse (ICPSR #3903); the 1999 National Gambling Impact Survey (ICPSR #2778); and the 1995 National

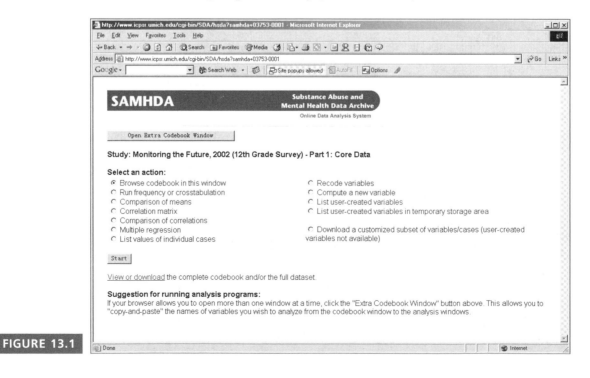

FIGURE 13.1

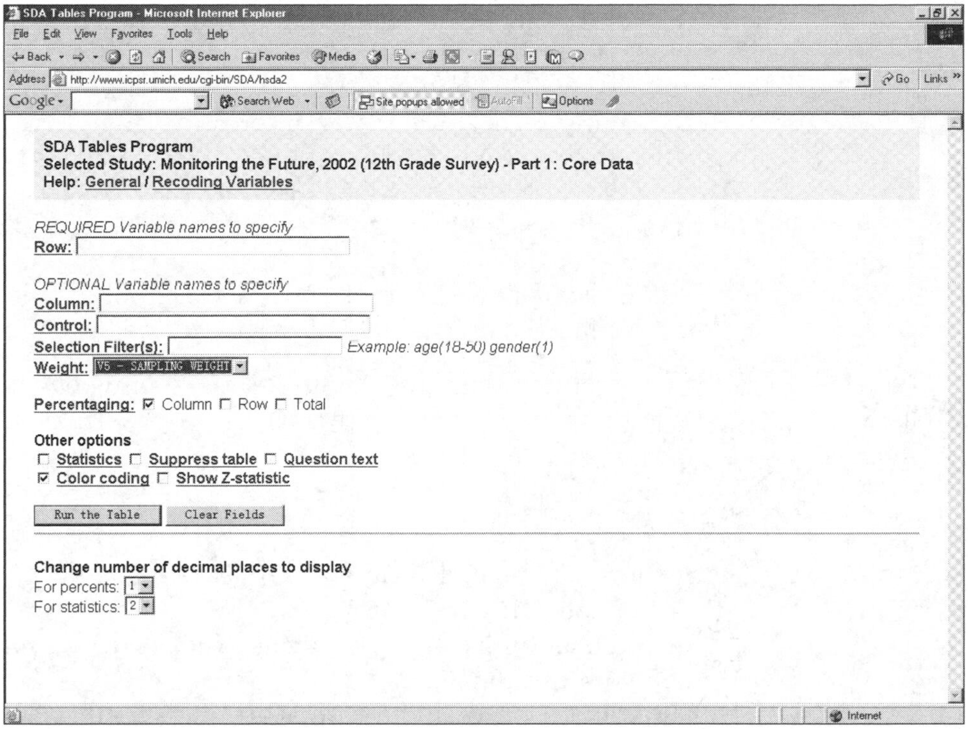

FIGURE 13.2

Survey of Adolescents (ICPSR #2833). Each of these studies will be accessed from the Inter-University Consortium for Social and Political Research at the University of Michigan (ICPSR) web site. To begin your analysis of problems with each of the above datasets, you will need to perform the following steps:

1. Go to the ICPSR home page at **www.icpsr.umich.edu**
2. You will see a box labeled "Web Site & Data Holdings". As you wish to proceed to the 2002 Monitoring the Future Survey, type **3753** in the blank box and select "study number" from the drop down menu to its right. Press the **Search** button.
3. The first option in the resulting list should be labeled "Monitoring the Future: A Continuing Study of American Youth (12th-Grade Survey), 2002." Below this will be four links—select **online analysis**.
4. A new page will appear, giving you information about this study; at the bottom of the page click **Monitoring the Future, 2002 (12th Grade Survey)—Part 1: Core Data**. This will open a familiar menu screen, much like the one at the SDA Berkeley website, which is shown in Figure 13.1.
5. As you analyze each of the remaining datasets in this chapter, you will enter the appropriate study number and go through these same steps, taking you to the correct menu page for your analyses.

Select "Run frequency or crosstabulation" and click **Start**. You will now see the layout shown in Figure 13.2.

In the middle of the page you will see a "Weight" option. The default setting for this option is: "V5 – SAMPLING WEIGHT." For the analyses with MTF and NHSDA in this chapter, you do *not* want to apply survey weights. To turn this option off, simply click on the "Weight" Box and select the "No weight" option.

We are now ready to do some interesting analyses. As a reminder, always use the recoded variables found at the end of this chapter when answering the following questions. Also, be sure to select "Statistics" and "Question Text" from "Other Options" before clicking **Run the Table**.

1. In 2002, what percentage of U.S. high school seniors were current smokers (i.e. had one or more cigarettes in the last month)? Type **v102** in the "Row" Box.
   a. 42 percent
   b. 58 percent
   c. 34 percent
   d. 66 percent
   e. 27 percent

2. Are there age-related differences (**V148**) to being a smoker? (Hint: crosstabulate **V102** by **V148**.)
   a. Differences are not statistically significant between the two groups and could be due to chance.
   b. Differences between the groups are statistically significant.
   c. Unclear results.
   d. Those who are under 18 years of age are more likely to be current smokers.

3. Does smoking differ by race (**V151**) and gender (**V150**)? (Hint: Run two separate analyses: **V102** by **V151** and **V102** by **V150**.)
   a. Males are less likely to be smokers than females and whites are more likely to be smokers than African Americans.
   b. Females are less to be smokers than males and African Americans are more likely to be smokers than whites.
   c. Males are less likely to be smokers than females and African Americans are more likely to be smokers than whites.
   d. Females are less likely to be smokers than males and whites are more likely to be smokers than African Americans.
   e. Differences are not statistically significant for the relationship between smoking and race.

4. Does it vary by maternal employment (**V165**), or father's educational attainments (**V163**)?
   a. Mother's employment is not related to children's smoking behavior.
   b. Father's education is not related to children's smoking behavior.
   c. Mother's employment is related to children's smoking behavior.
   d. Father's education is related to children's smoking behavior.
   e. a and d only.

Now let's work with the 2002 National Household Survey of Drug Abuse. Go to: www.icpsr.umich.edu/cgi-bin/SDA/hsda?samhda+03903-0001. Select "Run frequency or crosstabulation" and click **Start**. You will see the layout shown in Figure 13.3.

Again, you will need to change the default "Weight" option from "ANALWT_C . . ." to "No weight." To turn this option off, simply click on

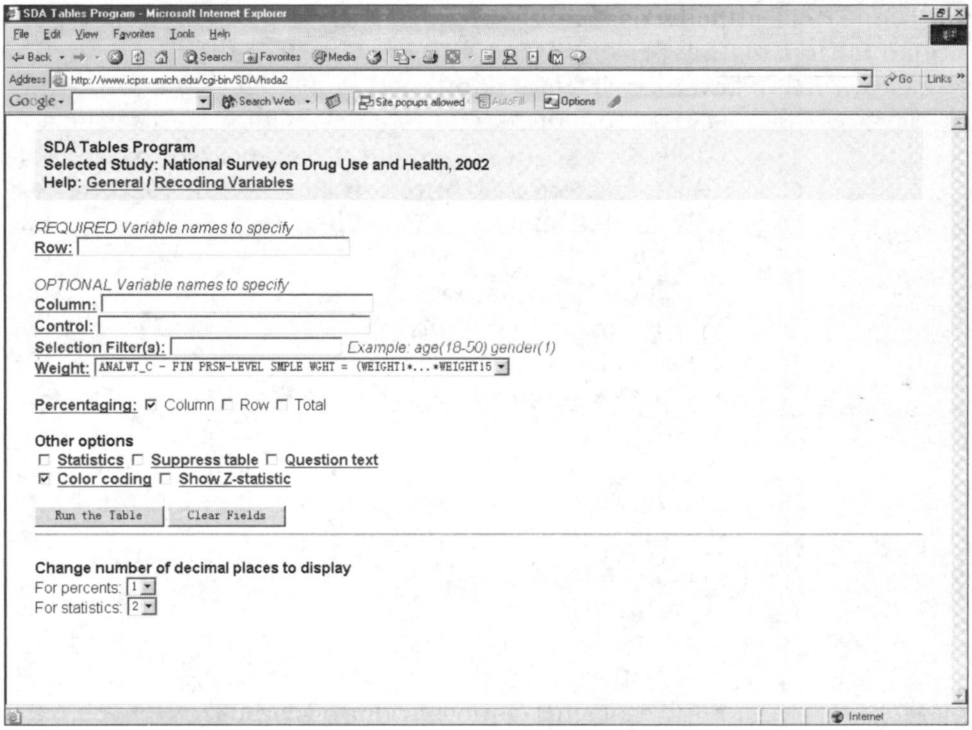

FIGURE 13.3

the "Weight" Box and select the "No weight" option. Also, be sure to select "Statistics" and "Question Text" from "Other Options" before clicking **Run the Table**.

5. Does the 2002 NHSDA data show that collegians smoke any more or less than high school seniors? (Hint: Refer to your answer for Question 1, or those from the 18–22 age group that do not attend college and use **CIGMON** as the dependent variable and **COLLENR2** for the independent variable.)
   a. College students are more likely to be smokers than high school seniors.
   b. College students are less likely to be smokers than high school seniors.
   c. College students are more likely to be smokers than those who do not attend college.
   d. The relationship between **CIGMON** and **COLLENR2** is not statistically significant.
   e. a and c only.

6. Getting drunk at least twice a month could be an indication of having a serious drinking problem. What percentage of high school seniors reported get drunk one or more times in the last two weeks? (Getting drunk was defined as having five or more drinks on each drinking occasion.) In MTF use V108 as your dependent variable.
   can't find in database
   a. 71 percent
   b. 61 percent
   c. 39 percent
   d. 29 percent
   e. 16 percent

7. In the NHSDA, binge drinking was counted on a monthly basis (BINGEDRK). Using the same standard of two or more binge drinking events within a month period, which of the following groups is most at-risk from drinking problems: high school seniors, full-time college students, part-time students, 18–22 year olds not going to college, or all other groups? (Hint: crosstabulate BINGEDRK by COLLENR2. You will need to compare this table with the one you created for Question 6.)
   a. High school seniors
   b. Full-time college students
   c. Part-time students
   d. 18–22 year olds not going to college
   e. All other groups

8. Which group of young people is most likely to drive while drunk (DRIVALC2)? (Hint: Type drivalc2 in the "Row" box and collenr2 in the "Column" Box.)
   a. Full-time college students
   b. Part-time student
   c. 18–22 year olds not going to college
   d. All other groups
   e. The relationship between DRIVALC2 and COLLENR2 is not statistically significant

In the NHSDA, questions were asked about the use of the following illegal drugs: marijuana (MJEVER); cocaine (COCFLAG); crack (CRKFLAG); LSD (LSDFLAG); PCP (PCPFLAG); inhalants (INHFLAG); heroin (HERFLAG); hallucinogens (HALFLAG); painkillers (ANLFLAG); tranquilizers (TRQFLAG); stimulants (STMFLAG); sedatives (SEDFLAG).

9. Of the above drugs, which is the least used among 18–22 year olds? (Hint: Simply run each variable and recode answers on a piece of paper so that you can compare them.)
   a. Heroin   1.3
   b. Inhalants   12.5
   c. LSD   10.8
   d. PCP   2.7
   e. Stimulants   8.7

10. What percentage of 18–22 year olds used it?
   a. 2.8 percent
   b. 1.6 percent
   c. 5.2 percent
   d. 3.5 percent
   e. 15.4 percent

11. Of the above drugs, which was the most used among 18–22 year olds?
   a. Cocaine   12.4
   b. Hallucinogens   15.9
   c. Marijuana   41.4
   d. Pain killers   15.3
   e. LSD   10.8

12. What percentage of 18–22 year olds used it?
    a. 24 percent
    b. 55 percent
    c. 41 percent
    d. 33 percent
    e. 16 percent

13. What percentage of 18–22 year olds had smoked marijuana in the last year? (Hint: Use the variable MRJYR to answer this question.)
    a. 18 percent   18.2
    b. 57 percent
    c. 10 percent
    d. 33 percent
    e. 25 percent

14. What percentage of young adults (18–22) smoked marijuana weekly (50 or more times) in the last year (MRJYDAYS)? (Hint: You will need to compute this statistic yourself by dividing the number of 18–22 year olds who used marijuana 50 or more times over the total number who ever used it among the population.)
    a. 58 percent   59,079
    b. 17 percent
    c. 9 percent   1.7511
    d. 46 percent
    e. 25 percent

15. Excluding marijuana use, what percentage of 18–22 year olds had tried any illegal drugs at any time during their life? (Hint: Use IEMFLAG to answer this question.)
    a. 13 percent
    b. 19 percent
    c. 32 percent   32.1
    d. 68 percent
    e. 25 percent

16. Using all illegal drug uses (excluding marijuana) as your dependent variable (IEMFLAG), which group (COLLENR2) is most at risk for all other illegal drug uses?
    a. Full-time college students
    b. Part-time college students
    c. 18–22 year olds not in college
    d. 18–22 years elsewhere
    e. There were no appreciable differences between these groups

17. Using marijuana (MJEVER) as your dependent variable, which group (COLLENR2) is most at risk for marijuana use?
    a. Full-time college students
    b. Part-time college students
    c. 18–22 year olds not in college
    d. 18–22 years elsewhere
    e. There were no appreciable differences between these groups

There has been a great deal of debate on the importance of having stay-at-home moms in helping kids assume conventional roles and shy away from drug use. It is charged that working moms, and the latchkey kids they spawn, are more independent and more inclined to use drugs. Of course, the issue is a very complex one. Income differences between families matter; parental divorce is still another factor complicating maternal work and drug uses, besides a mother's own use (or abstention) from drug use. Using the MTF 2002, let's run maternal employment (**V165**) against smoking (**V101**); binge drinking (**V108**); marijuana use (**V112**) to answer the following question. *(Not in database)*

18. How does mother's employment affect children's smoking, drinking, and marijuana use? (Hint: Run three separate analyses. Always put the independent variable (**V165**) in the "Column" Box and the dependent variable in the "Row" Box.)

   a. Children are less likely to smoke when their mother stays at home.
   b. Children are less likely to engage in binge drinking when their mother stays at home.
   c. Children are less likely to use marijuana when their mother stays at home.
   d. All of the above are true.
   e. Only a and b are true.

In the next question, we will investigate whether a mother's employment status affects their children's use of any other illegal drugs. To do this, we will need to compute a new variable from ever using any of the following drugs: LSD (**V118**); psychedelics (**V121**); cocaine (**V124**); amphetamines (**V127**); ice (**V130**); sedatives (**V133**); tranquilizers (**V136**); heroin (**V139**); other narcotics (**V142**); and inhalants (**V145**). You will need to perform the following steps to compute a new variable:

1. Go to **www.icpsr.umich.edu/cgi-bin/SDA/hsda?samhda+03753-0001**.
2. Select "Compute a new variable" and click **Start**.
3. Type the following syntax into the box labeled "EXPRESSION TO DEFINE THE NEW VARIABLE":
       illdrug=v118+v121+v124+v127+v130+v133+v136+v139+v142+v145
4. Select "Yes" for the option "Replace that variable, if it already exists?".
5. Click **Start Computing**.

The newly created variable, ILLDRUG, ranges from 10 to 65. The larger the value, the more likely the respondent is to use one of the various drugs listed above. To make the analysis easier, we will separate this variable into two groups by using the following recode:

illdrug(r: 10 "Never used illegal drugs"; 11-65 "Ever used illegal drugs")

To go back to the crosstabulation analysis, simply click the **Back** button within your browser twice. Then select "Run frequency or crosstabulation" and click **Start**. You can also go to the crosstabulation analysis by typing in the following URL: **www.icpsr.umich.edu/cgi-bin/SDA/hsda?samhda+03753-0001**.

19. How does mother's employment affect children's use of illegal drugs? (Hint: Put the recoded ILLDRUG is the dependent variable and V165 is the independent variable.)
    a. Children whose mothers stay at home are least likely to use other illegal drugs.
    b. Children whose mothers are working part time are least likely to use other illegal drugs.
    c. Children whose mothers are working full time are least likely to use other illegal drugs.
    d. The relationship between ILLDRUG and V165 is not statistically significant.

Drug abuse analysts often claim that cigarette and marijuana smoking are "gateway" drugs, leading their users into more serious illegal drug use. Focusing on the population of those who ever used any of the above illegal drugs other than marijuana, assess the correctness of this theory. Does it also apply to heavy alcohol use?

20. Run the crosstabs of illegal drug use (ILLDRUG) against cigarette smoking (V101); binge drinking (V108); and current marijuana use (V117). Which of the following statements most accurately reflects your findings? (Hint: Run three separate tables—type illdrug in the "Row" Box (dependent variables) and put each of the independent variables in the "Column" Box.)
    a. All three drugs appear to support the gateway theory, though by judging deltas (percentage differences), one would have to say that current marijuana use produces the largest gateway effect of all these drugs.
    b. There does not appear to be gateway effects for alcohol and cigarette use, only for marijuana.
    c. The gateway hypothesis is not supported by this data.
    d. Heavy alcohol use and marijuana use support the gateway hypothesis, but not cigarette smoking.

Is depression associated with all types of drug use? This is an important question that cannot be readily answered from the Monitoring the Future Study, but it can be answered from the National Household Study of Drug Abuse (NHSDA) where depression experienced in the last year was one of the questions asked (MDEDP2WK).

21. Using cigarette smoking (CIGMON), binge drinking (BINGEDRK), marijuana use (MJEVER), and any illegal drug use not including marijuana (IEMFLAG) as dependent variables is depression related to the use of these drugs?
    a. Depression is associated with only cigarette smoking, binge drinking, and marijuana use.
    b. Depression is associated with only binge drinking, marijuana use, and other illegal drug use.
    c. Depression is associated with cigarette smoking, binge drinking, marijuana, and other illegal drug use.
    d. Depression is associated with only marijuana and other illegal drug use.
    e. Depression is not associated with cigarette smoking, binge drinking, marijuana, or other illegal drug use.

Another serious youth problem is suicide. More than 30,000 suicides occur annually in the U.S. and suicide is the third leading cause of death (after accidental and homicide deaths) among people under the age of 25. The NHSDA survey did not investigate suicide directly but it did probe suicide attempts. Although there are hundreds to thousands of suicide attempts for the cases of completed suicides, attempted suicides nevertheless represent one of the best predictors of completed suicides. However, the suicide attempt question was not asked of those over 18 years of age in this survey, which was probably a big mistake. Nevertheless, it is still useful to see what other things are associated with suicide attempts among the 12–17 year old population, to whom the question was asked. The measure of suicide attempts in the NHSDA survey is a little different from the direct question usually asked in many national surveys, which typically show anywhere from 3 to 8 percent of this demographic subgroup attempting suicide within the previous 12 months. In the NHSDA, the question was asked in terms of whether people had ever sought care in any one of nine locations (such as with a doctor, therapist, hospital, or treatment center) because they thought they might want to kill themselves. A "0" response meant a person sought mental health care, but not because of suicidal thoughts. A "1" response meant someone sought care because of suicidal thoughts or attempts.

22. Run attempts to kill oneself (**REASSUIC**) by gender (**IRSEX**) to see whether males or females are more likely to attempt suicide. Which of the following statements is most accurate?

    a. Males are more likely to attempt suicide.

    b. Females are more likely to attempt suicide.

    c. There are no gender differences in the inclination to attempt suicide.

    d. Although females show somewhat elevated levels of suicide ideation, the differences are below the level of statistical significance.

Females: 22.2
Males: 13.7

23. Suicide attempts could be related to race and ethnic differences (**NEWRACE2**). Does the data support this hypothesis?

    a. African Americans attempt suicide appreciably more than whites.

    b. Native Americans show the highest attempted suicide rate.

    c. Asian Pacific Islanders have the highest attempted suicide rate.

    d. Hispanics show higher suicide attempts than all others.

    e. There are no appreciable differences in attempting suicide across the different races.

24. Suicide attempts could be related to immigrant status (**BORNINUS**). Does the data support this hypothesis?

    Not in data base

    a. Immigrants attempt suicide appreciably more than native born Americans.

    b. Native born Americans show a highest attempted suicide rate than immigrants.

    c. There are no appreciable differences in attempting suicide between immigrants and native born Americans.

    d. It looks as though immigrants attempt suicide more than native born Americans, but the differences fall slightly short of statistical significance.

25. Frequent residential mobility (MOVESPY2) could be related to suicide attempts. Does the data support this hypothesis?
    a. Those whose families moved often were more likely to attempt suicide than those whose families lived in the same places.
    b. There are statistically significant differences in attempting suicide with greater numbers of geographic moves.
    c. The data shows that geographic mobility has been vastly over rated as a destabilizing force among youth.
    d. a and b only.
    e. None of the above.

Another youth issue to be explored is the problem of gambling. Much gambling in society is normative, generally accepted and socially approved behavior—for example, buying occasional lottery tickets, having small stakes card games, playing bingo games at local churches, and/or betting on horse races or other sporting events. However, when people become compulsively committed to gambling—when they become preoccupied with it, spending much of their day planning out their future gambling activities, when they "chase" their bets (i.e. continue to make bets attempting to win back earlier loses), when they have discord with their friends or family members because of their gambling—then, we may speak of this kind of gambling as problem gambling. From responses to a 17-item check list of adverse effects from gambling asked in the most recent national study of American gambling, the 1999 National Gambling Impact Study, it was found that about one percent of the adult population (about 5,500,000 people) could be described as problem gamblers. Another 15,000,000 were judged to have the potential to be future problem gamblers.

Problem gambling is an under-appreciated issue in the United States. Yet, problem gamblers can do a great deal of damage, annually costing the nation billions of dollars from their gambling losses and from their inability to work at conventional jobs and their over-representation in criminal enterprises. Usually, problem gamblers harm other people when they gamble, often borrowing money under false pretenses and some times creating financial devastation for families when they quickly dissolve a family's lifetime capital accumulations from their gambling ventures.

The assessment of problem gambling from responses to the 17-item checklist of gambling problems was a well-proven assertion. The questions comprising that checklist had been extensively tested in many other studies conducted over the preceding 25 years. From these items, norms have been established in the United States and many other countries for normal and treatment populations. In the NGIS scale, someone indicating agreement with any one or more of the 17-item list would be termed an "at-risk" gambler, someone with the potential to be a future problem gambler. Those scoring positive on three or more of the checklist questions were termed problem gamblers.

In this exercise you will use the dataset of the1999 National Gambling Impact Study (NGIS), which can be accessed from **www.icpsr.umich.edu/cgi-bin/SDA/hsda?samhda+gibs1.**

We will begin by assessing if young adults are over- or under-represented in the ranks of problem gamblers. With the small sample size used in the NGIS, it is important to keep the default setting of weights in place on all subsequent analyses.

26. Are young adults more or less likely to have gambling problems than their elders? (Hint: Run **PROB12MO** by **A2_R**.)
    a. Young adults are slightly more likely to have gambling problems.
    b. Older adults are slightly more likely to have gambling problems.
    c. There are no appreciable age differences in gambling problems.

27. Are at-risk gamblers more likely to be depressed (**J23**)? (Hint: **J23** is the dependent variable and **PROB12MO** is the independent variable.)
    a. No
    b. Yes
    c. The results are unclear
    d. The relationship is not statistically significant

28. Are at-risk gamblers (**PROB12MO**) more likely to have suicidal thoughts (**J40**)?
    a. No
    b. Yes
    c. The results are unclear
    d. The relationship is not statistically significant

29. Are at-risk gamblers (**PROB12MO**) more likely to be using any of the following drugs: alcohol (**K1_**), marijuana (**K2_**), cocaine/crack (**K3_**), stimulants (**K4_**), tranquilizers (**K5_**)? (Hint: You need to run five crosstabulations. Use **PROB12MO** as your independent variable and the various drugs as the dependent variables.)
    a. At-risk gamblers do not use alcohol
    b. At-risk gamblers do not use marijuana
    c. At-risk gamblers do not use cocaine/crack
    d. At-risk gamblers do not use stimulants
    e. At-risk gamblers do not use tranquilizers

30. Are whites more likely to be at-risk gamblers (**PROB12MO**) than those from other races (**A4_R**)?
    a. Yes
    b. No
    c. The results are unclear
    d. The relationship is not statistically significant

31. Do at-risk gamblers (**PROB12MO**) have a history of having had school problems (**A10_**)?
    a. Yes
    b. No
    c. The results are unclear
    d. The relationship is not statistically significant

32. Do at-risk gamblers (**PROB12MO**) show any distinctive trends in moving from place to place (**A14_**)?
    a. Yes, although the percentage difference (delta value) is not substantial
    b. No
    c. The results are unclear
    d. The relationship is not statistically significant

33. Are there any gender differences (**A1_**) associated with at-risk gambling (**PROB12MO**)?
    a. Yes
    b. No
    c. The results are unclear
    d. The relationship is not statistically significant

In the final section of this chapter, we will explore another important youth problem: violent behavior. When young adults, males especially, join street gangs, they are known to attack and challenge one another. Sometimes, small disagreements about trivial things compound and become more serious in their consequences. Unfortunately, every year in the United States there are a significant number of killings and serious assaults that have snowballed from small simple fights and disagreements. In this section, we will attempt to explore the physically aggressive behavior of young people. There is probably no better dataset for probing the correlates of youth violence than the 1995 National Survey of Adolescents, based on a nationally representative sample of over 3,000 youths between the ages of 12 and 17.

In this analysis, we will focus our attention on getting into fights in response to being attacked. Five questions were asked to respondents assessing the frequency of whether they had ever been attacked by someone and thus challenged to fight back to defend themselves:

- whether they had ever been attacked by someone with a weapon
- whether they had ever been attacked by someone without a weapon
- whether they had ever been threatened with a knife or gun
- whether they had ever been beaten up with an object and hurt badly
- whether they had ever been beaten up with fists and hurt badly.

Most youths indicated that they had never been attacked in these ways. Yet, approximately 18 percent indicated agreement that they had been challenged in one or more of these five ways. We will use this five-item indicator as our barometer of getting into fights. To get started, you will need to perform the following steps:

1. Go to the 1995 National Survey of Adolescents SDA website, which can be found at: **www.icpsr.umich.edu/cgi/SDA/hsda?nacjd+nsa**.
2. Select "Compute a new variable" and click **Start**.
3. Type the following syntax into the box labeled "EXPRESSION TO DEFINE THE NEW VARIABLE":
    if(q18a eq 1 or q18b eq 1 or q18c eq 1 or q18d eq 1 or q18e eq 1)
        fights =1
    else
    fights = 0
4. Select "Yes" for the option "Replace that variable, if it already exists?".
5. Click **Start Computing**.

You have now created a new variable, **FIGHTS**. To go back to the crosstabulation analysis, simply click the **Back** button within your browser twice. Then select "Run frequency or crosstabulation" and click **Start**. You can also go to the crosstabulation analysis by typing in the following URL: **www.icpsr.umich.edu/cgi/SDA/hsda?nacjd+nsa**. For the following questions, you will need to use the following recode for FIGHTS: fights(r: 0 "no fights"; 1 "had fights").

34. Getting into fights (FIGHTS) could be linked with particular demographic correlates. Analyze the following: age (S1); sex (GENDER); race (Q64); hispanic status (Q63); and the number of people in the household (Q62). From analyzing the delta differences on the dependent variable FIGHTS, which of the above variables is apparently the strongest correlate to getting into fights?
    a. Age
    b. Gender
    c. Race
    d. Being Hispanic
    e. Number of people in the household

35. Getting into fights (FIGHTS) could be linked with particular family and household experiences. Analyze the following: frequent residential mobility (Q7A); parents divorced or separated (Q7D); a parent lost their job (Q7E); death of a family member (Q7F); and getting physically punished at home—i.e. being spanked so hard that one got marks (Q40C). From analyzing the delta differences on the dependent variable FIGHTS, which of the above variables is apparently the strongest correlate with getting into fights?
    a. Frequent residential mobility
    b. Parents divorced or separated
    c. A parent lost their job
    d. Death of a family member
    e. Getting physically punished at home

36. Getting into fights (FIGHTS) could be linked with certain traumatic experiences. Analyze the following: the death of a friend (Q7Q); having a serious accident (Q8A1); experiencing a natural disaster (Q8A2); being sexually assaulted—unwanted penile entry (Q10A); being sexually assaulted—the touching of private parts (Q13A); being suspended from school (Q7T); and being forced to repeat a grade (Q7O). From analyzing the delta differences on the dependent variable FIGHTS, which of the above variables is apparently the strongest correlate to getting into fights?
    a. Having a serious accident experience
    b. Being forced to repeat a grade
    c. Experiencing a natural disaster
    d. Being sexually assaulted (unwanted penile entry)
    e. Being suspended from school

37. Getting into fights could be linked with different kinds of drug use and being depressed. Analyze the following: ever smoking cigarettes regularly (Q27C); being a binge drinker (Q28D); tranquillizer use (Q30A1); sedative use (Q30A2); stimulant use (Q30A3); pain killer use (Q30A4); marijuana frequency (Q32BA); and being depressed (Q64). From analyzing the delta differences on the dependent variable FIGHTS, which of the above variables is apparently the strongest correlate to getting into fights?
    a. Smoking cigarettes regularly
    b. Tranquillizer use
    c. Sedative use
    d. Being a binge drinker
    e. Being depressed

38. Summing up the results of the last four short-answer questions and judging by the magnitude of the overall delta values, which factor(s) appear to have the strongest associations with getting into fights? (Hint to answer you will need to calculate an average delta value from each type of correlate: demographic, family experience, trauma, and drug use, and compare the averages with one another.)
    a. Demographic factors
    b. Family and household differences
    c. Traumatic experiences
    d. Drug uses and depression

38

2.63 → 37   = 97.31
2.69 → 1   → 100

ESSAY QUESTIONS

13-A   Compare the similarities and differences between the findings from the Monitoring the Future 2002 survey of high school seniors and the National Household Survey of Drug Abuse 2002 among the 18–22 year old population. Indicate convergences and divergences between their findings in the types and frequencies of drugs used. Keep a common frame of reference for the comparison of the following drug variables: smoking cigarettes, binge drinking, marijuana use, and all other illegal drugs. Present all relevant tables that document the similarities and differences you are displaying.

13-B   Both of the above mentioned studies have identified urban, suburban, small city and rural resident respondents. Using the same drug variables for this comparison, contrast the differences in drug use between large city and suburban residents within each data set as they are used by either high school seniors in MTF or 18–22 year olds in NHSDA. Do large city residents differ in their drug uses from suburbanites? If so, how? What do both studies show on this question? Present all relevant tables.

13-C   In answering some of the multiple choice questions, you have looked at a number of the correlates of attempted suicide. The 1995 National Survey of Adolescent Behavior also asked respondents a parallel question: Whether they had ever thought of killing themselves. Fourteen percent indicated that they had thought about killing themselves (q56a). Re-examine the findings obtained from the NHSDA study and try to replicate as many of their hypothesis tests as is possible with the National Survey of Adolescent Behavior data and compare the results. If certain findings in one study cannot be replicated in the other, try to explain why. Present all supporting data analysis tables.

13-D   Using the 1995 National Survey of Adolescent Behavior as your source material, try to develop a series of hypotheses explaining why young people would want to kill themselves. Make the tests, present the tables and develop the appropriate data-supported conclusions for your hypotheses.

13–E　In the array of multiple choice questions in this chapter, you explored a number of hypotheses related to using illegal drugs (besides marijuana), including: Growing up in a one-parent (vs. in a two-parent) family, being depressed, being male, use of marijuana and cigarettes. See if you can develop several additional hypotheses from any of the datasets you have worked with in this chapter (Monitoring the Future, National Survey of Adolescent Behavior, or the National Household Study of Drug Abuse) to enhance our understanding of illegal drug use. Once you have developed your hypotheses run the tables to test them, present all relevant tables and summarize your findings.

CHAPTER PROJECT

Evaluate whether the use of any type of drug increases the risk that one might try to kill oneself. This question can be analyzed using the National Household Study of Drug Abuse (NHSDA). Separately run each against suicide attempts (**REASSUIC**) to see if there are any differences in the strength of the associations between using the drug and attempting suicide. The drugs you will investigate are cigarette smoking (**CIGMON**); binge drinking (**DR5DAY**); marijuana use (**MJEVER**); and all other illegal drug uses(**IEMFLAG**). You will compare delta values to see whether the associations are strong or weak associations. Remember, when looking across the differences in the independent variable, when one sees the dependent variable changing 15 percent or more across different values of the independent variable, we are witnessing a more substantial association. And when delta differences show a variability of five percent or less, this indicates a weaker association. Of the four types of drugs mentioned, which is clearly producing the strongest association with suicide attempts? Which one has the least association? Present all your results in a table showing all delta comparisons and computations.

SYNTAX GUIDE

2002 MONITORING THE FUTURE SURVEYS (MTF)
Go to: www.icpsr.umich.edu/cgi-bin/SDA/hsda?samhda+03753-0001
Select "Run frequencies or crosstabulation"
Click **Start**

2002 Monitoring the Future Surveys (MTF) Recodes
Please note that all recodes can also be copied and pasted from either www.ncc.edu/users/feigelb/sda.htm or www.ablongman.com/feigelman3e. If you type the recode syntax in, make sure that you type *exactly* what is shown below.

illdrug(r: 10 "Never used illegal drugs"; 11-65 "Ever used illegal drugs")

v101(r: 1 "Never"; 2-5 "Ever smoked")

v102(r: 1 "non-smoker"; 2-7 "current smoker")

v108(r: 1 "None"; 2-6 "Once or more")

v112(r: 1 "Never"; 2-7 "Ever used marijuana")

v117(r: 1 "Never"; 2-7 "Used marijuana over the past 30 days")

v165(r: 1 "Stay home mom"; 2-3 "Worked part-time"; 4 "Worked full-time")

No recode needed: V148; V150; V151; V163

2002 NATIONAL HOUSEHOLD SURVEY OF DRUG ABUSE
Go to: www.icpsr.umich.edu/cgi-bin/SDA/hsda?samhda+03903-0001
Select "Run frequencies or crosstabulation"
Click **Start**

2002 National Household Survey of Drug Abuse Recodes
Please note that all recodes can also be copied and pasted from either
www.ncc.edu/users/feigelb/sda.htm or www.ablongman.com/feigelman3e.
If you type the recode syntax in, make sure that you type *exactly* what is
shown below.

borninus(1-2)

collenr2(r: 1 "Full-time college student aged 18-22"; 2 "Part-time college
    student aged 18-22"; 3-4 "Non college students aged 18-22"; 5 "Persons
    aged 12-17, or 23 or Older")

dr5day(r: 0 "None"; 1-25 "At least one day")

drivalc2(r: 1 "Yes"; 2, 4 "No")

mrjydays(1-5)

No recode needed: ANLFLAG; BINGEDRK; CIGMON; COCFLAG; CRKFLAG;
    HALFLAG; HERFLAG; IEMFLAG; INHFLAG; IRSEX; LSDFLAG; MDEDP2WK;
    MJEVER; MOVESPY2; MRJYR; NEWRACE2; REASSUIC; PCPFLAG; SEDFLAG;
    STMFLAG; TRQFLAG

1999 NATIONAL GAMBLING IMPACT STUDY
Go to: www.icpsr.umich.edu/cgi-bin/SDA/hsda?samhda+gibs1
Select "Run frequencies or crosstabulation"
Click **Start**

1999 National Gambling Impact Study Recodes

Please note that all recodes can also be copied and pasted from either
www.ncc.edu/users/feigelb/sda.htm or www.ablongman.com/feigelman3e.
If you type the recode syntax in, make sure that you type *exactly* what is
shown below.

a2_r(r: 1 "18-29"; 2-5 "30 and older")

prob12mo(r: 0 "No"; 1-9 "Yes")

No recode needed: A1_; A4_R; A10_; A14_; J23; K1_; K2_; K3_; K4_; K5_

1995 NATIONAL SURVEY OF ADOLESCENTS SDA
Go to: www.icpsr.umich.edu/cgi/SDA/hsda?nacjd+nsa
Select "Run frequencies or crosstabulation"
Click **Start**

1995 National Survey of Adolescents SDA Recodes

Please note that all recodes can also be copied and pasted from either www.ncc.edu/users/feigelb/sda.htm or www.ablongman.com/feigelman3e. If you type the recode syntax in, make sure that you type *exactly* what is shown below.

fights(r: 0 "no fights"; 1 "had fights")

q10a (1,2)

q13a(1,2)

q27c(1,2)

q28d(r: 0 "0"; 1 "1"; 2 "2"; 3-350 "3 or more")

q30a1(1,2)

q30a2(1,2)

q30a3(1,2)

q30a4(1,2)

q32ba(1,2)

q40c(1,2)

q62(r:1-2 "1-2 people"; 3 "3 people"; 4-43 "4 or more")

q64(1,2)

q7a(1,2)

q7d(1,2)

q7e(1,2)

q7f(1,2)

q7o(1,2)

q7q(1,2)

q7t(1,2)

q8a1(1,2)

q8a2(1,2)

No recode needed: GENDER; Q30A2; Q63; Q64; S1

Chapter 14

Population

In this chapter, we will be using the 2000 U.S. Census, the One Percent Public Use Microdata Sample, the GSS, and the National Survey of America's Families data to examine population-related questions. The U.S. Census Bureau conducts a census every ten years to collect data on household and population characteristics. This is required by Article I of the U.S. Constitution for the purpose of reapportioning the U.S. House of Representatives. According to the Census Bureau, the census is "a complete enumeration, usually of a population, but also of businesses and commercial establishments, farms, governments, and so forth." The decennial census is "the census of population and housing," taken by the Census Bureau in years ending in zero. The One Percent Public Use Microdata Sample (PUMS) file is a computerized file containing one percent of the individual records from the census long form. The SDA 2000 U.S. 1% PUMS contains 2.8 million cases. One can readily conduct empirical studies making use of this rich dataset. We'll start our analysis using the PUMS data to explore issues related to population distribution, family composition, race and ancestry identification, aging, migration, language use in the home, and whether grandparents were responsible for caring for their grandchildren.

1. Go to the University of California's SDA site at http://sda.berkeley.edu.
2. Click on **SDA Archive** on the upper left corner of the page.
3. Under the subtitle "U.S. Census Microdata" click on **2000 U.S. 1% PUMS**.
4. Select "**Frequencies or crosstabulation**".
5. Click the **Start** button.

For all questions, be sure to use the recoded variables (which can be found at the end of this chapter). Also remember to put the dependent variable in the Row Box and the independent variable in the Column Box. If only one variable is involved in a question, simply enter that variable in the Row Box. Always select **Statistics** and **Question Text** from "Other Options" before clicking **Run the Table**.

1. Which region of the country (**REGION**) has the largest percentage of the country's total population?
   a. Northeast
   b. Midwest
   c. South
   d. West
   e. None of the above

2. Which state (STATE) has the largest population and which has the smallest?
   a. California and New Jersey
   b. California and Wyoming
   c. California and Alaska
   d. New York and Wyoming
   e. New York and Vermont

The next few questions examine the household family composition of the United States.

3. Which state has the highest percentage of families composed of married couples (HHT)?
   a. Idaho
   b. Iowa
   c. Nebraska
   d. Kentucky
   e. Utah

4. What percentage of all U.S. family households are female-headed (HHT) and what percentage are family households that consist of married couples?
   a. 14% and 66%
   b. 24% and 75%
   c. 24% and 41%
   d. 18% and 57%
   e. 28% and 47%

5. What percentage of all U.S. households are potentially gay or lesbian headed households? (Hint: Use HHT to answer this question.)
   a. 1.9%
   b. 2.9%
   c. 4.8%
   d. 7.5%
   e. 8.7%

6. Run HHT by race (RACE1). Which race/ethnic group has the lowest percentage of households with married couples?
   a. Asian
   b. African American
   c. White
   d. American Indian
   e. None of the above

7. Which of the following groups is currently the most numerous in the U.S. population? (Hint: use both RACE1 and HISPAN to answer this question and do two separate frequency distributions.)
   a. African Americans
   b. Asians
   c. Native Americans
   d. Hispanics
   e. Other and/or people who identified themselves as multiracial

8. Which types of household units have the highest percentage of house-holders with advanced degree holders (i.e. with a masters degree or higher)? (Hint: Run education (EDUC) by (HHT) for this analysis.)
   a. Married couple households
   b. Non-family males living alone
   c. Non-family females living alone
   d. Family households of females without husbands

We will next use the Census 2000 PUMS data to look at some questions on aging. As you may know, the proportion of the elderly population in Western industrialized nations is much higher than that of the developing world. The "graying of America" is an important social issue facing us today. Let's now examine some important questions on aging.

9. What percentage of the population is age 65 and over? (Hint: Enter age in the SDA Row Box [be sure to use the recoded variable].)
   a. 4%
   b. 8%
   c. 12%
   d. 16%
   e. 20%
10. Run AGE by STATE and identify the top three states with the greatest proportion of the elderly.
    a. Florida, California, and Pennsylvania
    b. Florida, Pennsylvania, and West Virginia
    c. California, Florida, and Iowa
    d. California, Florida, and Nebraska
    e. New York, Texas, and Florida
11. Which state has the lowest percentage of the population aged over 65?
    a. North Dakoka
    b. Minnesota
    c. Hawaii
    d. Alaska
    e. Utah
12. What percentage of the sample identified themselves as being multi-racial? (Hint: You will need to use the variable NUMRACE—number of major race groups marked by the respondent—to answer this question.)
    a. None
    b. 1%
    c. 2.5%
    d. 10%
    e. 25%
13. What is the average household size (PERSONS)?
    a. 2.4
    b. 3.4
    c. 4.4
    d. 5.4
    e. 6.4

Now let's examine the average household size (PERSONS) by race (RACE1). To do this, you will need to perform the following steps:

1. Go to the University of California's SDA site at http://sda.berkeley. edu.
2. Click on **SDA Archive** on the upper left corner of the page.
3. Under the subtitle "U.S. Census Microdata" click on **2000 U.S. 1% PUMS**.
4. Select "Comparison of means" (instead of "Frequencies and Crosstabulations").
5. Click the **Start** button.
6. Type **persons** in the "Dependent" Box and **race1** in the "Row" Box.
7. Select "ANOVA stats" under "Other options".
8. Click **Run the Table**.

You are now ready to answer the following questions.

14. Which racial group has the lowest average household size?
    a. Asians
    b. African Amerians
    c. Whites
    d. American Indians
    e. None of the above

15. Repeat the ANOVA analysis with household size (PERSONS) as your dependent variable and education (EDUC) as your row variable. Which education group has the highest average household size?
    a. Less than high school
    b. High school
    c. Some college
    d. Bachelor's degree
    e. Master's degree and higher

16. In the 2000 census, respondents were asked their self-identified ancestry origins. Which was the single highest foreign national source? (Hint: Run **ANCFRST** to answer this question.)
    a. English
    b. German
    c. Italian
    d. Irish
    e. Mexican

17. Now let's examine language used in household (HHL) by region (REGION). Which of the following statements is most accurate?
    a. Spanish is mostly spoken in the South
    b. Spanish is mostly spoken in the West
    c. English-only households are found more in the Midwestern region than other parts of the country
    d. a and c only
    e. b and c only

18. Run residence five years ago (MOB) by household total income (FINC). Which of the following statements is most accurate?
   a. The relationship between MOB and FINC is not statistically significant.
   b. Those with the highest incomes are most likely to have stayed in the same house during the past five years.
   c. Those with the lowest household total income are most likely to have stayed in the same house during the past five years.
   d. None of the above.
   e. a and c.

19. Run MOB by REGION. In what region are people most likely to stay in the same house during the past five years?
   a. Northeast
   b. Midwest
   c. South
   d. West
   e. None of the above

20. Run MOB by STATE. In what state are people most likely to stay in the same house for five years? In what state are people least likely to stay in the same house for five years?
   a. Pennsylvania and Nevada
   b. Florida and New Jersey
   c. California and Nebraska
   d. Nebraska and South Dakota
   e. New York and Texas

21. Run MOB by AGE. In what age group are people most likely to have stayed in the same house during the past five years?
   a. Below 15 years old
   b. 15–64
   c. 65 and over
   d. There is no difference
   e. None of the above

The next few questions examine the pattern of having people live in the same households as their grandparents. As U.S. families continue to experience high levels of divorce and an ever increasing need to have both parents work outside the home, it is not surprising the latest census would investigate this issue. First, let's look at the percentage of people who live in the same homes as their grandparents.

22. What percentage of U.S. households have grandchildren and grandparents living together in the same homes? (Hint: Use GRANDC to answer this question and make sure to apply the selection filter "hht (1-3)" to ensure that only family households are counted.)
   a. 2%
   b. 3%
   c. 5%
   d. 7%
   e. 12%

23. Which race or ethnic group (RACE1) has the highest percentage of people living in the same homes as their grandparents (GRANDC)? (Hint: Make sure to apply the selection filter "hht (1-3)" to ensure that only family households are counted.)
    a. Native Americans
    b. Blacks
    c. Whites
    d. Asians

24. Which income group (FINC) has the highest percentage of people living in the same homes as their grandparents (GRANDC)? (Hint: Make sure to apply the selection filter "hht (1-3)" to ensure that only family households are counted.)
    a. Lower income groups
    b. Moderate income groups
    c. Higher income groups
    d. Although the relationship is statistically significant, the percentage points difference between the income groups is extremely small (less than 1 percent)
    e. None of the above

25. Does people living in the same homes as their grandparents (GRANDC) have any association with someone in the family having a mental (MENTAL) or physical disability (PHYSCL)? (Hint: Make sure to apply the selection filter "hht (1-3)" to ensure that only family households are counted. Also, you will need to run two tables to answer this question: GRANDC by MENTAL and GRANDC by PHYSCL.)
    a. Having people live in the same homes as their grandparents is associated with having someone in the family have a mental, but not a physical disability.
    b. Having people live in the same homes as their grandparents is associated with having someone in the family have a physical, but not a mental disability.
    c. Having people live in the same homes as their grandparents is not associated with neither mental nor physical disability.
    d. Having people live in the same homes as their grandparents is associated with both having someone in the family with a mental and a physical disability.
    e. None of the above.

We will now turn to the GSS data to examine questions on preferences for family size. First, go to http://sda.berkeley.edu/cgi-bin/hsda?harcsda+gss02. Select "Frequencies or crosstabulation" and click **Start**. Enter chldidel as your "Row" variable and **year** as your "Column" variable. Be sure to select "Statistics" and "Question Text" from "Other options" before clicking **Run the Table**.

26. How would you describe the trend of family size preference?
    a. There is an increasing trend of preferring childless families.
    b. There is a decreasing trend for preferring to have one to two children.
    c. There is a decreasing trend for preferring to have three to four children.
    d. The preference for 5 or more children has increased significantly from the 1970s to 2002.
    e. Both a and c.

27. Now let's crosstabulate the actual number of children one has ever had (CHILDS) by YEAR. How would you describe this trend?
    a. There is an increasing trend for a large family size.
    b. There is a decreasing trend for a large family size.
    c. The relationship between family size and year is statistically significant.
    d. b and c only.
    e. a and c only.

28. Is the actual number of children one has ever had (CHILDS) related to one's education (EDUC)? Hint: Crosstabulate CHILDS by education (EDUC).
    a. Those with a low level of education tend to have a higher number of children.
    b. The relationship between CHILDS and EDUC is statistically significant.
    c. Among those with a college education, more than one third have no children.
    d. All of the above.
    e. a and c only.

29. Crosstabulate CHILDS by religion (RELIG). What do you find?
    a. The religiously non-affiliated are most likely to have larger families.
    b. Jews are most likely to have larger families.
    c. Protestants are most likely to have no children.
    d. The relationship between CHILDS and RELIG is not significant.
    e. None of the above.

30. Crosstabulate CHILDS by race (RACE). What do you find?
    a. African Americans are most likely to have larger families (four or more children).
    b. Whites are most likely to have larger families.
    c. Those who belong to "Other race" are most likely to have larger families.
    d. The relationship between CHILDS and RACE is not statistically significant.
    e. None of the above.

31. Crosstabulate CHILDS by ethnic group (ETHNIC). What do you find?
    a. Asians are most likely to have larger families (four or more children).
    b. Italians are most likely to have larger families.
    c. Irish are most likely to have larger families.
    d. Hispanics are most likely to have larger families.
    e. Africans are most likely to have larger families.

In addition to the actual number of children one has, the GSS also asks respondents a question on their conceptions of the ideal family size (CHLDIDEL). We will now do some interesting analyses on people's ideal family size preferences.

32. Run CHLDIDEL by AGE, what do you find?
    a. Older women prefer to have four or more children.
    b. The majority of younger women prefer to have two children.
    c. The relationship between CHLDIDEL and AGE is statistically significant.
    d. All of the above.
    e. There is no age difference when considering ideal family size.

33. Run ideal family size (CHLDIDEL) by immigration status (BORN). Are immigrants more likely to prefer a larger family (four or more children)?
    a. Yes, although there is a significant relationship the percentage difference is actually small
    b. No
    c. This can not be determined

34. Let's compare one's ideal family size against one's actual family size. Crosstabulate CHILDS by CHLDIDEL. What do you find?
    a. Family size preference is not related to actual number of children.
    b. Those who prefer large family size tend to have more children.
    c. Among those who prefer to have no children, over 50% of them have two children or more.
    d. All of the above are true.
    e. Only b and c are true.

Our final task in this chapter is to examine the *National Survey of America's Families*. This source is managed by the Urban Institute and use is free to anyone as long as they register, which is easily done. Once you have registered, you will have access to a dataset based on the results of a survey of over 34,000 children. To register to use the data file, go to: www.urban.org/content/Research/NewFederalism/NSAF/OnlineAnalysis/ AnalysisPrelogin.htm. Once you are registered, you can access the actual dataset and start an online analysis from this website: http://anfdata. urban.org/sdaweb/cgi-bin/hsda.exe?/sdaweb/cgi-bin/harcsda+NSAF7.

35. We will start by examining the living arrangements of children (UFAMSTR). What percentage of children do not live with two biological/ adoptive parents?
    a. 37%
    b. 4%
    c. 25%
    d. 8%
    e. 63%

36. Now run living arrangements of children (**UFAMSTR**) by race (**UBRACE4**). Which of the following statements is most accurate?
    a. White children are most likely to be living with two biological/adoptive parents.
    b. African American children are least likely to be living with two biological/adoptive parents.
    c. Asian children are most likely to be living with two biological/adoptive parents.
    d. a and b only.
    e. b and c only.

37. What percentage of children live in families on or below the 100% poverty line (**UINCRPOV**)?
    a. 7%
    b. 10%
    c. 17%
    d. 28%
    e. 43%

38. Which race (**UBRACE4**) is least likely to be living on or below 100% poverty line (**UINCRPOV**)? (Hint: Crosstabulate **UINCRPOV** by **UBRACE4**.)
    a. White
    b. African American
    c. American Indian
    d. Asian
    e. The relationship between poverty and race is not statistically significant

ESSAY QUESTIONS

14–A   Multiple choice question 28 examines the relationship between education and family size. Consult prior sociological or demographic research and explain the mechanisms in which education affects one's level of fertility.

14–B   Multiple choice question 30 examines the relationship between race and fertility. Consult sociological or demographic literature and explain why there is a racial difference.

14–C   Multiple choice question 18 looks at the extent of migration (**MOB**) within the previous five years. Would you expect to see a relationship between marital status (**MARSTAT**) and migration? According to the PUMS classification, there are five categories for marital status: Currently married, widowed, divorced, separated, and never married (includes under 15 year olds). Before examining the PUMS data, which groups of respondents would you expect to be most and least likely to move within the past five years? Explain your rationale. Now go to the PUMS 1% website and run **MOB** by

MARSTAT. Do the findings support your earlier hypotheses? For extra credit examine the sociological literature on mobility and marital status differences and comment on how your findings mesh with the findings from this research.

14–D   Multiple choice question 16 investigated the percentage of respondents who identified their foreign ancestries (ANCFRST). Combining similar groups (such as British and English) list the five leading foreign national memberships of Americans. How much do they account for totally? Make a table showing a summary total. Make sure to turn off the weight option when you are assembling your list of important foreign ancestry sources.

CHAPTER PROJECT

Using the PUMS 1% data, run the crosstabulation for female-headed households (HHT) by race (RACE1). (To do this analysis, you will need to provide a recode for HHT of 2 for female headed household vs. 1 for married couple household.) What do you find? What are the associated demographic characteristics associated with female headed families: the differences in incomes, race and ethnic differences, educational attainment differences, differences in urban vs. rural living patterns, geographical mobility, etc.? Review the past research literature on this subject. Present all tables showing the differences between female-headed and married couple households. Summarize your findings and note any discrepancies between your findings and what past research showed.

SYNTAX GUIDE

PUMS 1% DATASET
Go to: http://sda.berkeley.edu/cgi-bin/hsda?harcsda+uspums00
Select "Frequencies or crosstabulation"
Click **Start**

PUMS 1% Recode List

Please note that all recodes can also be copied and pasted from either www.ncc.edu/users/feigelb/sda.htm or www.ablongman.com/feigelman3e. If you type the recode syntax in, make sure that you type *exactly* what is shown below.

age(r: 0-14 "Below 15"; 15-64 "15-64 years old"; 65-94 "65 and over")

educ(r: 1-8 "Less than high school"; 9 "High school"; 10-12 "Some college"; 13 "Bachelor degree"; 14-16 "Master and above")

finc(r: *-15000;15001-40000;40001-65000;65001-90000;90001-*)

hispan(r: 1"nonhispan"; 2-24 "hispan")

race1(r: 1 "White"; 2 "Black"; 3,4,5,7 "NativeAmer"; 6 "Asian"; 8,9 "Other/ Multi")

No recode needed: ANCFRST; GRANDC; HHL; HHT; MENTAL; MOB; NUMRACE; PERSONS; PHYSCL; REGION; RSPNSBL; STATE

GSS DATASET

Please note that all recodes can also be copied and pasted from either www.ncc.edu/users/feigelb/sda.htm or www.ablongman.com/feigelman3e. If you type the recode syntax in, make sure that you type *exactly* what is shown below.

Go to: http://sda.berkeley.edu/cgi-bin/hsda?harcsda+gss02
Select "Frequencies or crosstabulation"
Click **Start**

GSS Recode List

Please note that all recodes can also be copied and pasted from either www.ncc.edu/users/feigelb/sda.htm or www.ablongman.com/feigelman3e. If you type the recode syntax in, make sure that you type *exactly* what is shown below.

age(r: 18-29 "18-29"; 30-39 "30-39"; 40-49 "40-49"; 50-99 "50 and over")

childs(r: 0 "0"; 1 "1"; 2 "2"; 3 "3"; 4-* "4 or more")

chldidel(r: 0 "0"; 1 "1"; 2 "2"; 3 "3"; 4-* "4 or more")

educ(r: *-11 "Less than high school"; 12 "High School"; 13-* "Some College or higher")

ethnic (r:1,39 "Af"; 4,8,24 "En"; 14 "Iri";15 "Ita"; 2,6,13,21,23,33-35 "EEu"; 11 "Ger"; 7,9,19,26 "Sca"; 17,22,25,28,38 "His"; 3,10,18,27,36 "WEu"; 5,16,20,31,37,40 "As"; 97 "US"; 30 "AIn"; 12,29,32,41 "Otr")

region(r:1-2 "Northeast"; 3-4 "Central"; 5-7 "South"; 8-9 "West")

relig(r: 1 "Protestant"; 2 "Catholic"; 3 "Jewish"; 4 "None"; 5-13 "Other")

year(r: 1972-1979 "1972-79"; 1980-1984 "1980-84"; 1985-1989 "1985-89"; 1990-1994 "1990-94"; 1995-20002"1995-2002")

No recode needed: BORN

NATIONAL SURVEY OF AMERICA'S FAMILIES

Go to: http://anfdata.urban.org/sdaweb/cgi-bin/hsda.exe?/sdaweb/cgi-bin/ harcsda+NSAF7

Select "Frequencies or crosstabulation"

Click **Start**

National Survey of America's Families Recode List

No recode needed: UBRACE4; UFAMSTR; UINCRPOV

CHAPTER 15

Dealing with Continuous Data and Still More Complex Data Analysis Problems

This introductory exploration of the quantitative dimensions of doing sociological analysis wouldn't be complete without discussing some of the many alternative statistical tests researchers use to explain their data. Researchers usually employ one or a number of tests to extract the greatest possible interpretative value from their data. In this chapter, we will demonstrate several statistical tests for use with continuous data. We will also introduce the idea of doing multivariate data analysis. As researchers have a wider array of statistical analyses they can apply, they are able to extract the greatest possible meaning and value from their data.

As you may have noted from doing many of the workbook exercises, crosstabular analyses with Chi-Square significance tests have some serious limitations. For one, significance tests say little about the strength of associations between variables, and whether one causal influence may be stronger than another. Chi-Square tests simply indicate whether associations between hypothesized variables are likely (or not) to occur by chance. As we have shown in Chapter 6, although delta values can facilitate estimations of the strength of causal forces, delta value comparisons should not be overextended. For example, on some occasions—especially where the categorical designations between different independent variables are not directly comparable to one another—computing delta values and making comparisons among different independent variables would be misleading or inappropriate.

A second and more serious difficulty with crosstabular analysis is in dealing with the problem of spuriousness. You may recall we defined a spurious relationship in Chapter 6 as a coincidental and causally meaningless association. By generating control variable subtables (to eliminate and adjust for the effects of confounding causal influences), and slicing one's sample into smaller subsamples, there is always the risk of depleting the sample of sufficient numbers of cases. Remember too that statisticians apply inferences based upon the chance occurrence of events. If you generate many crosstabular tables, some will attain statistical significance by sheer chance alone. Thus, researchers employing crosstabular analysis will need to have extra large samples to be able to make many subdivisions of their data. They may also need to apply more demanding tests, such as the .01 probability level, for significance.

Alternatively, statisticians may employ other statistical tests to deal with the above problems, if the required assumptions for employing these tests are found within their data. Many alternative statistical tests presume that the analysis being conducted is with continuous data. Continuous data can be scaled; you can have none, some, or a great deal of a quality that is continuous. Age is a good example of a continuous variable. Another example to be used throughout this chapter will be educational attainments.

Receiving a lot or a little education, as all of us know, is a crucial social issue. For this reason, this subject comprises a worthy problem (or dependent variable) to focus upon in much of the remainder of this chapter. Why do some people complete a great many years of schooling, twenty or more perhaps, while others complete next to none? First, we will highlight the 43,559 respondents who have participated in the General Social Surveys over their thirty year history from 1972 to 2002. We will examine the range of educational attainments of this very large group of respondents. Later in this chapter, we will investigate why some went on to do postgraduate study, while others barely finished elementary school. We will begin by looking at the educational attainments of all GSS respondents.

Figure 15.1 shows that most completed intermediate amounts of education and the histogram also reveals that the educational attainments of GSS respondents are somewhat normally distributed. That is to say most responses fall within the middle ranges, and are below the normal curve outline. However, this isn't a perfectly normal distribution, with most responses under the line: Two bulges are noted, one where most respondents completed high school degrees, and a second where a smaller number completed four-year college programs. We can see that the overwhelming majority of responses are dispersed closely around the mean of 12.54 years.

If we were interested in investigating whether region is related to educational attainments, we could, as we've done many times before, use the

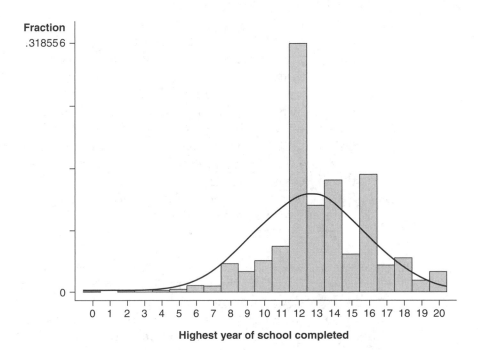

FIGURE 15.1

Highest year of school completed

Chi-Square significance test. If we were to use this measurement, we could compare whether the percentage of college graduates and postgraduates was any higher or lower in different regions of the country. Alternatively, we could compare whether the high school dropout rate was any smaller or larger in different places. However, since we are dealing with a continuous dependent variable—educational attainments, which is also assumed to be normally distributed—we can apply another test based around differences in the means of subgroups. Statisticians frequently test means to assess whether there are indeed group differences. A widely employed test that we will discuss here is a *One-Way ANOVA* (or single-factor ANOVA). The null hypothesis presupposes that subgroup means (and variances) of hypothesized independent variables will be similar to one another, if there is no relationship or significant differences between them. Thus, if region does not matter as a decisive force affecting educational attainments, the means of respondents from different regions will be similar to one another with respect to their educational attainments. It has been said that the South lags behind other regions in educational accomplishments. Let's try to determine if this assertion is correct.

If you reflect on it for a moment you will see that comparing and contrasting means with one another, is a different way of comparing percentage differences. Actually, continuous data comparisons, when it is possible to perform them, represent a more desirable alternative. We can speak of differences being twice or three times greater than another, which cannot be done with Chi-Squares. Yet, the present technique bears some similarity to the familiar Chi-Square significance test.

TESTS OF MEANS: ONE-WAY ANOVA TESTS

Doing a one-way ANOVA is very straightforward with the SDA statistical platform:

1. Go to the GSS 1972–2002 cumulative data file available online from http://sda.berkeley.edu/cgi-bin/hsda?harcsda+gss02.
2. Select "Comparison of means" and click **Start**.
3. Use educational attainments (**EDUC**) as the dependent variable.
4. Use **REGION** as the independent variable, typing the following recode language into the "row" box: **region(r:1-2 "Northeast"; 3-4 "Midwest"; 5-7 "South"; 8-9 "West")**. Note that the row variable here has a different meaning than it has in the Chi-Square crosstabulation test: Here it is the *independent* variable.
5. Finally, select the option for "ANOVA statistics". One-way ANOVA tests enable the data analyst to examine differences among several means.

We will now run the One-Way ANOVA test to see if the mean educational attainments of the four regions of the country show similar or different levels of educational attainments.

Table 15.1 displays the results from running this analysis. It shows the highest educational attainments in the West with 13.26 as the mean for all GSS surveys. The lowest level of educational attainment was found in the South, with a mean of 12.06 years. The table also shows that the Northeast and Midwest trail behind the West in average educational attainments. The most crucial result in a one-way ANOVA test is the F statistic, which is based upon a comparison of the variations of all cases

---

SDA 1.3: Means

GSS 1972-2002 Cumulative Datafile

Sep 14, 2004 (Tue 09:17 AM PDT)

Variables					
Role	**Name**	**Label**	**Range**	**MD**	**Dataset**
Dependent	**educ**	HIGHEST YEAR OF SCHOOL COMPLETED	0-20	97,98,99	1
Row	**region(Recoded)**	REGION OF INTERVIEW	1-4		1

Main Statistics

Cells contain:
-Means
-N of cases

region	1: Northeast	**12.68** 8,899
	2: Midwest	**12.54** 11,618
	3: South	**12.06** 14,937
	4: West	**13.26** 8,105
	COL TOTAL	*12.54* *43,559*

Color coding:	<-2.0	<-1.0	<0.0	>0.0	>1.0	>2.0	**T**
Mean in each cell:	Smaller than average			Larger than average			

Analysis of Variance						
	SSQ	Eta_sq	Df	MSQ	F	P
region	7,773.101	.018	3	2,591.034	262.306	.0000
Residual	430,232.065	.982	43,555	9.878		
Total	438,005.165	1.000	43,558			

Recode for 'region'
1 = 1-2 "Northeast"; 2 = 3-4 "Midwest"; 3 = 5-7 "South"; 4 = 8-9 "West"

Allocation of cases

Valid cases	43,559
Cases with invalid codes on dependent variable	139
Total cases	*43,698*

TABLE 15.1

around the mean (known as within-group variability) and variability between each subgroup's mean. The F statistic is actually the ratio of between group variability to within group variability. Without getting into the formulas used to compute the F statistic, the question the one-way ANOVA test answers is whether the subgroup differences in means are within chance variations of one another, or whether any one (or several) are significantly different from the rest. In this case, the probability of F is reported to be .0000, or 1 in 10,000 samples, indicating that these mean

---

SDA 1.3: Means

GSS 1972-2002 Cumulative Datafile

Sep 14, 2004 (Tue 09:21 AM PDT)

Variables					
Role	Name	Label	Range	MD	Dataset
Dependent	**educ**	HIGHEST YEAR OF SCHOOL COMPLETED	0-20	97,98,99	1
Row	**racecen1(Recoded)**	WHAT IS RS RACE 1ST MENTION	1-6		1

Main Statistics		
Cells contain: -Means -N of cases		
racecen1	1: White	**13.50** 3,261
	2: Black	**12.44** 596
	3: Nativ Ame	**11.94** 49
	4: AsianPac	**14.87** 102
	5: Other	**13.52** 23
	6: Hispan	**12.61** 114
	COL TOTAL	*13.34* *4,145*

Color coding:	<-2.0	<-1.0	<0.0	>0.0	>1.0	>2.0	T
Mean in each cell:	Smaller than average			Larger than average			

Analysis of Variance					
	SSQ	Eta_sq	df	MSQ	F	P
racecen1	972.078	.027	5	194.416	23.241	.0000
Residual	34,622.922	.973	4,139	8.365		
Total	35,595.000	1.000	4,144			

TABLE 15.2

differences would not occur this way by chance alone. Thus, this one-way ANOVA test says that the group means are significantly different from one another. However, the one-way test alone simply says the means are unequal to one another; it doesn't pinpoint which mean(s) is/are unique. Nevertheless, we have proven the assertion that the South lags behind all other regions in educational attainment.

Let's try to do another comparison of means test on educational attainments. This time we will run racial and ethnic differences (**RACECEN1**) as the independent variable against educational attainments. This particular race/ethnic self-classification question was only asked in the 2000 and 2002 surveys. You will need to enter the following recode for race/ethnic membership into the "Row" box: **racecen1(r:1 "White"; 2 "Black"; 3 "NativAme"; 4-14 "AsianPac"; 15 "Other"; 16 "Hispan")**. If you did your analysis correctly, you should see the results shown in Table 15.2.

You will note that Asian-Pacific Islanders have the highest average level of education with almost 15 years (14.87 to be exact) and Native Americans the lowest level, which at 11.94 years is approximately equivalent to high school graduates. African Americans and Hispanics show similar educational attainments and whites show higher educational levels.

Therefore, we have established that racial and ethnic differences are associated with differences in educational attainments. But we've created a perplexing problem for ourselves because we already knew that race and ethnicity were confounded with social class and educational differences. If we are going to state with confidence that race is related to educational differences, we will have to disentangle race from social class and parental educational differences.

A question we will now have to answer is: How can we disentangle the factors related to the completion of educational attainments—parents' social status, educational accomplishments and a person's race or ethnic membership—from one another? We should mention the other specific associated factors that could be linked with a person's educational attainments, which include: father's educational attainments; mother's educational attainments; and parental social class position. We'll work with these. By the time you finish reading this chapter, you should be able to discern which factors are most important in their association with education, which are less important ones, and which may be simply coincidental factors.

SIMPLE CORRELATIONAL ANALYSIS

Before we proceed any further, let us introduce another method used to measure associations between hypothesized variables called *correlation coefficients*. However, before we say anything more about correlation, we need to discuss *scatter plots*. A scatter plot shows you the distribution of the values of one variable, while at the same time displaying the values of its presumed correlate (the other variable you think it might be related to).

On the following pages, you will see three scatter plots. Each was drawn from a survey done by the World Bank in the late 1990s of attributes of the nations of the world. Figure 15.2 shows differences in life expectancies in different societies by their rates of literacy. Figure 15.3

shows life expectancy differences by birth rate differences. Figure 15.4 shows life expectancy data plotted against the percentage of males in each population. Each plot shows a different pattern.

In Figure 15.2, as life expectancies rise so do literacy rates. Conversely, lower literacy rates are found with shorter life expectancies. In societies with more resources, people live longer due to more abundant health resources. These societies also furnish better educational advantages to their members. It works the other way, too: Better-educated people are in a more advantaged position to facilitate their own longevity. We could call this a positive association. You will also note that a line has been drawn on the plot, but we won't discuss its significance just yet. Figure 15.3 shows increased life expectancies associated with lower birth rates. When people are living longer, they tend to reduce the number of children they have. We could call this a negative association. In the societies where people live the longest, birth rates are lowest; where people live for shorter periods, birth rates are highest. In Figure 15.4, we do not see any discernible pattern of association life expectancy and percentage of males in the population: They are simply scattered about on the plot of longevity. Most societies hover at the 50 percent mark, with an evenly divided sex ratio and no clustering of responses in any way with differences in life expectancy.

We will now discuss correlation. To be more precise, we will be employing the Pearson correlation coefficient, which is based on the assumption of normally distributed, continuous data variables. Correlation coefficients not only tell you whether an independent variable is significantly related to a dependent variable; they tell you whether they are strongly related or not. Coefficients can vary anywhere between $+1.0$ and -1.0. A relationship of $+1.0$ would mean a perfect match: when the independent variable increases, the dependent variable increases in exactly the same way. This is a lot like the plot of life expectancy and literacy shown in Figure 15.2, which correlated at a value of .74.

In a negative association, when one rises, the other falls, yielding a maximal value of -1.0. Figure 15.3 shows this pattern, with birth rates

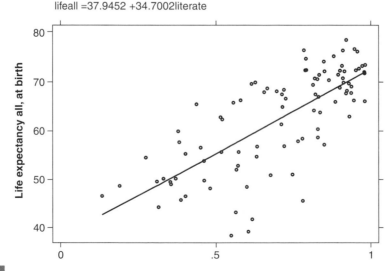

FIGURE 15.2

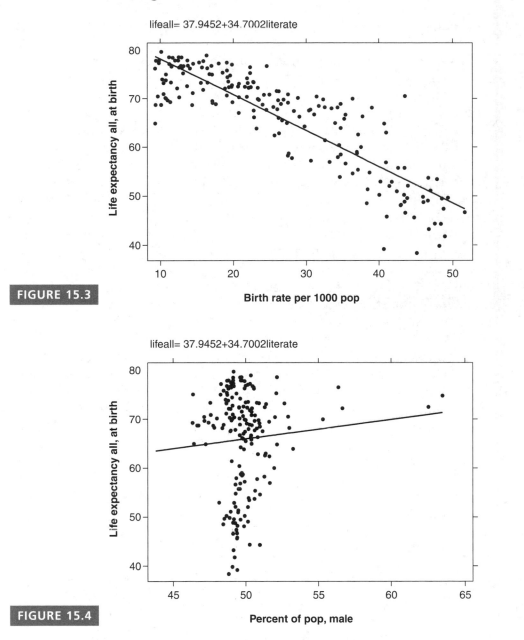

lifeall= 37.9452+34.7002literate

FIGURE 15.3

Birth rate per 1000 pop

lifeall= 37.9452+34.7002literate

FIGURE 15.4

Percent of pop, male

falling when life expectancies rise; the value for this correlation was −.86. If the two variables are perfectly unrelated to one another, then the correlation coefficient would be zero. This reflects the pattern shown in Figure 15.4, which shows no association between a society's percentage of men and its life expectancies. This yielded a correlation of .07. Thus, correlation coefficients of .60 or more would indicate a strong degree of association, while a .30 would signify a moderate association, and a .15 represents a weak affiliation.

Now let's give some attention to the lines that were drawn across the scatter plots. Figure 15.5 shows life expectancy plotted against the percentage of each society living in cities. This plot looks much like that for life expectancies and literacy. Instead of putting little circles at each observation point, however, the name of each country appears, showing you each country's place among the other values in the data set. Incidentally, the correlation for urbanization and life expectancy is .68. But what do the lines across the scatter plots signify and how can they guide us to identify strong and weak correlations?

In Figure 15.5, several possible lines that could be drawn to best summarize all the observations are shown. In fact, only one of the three lines—line A—is the best-fitting line; it is called the least-squares regression line. It has the smallest sum of squared vertical distances between itself and all the observation points. If you refer to Figure 15.6, you will see how the least-squares regression line is computed from several of the vertical lines that have been drawn in to illustrate it. Also shown in Figure 15.6 is the intercept point, the predicted value for one variable when the other variable equals zero. In the present example, the intercept for zero percent living in cities is roughly at the 50-year life expectancy point (49 years to be exact). The least-squares line also displays a slope, where a rate of change for one variable matches changes that occur in the other variable. Without going into mathematical formulas, you will note in the present example that for each percentage increase in urbanization there will be a .31 percent yearly increase in life expectancies.

If there was a perfect positive correlation between these (or any other two) variables, the least-squares regression line would form a perfect 45 degree angle at the zero points of both variables and would rise, showing corresponding changes to both. A perfect negative correlation would show a regression line that began in the upper left corner of the scatter plot and fell off to the lower right side of the grid (like the life expectancies, birth rates scatter plot did). The absence of any association is demonstrated by a least-squares line that has no slope. Such a horizontal line suggests that a change in one variable has no effect on the other (much like the life expectancy to percentage of males scatter plot showed).

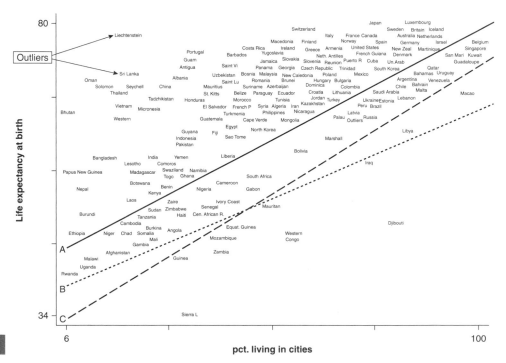

FIGURE 15.5

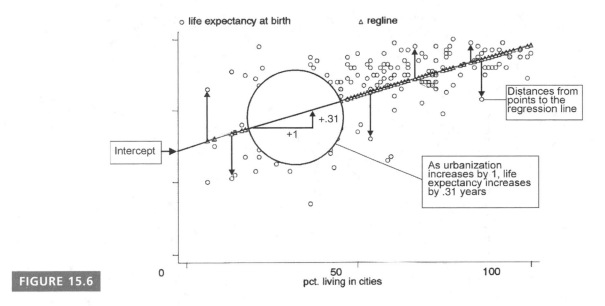

o life expectancy at birth   △ regline

Intercept

+.31
+1

Distances from points to the regression line

As urbanization increases by 1, life expectancy increases by .31 years

0   50   100
pct. living in cities

FIGURE 15.6

A final point to mention about scatter plots are the potential outliers: There may be some extreme or unusual cases. These observations are way off from the regression line. The case of Sri Lanka is shown in Figure 15.5 as a relatively less urbanized society (with only 22 percent of its citizens living in cities), but which, uncharacteristically of rural societies, has a relatively high life expectancy of 72 years. Such unique cases can influence associations by reducing (or increasing) correlation coefficients, especially when sample sizes are small. In large samples like the GSS samples, such cases affect coefficients negligibly. Yet, such cases could be very interesting for their uniqueness, and worthy of examination in greater detail. At other times, such cases could signify serious data entry errors.

Figures 15.7 and 15.8 display scatter plots with data taken from the 2002 GSS. Figure 15.7 displays a respondent's level of education by their mother's educational attainments, which yielded a correlation coefficient of .38. Figure 15.8 shows the distribution of responses between a respondents' education and their father's occupational prestige score, with a coefficient of .30. Since these two results showed a similar level of association, it should come as no surprise that, looking over the scattering of circles on both drawings, they seem much alike. A third scatter plot, showing the relationship between a person's education and the size of the community they lived in, is shown in Figure 15.9. This correlation yielded a coefficient of −.15, indicating a slight negative association.

In Figure 15.7, we have plotted the values of people's educational attainments against those of their mother's attainments. Years of school completed are plotted along a twenty-point scale. The plot of an individual respondent's educational attainment, shown on the left side of the figure, is related to their mother's educational attainment, shown across the bottom of the figure. The graph shows most responses clustered around the middle response ranges—high school graduates and those who had completed some college. If we were to match each case carefully along these two axes we would discover that respondents with high educational attain-

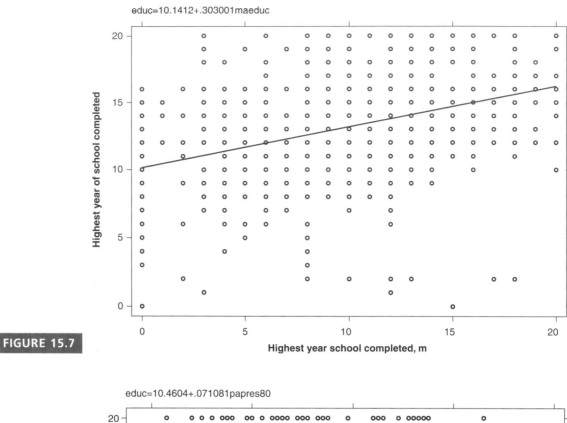

FIGURE 15.7

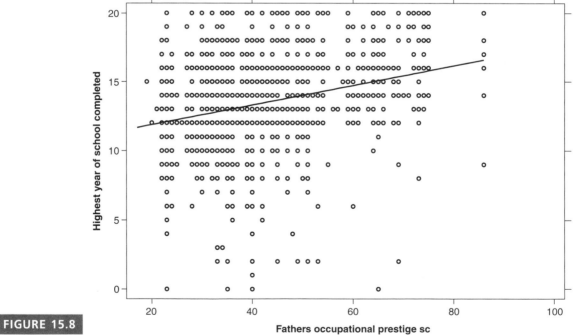

FIGURE 15.8

ments tended to have mothers who also completed a high level of schooling. Those respondents with intermediate educational attainments tended
to have mothers with similar (i.e. intermediate level) educations. Similarly,
those respondents completing little education, tended to have mothers who
had little schooling themselves. This also makes sense. Families where
mothers complete more education usually share values and expectations

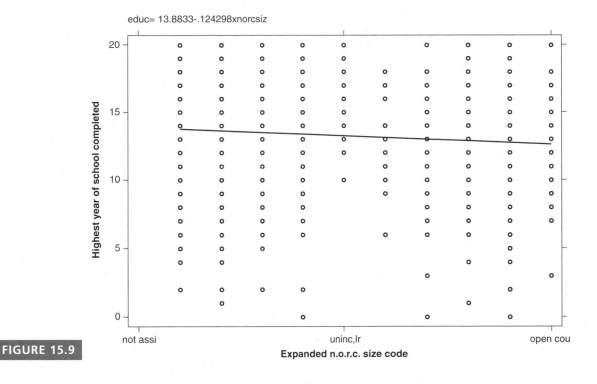

educ= 13.8833-.124298xnorcsiz

FIGURE 15.9

that children should be highly educated as well. They also usually possess resources to encourage their children's education. Similarly, at the other end of the spectrum, where mothers' complete little education themselves, they are likely to feel intimidated by schools and less equipped to offer their children substantial aid to solve their school problems, such as helping them with homework or helping them to plan their future educational goals. Thus, where a parent completes little schooling there is a diminished likelihood that their child will complete much schooling too. With the 2002 GSS data, we have obtained a modest positive association, of .38, between mother's education and a respondent's education.

In Figure 15.8, with the same GSS 2002 data, we have plotted a respondent's educational attainment by their father's occupational prestige score. Prestige scale scores are ranged on a scale of 100 at the very top for highest ranked occupations like judges, physicians, or scientists down to a low of 0 for low status positions like laborer, stock handler, or garbage collector. Thus, this association produced another modest positive correlation of .30. Here too we can readily understand that a professional father would be better able to advance their child's educational attainments than a father who held a less elevated position, such as auto-mechanic or roofer. In higher status families, there is more money available to finance the education of family members, more direct assistance available for navigating the complexities of the educational system, and more expectations that all family members will complete their education to at least the level of a baccalaureate degree.

A final plot, presented in Figure 15.9, shows years of education completed plotted against urbanicity. The urbanity codes follow U.S. Census classifications rating people's residences on a 10 point scale, applying a "1" to large city residents such as those living in New York City or Boston. Suburbs around the largest cities were given numeric ranks of 3 or 4. Residents of small, unincorporated farming communities were given numeric ratings of 9 or 10 for their places of residence. There is some slight correspondence between the amount of education one receives and whether one lives in a large or small community. Someone living in a big city such as Chicago will usually find it easier to get educated than someone living in a small farming hamlet in Nebraska. The correlation coefficient in this case was –.15, indicating a small negative association.

Unfortunately, the SDA software will not generate the scatter plots that we've shown here. More importantly, however, it will calculate the correlation coefficients of variables potentially related to your dependent variable of interest. It will also generate what we call a correlation table or matrix—showing how several hypothesized factors correlate with each other and the dependent variable. Doing a correlation matrix can save a researcher much time. With a table of coefficients (or a matrix, as statisticians refer to them), one can see at a glance how a set of hypothesized variables correlate with each other and with the primary dependent variable of interest. If, for example, we wanted to see whether a mother's educational attainments had more of an impact upon a respondent's educational attainments than their father's attainments, we can correlate both against the respondent's educational attainments and examine the differences.

The SDA procedure for getting a correlation matrix is simple and straight-forward: From the page at http://sda.berkeley.edu/cgi-bin/hsda?harcsda+gss02, select the "Correlation matrix" option and click **Start**. Then enter the variables that you want to correlate into the input fields under the heading "Variables to Correlate" and click **Run Correlations**. The SDA statistical software will then calculate all correlation coefficients of variables potentially related to your dependent variable of interest and will produce a neat grid displaying all results. All that will be left for you to do is identify the most powerful correlates of your dependent variable of interest.

Let us now assume we are interested in the dependent variable of educational attainments and that we want to identify what other correlates are associated with getting more (or less) schooling. Possible factors that immediately come to mind as having some impact on this variable include: father's educational attainments, mother's attainments, family's economic and social status (especially during one's young adult years), urbanicity, minority group membership, and parents' occupations. If you are conversant with the sociological literature on education and social mobility, you might also add several other potentially important correlates: whether one's parents stayed married or got divorced during one's adolescence or earlier, whether one was a member of a large or small family, a first born or latter born child, or an only child. (Past studies have often found that first born children from smaller families where parents stayed married usually get more schooling than their counterparts growing up in larger families where parents divorced.)

The only hitch, and this is not a trivial one, is to make sure all variables in the matrix are numeric and capable of being scaled. There are two important concerns that we need to be mindful of in making sure variables are scalar. If you do a frequency distribution of education (EDUC), you will note that its values extend from a low of "0" to a high of "20." This is perfect—it is numeric and scalar. Another example that seems appropriate at first glance is one's age at their first marriage (AGEWED), which extends from age 12 and upward. Yet, if one examines this variable carefully, you will note that the numbers "98" and "99" have been reserved for the responses "Don't Know" and "Not Applicable." The SDA software will usually exclude these analytically irrelevant responses from your analyses automatically. But before you can use some intentionally created variables in correlational analyses, you may have to follow the SDA recoding instructions to treat certain analytically meaningless cases like these 98 and 99 responses as missing data. Otherwise, we would be counting these cases as meaningful data, which would be very much a mistake. Thus, our first concern is to make sure all omitted cases in any analysis are treated as missing data.

The second concern is to make sure your variable can form a scale. This is very easy to do in some cases in agree/disagree type questions, such as one's support or opposition of capital punishment, abortion on demand, or some other controversial social question. It could be rated on a three-, five-, or seven-point scale, depending on the number of points on the scale. Variables like these are readily scalable. Yet, other categorical variables, such as a person's race, religion or the region of the country in which they live, are not clearly scalable at all. There are no easy ways of turning these variables into scales. For race, for example, the best we can do would be to create a contrast case of whites (scored as 1) vs. all others (scored as 0); you could call this variable "Whiteness". Alternatively, the variable we create could be called "Asianness" if we regrouped it to be Asian (scored as 1) vs. all others (scored as 0). For region, as another example, we may have Westness, people living in western states (scored as 1) vs. those of all other places (scored as 0). Alternatively, we could call the variable "Southernness" for people living in the southern states (scored as 1) vs. all others (scored as 0). The transformation of a categorical variable into a 0 vs. 1 scalar variable is known as creating a dummy variable.

Let's now try to set up the correlation matrix to examine the relationships we mentioned before. Below we list all the GSS variables we will be examining in the matrix and their appropriate recodes:

Variable	GSS Name	Recode
Respondent's educational attainment	educ	
Mother's educational attainment	maeduc	
Father's educational attainment	paeduc	
Father's occupational grouping at 16	paocc16	
Father's prestige at 16	papres16	
Urbanicity	xnorcsiz	
Race	racecomb	racecomb(d:1)
Size of family	sibs	
Whether parents stayed married	family16	family16(d:1)
Only child status	Does not exist in GSS (only)	

As you can see from this list, you will need to create a new variable for "only child status." To do this, perform the following steps:

1. Go to: http://sda.berkeley.edu/cgi-bin/hsda?harcsda+gss02.
2. Select the "Compute a new variable" option and click **Start**.

3. Enter the following text in the "Create variable" field:
   if (sibs eq 0) only = 1
   else only = 0
4. Select "Yes" for the option "Replace that variable, if it already exists?".
5. Click **Start Computing**.
6. You are now ready to create your correlation matrix for education.
7. Return to http://sda.berkeley.edu/cgi-bin/hsda?harcsda+gss02, select the "Correlation matrix" option and click **Start**.
8. Enter the variables that you want to correlate into the input fields under the heading "Variables to Correlate." You will want to type **educ** in the first box and the nine other variables in the subsequent boxes.
9. Click **Run Correlations** and compare your results with ours (shown in Table 15.3).

The correlation matrix in Table 15.3 shows five moderate to strong correlates of education variability: mother's education, .50; father's education, .50; father's occupational type at age 16, –.37; number of siblings, –.33; and father's occupational prestige at age 16, .30. All remaining correlates are weakly associated with educational variability: urbanicity, –.16; white vs. all others, .10; parent's marital stability, .06; and being an only child, .08.

These correlational analyses could also have been completed with Chi-Square crosstabulation tests. Had we used the Chi-Square significance tests, however, each of the clearly numeric variables that we examined would have had to have been converted into categorical variables. In other words, we would have needed to reduce the many positions along the education scale (20) into a smaller array of three or four subgroups, such as: those with high school or less education, those with some college, and those with college degrees and more education. Making these data transformations would have glossed over some potentially important attributes in our data; and it would also have taken additional time to make all the necessary data transformations. Thus, correlational analyses enable us to best preserve the richness of detail in our data; in addition, they enable us to very efficiently test a large body of presumed correlates with extreme rapidity. And most important of all, they enable use to gauge the magnitude of correlations, a feature that is often not permitted with crosstabular tests.

MULTIPLE REGRESSION ANALYSIS

Helpful as correlation matrices are for gaining a perspective of the strength of related associations, they tell us very little about the overlap between associated variables. Sometimes, associated variables may be redundant with other variables already in our explanatory models. We need another analytic technique to help us identify when associated variables simply duplicate the influence of other variables that we are already aware of in our analyses. Multiple regression analysis helps us to build the most efficient and parsimonious models to account for a dependent variable of interest.

Correlation Matrix										
	educ	maeduc	paeduc	paocc16	papres16	xnorcsiz	racecomb(d:1)	sibs	family16(d:1)	only
educ	1.00	.50	.50	-.37	.30	-.16	.10	-.33	.06	.08
maeduc	.50	1.00	.68	-.39	.34	-.11	.12	-.33	.01	.04
paeduc	.50	.68	1.00	-.50	.48	-.15	.13	-.32	.01	.04
paocc16	-.37	-.39	-.50	1.00	-.68	.16	-.16	.26	-.02	-.05
papres16	.30	.34	.48	-.68	1.00	-.07	.15	-.18	.03	.04
xnorcsiz	-.16	-.11	-.15	.16	-.07	1.00	.17	.07	.03	-.02
racecomb(d:1)	.10	.12	.13	-.16	.15	.17	1.00	-.21	.06	.00
sibs	-.33	-.33	-.32	.26	-.18	.07	-.21	1.00	-.07	-.30
family16(d:1)	.06	.01	.01	-.02	.03	.03	.06	-.07	1.00	-.03
only	.08	.04	.04	-.05	.04	-.02	.00	-.30	-.03	1.00

Missing data excluded: **Listwise**

Color coding:	<-0.45	<-0.30	<-0.15	<0.00	>0.00	>0.15	>0.30	>0.45

Recode for 'racecomb'
1 = 1; 0 = *-*

Recode for 'family16'
1 = 1; 0 = *-*

Allocation of cases

Valid cases	17,193
Cases with invalid codes on variables correlated	26,505
Total cases	*43,698*

Datasets

1	/7502docs/D3/GSS02
2	/7502docs/Npubvars/GSS02

CSM, UC Berkeley

TABLE 15.3

In multiple regression analyses, we include all important hypothesized independent variables against the dependent variable to see how well all predictors simultaneously explain variations in the dependent variable. Regression equations assume that the so-called predictors are additive and make unique contributions to explaining variations in the dependent variable of interest. We also use Beta weights, which are standardized from +1.0 to –1.0, to assess the relative strengths of each potential explanatory influence.

With regression analysis, we can assess whether a large array of potentially linked correlates is any better than it might be if compared to knowing only one or two of the presumed causal factors. With regression analysis, we can also assess how valuable our regression equation (or model) is for predicting the variability in our dependent variable of interest. It should be noted that in regression analysis only those cases where each and every variable in the analysis has a value will be counted. If there is a missing value for any one of the variables in the equation, that case will be excluded.

Now let us perform a multiple regression analysis of all the variables we just examined in our correlation matrix (i.e. on all the correlates we hypothesized as being linked to educational attainments in the General Social Surveys). To do a multiple regression analysis with the SDA software, you will need to perform the following steps:

1. Return to http://sda.berkeley.edu/cgi-bin/hsda?harcsda+gss02, select the "Multiple regression" option and click **Start**.
2. Type **educ** in the "Dependent" box.
3. Enter each of the nine variables that you want to consider into the input fields under the heading "Independent." the nine other variables in the subsequent boxes. Remember to apply the suggested recode language for all dummy variables.
4. Click **Run Regression** and compare your results with ours (shown in Table 15.4).

These results closely follow the results obtained from the correlation matrix procedure. The highest Beta weights are for mother's education, .26; father's education, .20; father's occupational category rating at age 16, –.11; and the number of siblings, –.15. For all other variables, the Beta weights showed lower values. You probably can use + or – .08 as the lower Beta weight cutoff limit; values below that number will usually be weak or ineffectual predictors of the dependent variable. The last five variables appeared to contribute negligibly to the overall explained variability. This matches exactly what we found for the correlation matrix. Thus, race, urbanicity, parental divorce, being an only child, and even a father's occupational prestige at age 16 appeared to be redundant to this model. This does not mean that these factors are unrelated to educational differences, but rather that in the presence of the other stronger correlates, these correlates contribute almost nothing to the explained variance.

The regression analysis also shows another very important statistic called the adjusted R-square value. This figure says how much the regression equation enables one to predict variability in the dependent vari-

SDA 1.3: Regression
GSS 1972-2002 Cumulative Datafile

Oct 01, 2004 (Fri 08:18 AM PDT)

Variables					
Role	Name	Label	Range	MD	Dataset
Dependent	educ	HIGHEST YEAR OF SCHOOL COMPLETED	0-20	97,98,99	1
Independent	maeduc	HIGHEST YEAR SCHOOL COMPLETED, MOTHER	0-20	97,98,99	1
Independent	paeduc	HIGHEST YEAR SCHOOL COMPLETED, FATHER	0-20	97,98,99	1
Independent	paocc16	FATHERS CENSUS OCCUPATION CODE (1970)	1-984	0	1
Independent	papres16	FATHERS OCCUPATIONAL PRESTIGE SCORE (1970)	9-82	0	1
Independent	xnorcsiz	EXPANDED N.O.R.C. SIZE CODE	1-10	0	1
Independent	racecomb(d: 1)	Race combination variable (race and racecen1)	0-1		1
Independent	sibs	NUMBER OF BROTHERS AND SISTERS	0-68	98,99	1
Independent	family16(d: 1)	LIVING WITH PARENTS WHEN 16 YRS OLD	0-1		1

	Regression Coefficients				Test That Each Coefficient = 0	
	B	SE(B)	Beta	SE(Beta)	T-statistic	Probability
maeduc	.215	.007	.258	.009	29.795	.000
paeduc	.144	.007	.202	.009	21.650	.000
paocc16	-.001	.000	-.109	.009	-12.073	.000
papres16	.003	.002	.012	.009	1.398	.163
xnorcsiz	-.075	.006	-.075	.006	-11.559	.000
racecomb(d:1)	.055	.063	.006	.007	.864	.388
sibs	-.148	.007	-.146	.007	-21.414	.000
family16(d:1)	.495	.071	.044	.006	6.984	.000
Constant	10.092	.165			61.001	.000

Color coding:	<-2.0	<-1.0	<0.0	>0.0	>1.0	>2.0	T
Effect of each variable:		Negative			Positive		

Multiple R = .580   R-Squared = .337   Std Error of Estimate = 2.493

Recode for 'racecomb'   1 = 1; 0 = *-*
Recode for 'family16'   1 = 1; 0 = *-*

TABLE 15.4

able. The adjusted R-square value for this 9-variable equation was 34%, which means that knowing these nine variables enabled one to make a 34% better prediction of the dependent variable than would have been possible without having this knowledge. It is therefore useful to know these nine variables if one wants to make better predictions of educational differences. If you removed the weaker correlates to educational differences, and re-ran the model, you would notice that the adjusted R-square only declines by one percent to 33%. Thus, this is another way of showing that the other variables—race, urbanicity, parental divorce, being an only child and father's occupational prestige at age 16—don't add much to improving our prediction of educational differences. In fact, their absence only brings about a 1% loss of predictive power.

Another point we mentioned at the outset of this chapter was the findings showing race related to educational differences, with Asians showing the highest average educational attainments and Native Americans showing the least. We cannot apply the race variable in the multiple regression analyses the way that it appeared in the one-way ANOVA, except in the form of a dummy variable. However, if you compared whites to all other minorities in a separate ANOVA test, you will find that whites show significantly higher educational attainments than all other minorities taken together. Yet, in our multiple regression model, the other stronger correlates, such as parents' educational attainments and class, showed race to be redundant when it was included with these more powerful causal influences. Thus, multivariate modeling enables us to identify theoretical redundancies.

Just as you might say that knowing the four predictors—mother's and father's education, number of siblings, and father's occupational category grouping at age 16—helps to predict people's educational attainments by 34 percent, you could also say that 66 percent of the variance to predict this outcome remains undetermined or uncertain. So there is still a lot that we don't know in attempting to predict this outcome. If the General Social Survey had been focused on people's early life experiences, we probably could have included a number of other relevant factors that would increase our ability to predict longer-term educational attainments. Had this data been collected, we would have liked to include any number of the following variables: having had the benefit of tutors, after-school programs as a pre-teen, foreign travel opportunities, close and positive relationships with teachers, class rank in one's high school, high school GPA, receiving awards during high school, clique memberships in high school, and being "popular" in high school (especially in academically oriented groups). Any of these experiences should help to improve our ability to predict longer-term educational attainments. Unfortunately, the GSS was not focused this way. But if one wished to pursue this question in greater depth, there are many other studies that one could investigate in an effort to improve predictions of the unexplained variance of educational attainments.

We will now turn our attention on another survey which we have examined at several points in this volume, the 1995 National Survey of Adolescents (www.icpsr.umich.edu/cgi/SDA/hsda?nacjd+nsa) in the U.S. This study has a nationally representative population of some 3,000 adolescents between the ages of 12 and 17. Let us focus on the variability of acting delinquently in this study. Respondents were asked a variety of questions about their delinquent behavior:

- had they ever stolen something with a value greater than $100
- had they ever stolen a motor vehicle
- had they ever broken into and entered a property that did not belong to them
- had they ever been involved in gang fights
- had they ever used force against someone in a robbery
- had they ever had sex with someone against their will
- had they ever attacked someone with the idea of hurting or killing them

We created a scale with these seven items. Eighty-seven percent of respondents reported doing none of these seven delinquent or criminal misdeeds; 8 percent reported doing one misdeed; 3 percent reported doing two misdeeds; and the remaining 2 percent reported doing three or more misdeeds.

You can create the same scale we did called **TOTDLINK** by using the SDA "Compute a new variable" command. For each of the following eight statements, you will need to enter the correct coding into the "Expression to define the new variable" field, select "Yes" from the option "Replace that variable, if it already exists?" and click **Start Computing**. Do *not* attempt to enter all of the variables in one go, as it will not work!

```
if (q49aa eq 1) dlink1 = 1
else dlink1 = 0

if (q49ab eq 1) dlink2 = 1
else dlink2 = 0

if (q49ac eq 1) dlink3 = 1
else dlink3 = 0

if (q49ad eq 1) dlink4 = 1
else dlink4 = 0

if (q49ae eq 1) dlink5 = 1
else dlink5 = 0

if (q49ae eq 1) dlink6 = 1
else dlink6 = 0

if (q49af eq 1) dlink7 = 1
else dlink7 = 0

if (q49ag eq 1) dlink8 = 1
else dlink8 = 0
```

After each of these eight variables has been created, make one final variable adding them all together:

```
totdlink = sum (dlink1, dlink2, dlink3, dlink4, dlink5, dlink6, dlink7,
    dlink8)
```

Once we have created this new variable, we are ready to investigate its correlates in the adolescent survey data. Let's begin by doing a correlation matrix running a number of potential correlates against delinquency: age (S1); sex (GENDER); being suspended from school (Q7T); parental divorce (Q7D); death of a friend (Q7G); repeating a grade (Q7O); being physically assaulted (PA); being physically assaulted or abused (PAAB); being a post-traumatic stress disorder victim (PTSDL), being a regular smoker (Q27C); frequently getting drunk(Q28F); drinking problems at home (Q41), drug problems at home (Q43); friends have destroyed property (Q48AA); friends have used marijuana (Q48AB); friends have threatened to hit people without good reason (Q48AD); friends have broken into a vehicle or house to steal things (Q48AF); friends have sold hard drugs (Q48AG); friends have stolen things with a value greater than $50 (Q48AH); friends suggesting you do something against the law (Q48AI). Any or all of these factors could be related to delinquent activities. You will find that the correlation matrix program will only accept 16 variables at one time for the matrix, making it necessary to complete the matrix in two passes. As you examine the matrix output, you will notice that age and parental divorce experience produced very low correlation coefficients, making it possible to discard these variables from any further consideration. The result is shown in Table 15.5.

Correlation Matrix															
	TOTDLINK	S1	GENDER	Q7T	Q7D	Q7G	Q7O	PA	PAAB	PTSDL	Q27C	Q28F	Q41	Q43	Q48AA	Q48AB
TOTDLINK	1.00	-.01	-.20	-.34	-.09	-.11	-.19	.38	.36	.22	-.20	.26	-.24	-.22	-.29	-.18
S1	-.01	1.00	-.14	.07	.03	-.03	.04	-.03	-.05	-.11	-.08	.08	-.01	.12	.09	-.08
GENDER	-.20	-.14	1.00	.15	-.03	-.08	.06	-.02	.00	.16	-.08	.00	-.13	-.11	.11	-.05
Q7T	-.34	.07	.15	1.00	.12	.08	.17	-.18	-.19	-.09	.20	-.11	.10	.09	.14	.07
Q7D	-.09	.03	-.03	.12	1.00	-.04	.15	-.11	-.11	-.07	.08	.01	.10	.04	.07	.04
Q7G	-.11	-.03	-.08	.08	-.04	1.00	.07	-.14	-.14	-.05	.04	-.04	.10	.03	.11	.05
Q7O	-.19	.04	.06	.17	.15	.07	1.00	-.09	-.11	-.04	.06	-.13	.09	.04	.09	-.05
PA	.38	-.03	-.02	-.18	-.11	-.14	-.09	1.00	.88	.31	-.17	.14	-.25	-.21	-.20	-.11
PAAB	.36	-.05	.00	-.19	-.11	-.14	-.11	.88	1.00	.30	-.17	.16	-.20	-.25	-.22	-.15
PTSDL	.22	-.11	.16	-.09	-.07	-.05	-.04	.31	.30	1.00	-.14	.02	-.13	-.18	-.18	-.08
Q27C	-.20	-.08	-.08	.20	.08	.04	.06	-.17	-.17	-.14	1.00	-.16	.13	.14	.16	.15
Q28F	.26	.08	.00	-.11	.01	-.04	-.13	.14	.16	.02	-.16	1.00	-.13	-.09	-.08	-.09
Q41	-.24	-.01	-.13	.10	.10	.10	.09	-.25	-.20	-.13	.13	-.13	1.00	.25	.07	.16
Q43	-.22	.12	-.11	.09	.04	.03	.04	-.21	-.25	-.18	.14	-.09	.25	1.00	.13	.14
Q48AA	-.29	.09	.11	.14	.07	.11	.09	-.20	-.22	-.18	.16	-.08	.07	.13	1.00	.23
Q48AB	-.18	-.08	-.05	.07	.04	.05	-.05	-.11	-.15	-.08	.15	-.09	.16	.14	.23	1.00

Correlation Matrix					
	TOTDLINK	Q48AD	Q48AF	Q48AG	Q48AH	Q48AI
TOTDLINK	1.00	-.31	-.40	-.32	-.37	-.35
Q48AD	-.31	1.00	.26	.23	.29	.32
Q48AF	-.40	.26	1.00	.37	.55	.35
Q48AG	-.32	.23	.37	1.00	.37	.26
Q48AH	-.37	.29	.55	.37	1.00	.40
Q48AI	-.35	.32	.35	.26	.40	1.00

TABLE 15.5

Once you have performed all of these calculations, you are now ready to run the multiple regression equation. The output is shown in Table 15.6.

The regression output shows that our equation does a reasonably good job of predicting the variability in delinquency; the adjusted R-square

Variables					
Role	**Name**	**Label**	**Range**	**MD**	**Dataset**
Dependent	**TOTDLINK**		.00-7.00		2
Independent	**GENDER**	GENDER 1-2			1
Independent	**Q7T**	BEING SUSPENDED FROM SCHOOL	1-3	9	1
Independent	**Q7G**	DEATH OF A CLOSE FRIEND	1-4	9	1
Independent	**Q7O**	HAVING TO REPEAT A SCHOOL GRADE	1-3	9	1
Independent	**PA**	PHYSICALLY ASSAULTED	0-1		1
Independent	**PAAB**	PHYSICALLY ASSAULTED OR ABUSED	0-1		1
Independent	**PTSDL**	LIFETIME PTSD DSM-IV	0-1		1
Independent	**Q27C**	EVER SMOKED REGULARLY	1-3	9	1
Independent	**Q28F**	NUMBER OF DAYS PAST YEAR GOTTEN DRUNK	0-366	999	1
Independent	**Q41**	FAMILY MEMBER-- DRINKING PROBLEM	1-4	9	1
Independent	**Q43**	ANYONE IN FAMILY USE HARD DRUGS	1-4	9	1
Independent	**Q48AA**	FRIENDS: PURPOSELY DESTROYED PROPERTY	1-5	9	1
Independent	**Q48AB**	FRIENDS: USED MARIJUANA OR HASHISH	1-4	9	1
Independent	**Q48AD**	FRIENDS: HIT/THREATENED TO HIT SOMEONE	1-4	9	1
Independent	**Q48AF**	FRIENDS: BROKEN IN TO STEAL SOMETHING	1-4	9	1
Independent	**Q48AG**	FRIENDS: SOLD HARD DRUGS	1-4	9	1
Independent	**Q48AH**	FRIENDS: STOLEN SOMETHING MORE THAN $50	1-5	9	1
Independent	**Q48AI**	FR: SUGGESTED YOU DO SOMETHING AGNST LAW	1-3	9	1

TABLE 15.6

Regression Coefficients				Test That Each Coefficient = 0	
	B	**SE(B)**	**Beta**	**SE(Beta)**	**T-statistic**	**Probability**
GENDER	-.601	.098	-.205	.033	-6.165	.000
Q7T	-.452	.112	-.134	.033	-4.043	.000
Q7G	.011	.099	.003	.032	.109	.913
Q7O	-.315	.164	-.061	.032	-1.917	.056
PA	.479	.208	.157	.068	2.304	.022
PAAB	-.008	.201	-.003	.068	-.038	.970
PTSDL	.273	.134	.069	.034	2.036	.042
Q27C	-.103	.094	-.035	.033	-1.087	.278
Q28F	.002	.001	.100	.032	3.086	.002
Q41	-.226	.117	-.065	.034	-1.924	.055
Q43	-.221	.123	-.060	.034	-1.789	.074
Q48AA	.043	.103	.015	.036	.414	.679
Q48AB	-.043	.125	-.012	.033	-.348	.728
Q48AD	-.543	.104	-.184	.035	-5.224	.000
Q48AF	-.509	.123	-.167	.040	-4.131	.000
Q48AG	-.371	.113	-.118	.036	-3.277	.001
Q48AH	-.131	.110	-.048	.041	-1.182	.238
Q48AI	-.120	.104	-.041	.036	-1.150	.251
Constant	6.514	.514			12.663	.000

Color coding:	<-2.0	<-1.0	<0.0	>0.0	>1.0	>2.0	T
Effect of each variable:		Negative			Positive		

Multiple R = .673   R-Squared = .453   Std Error of Estimate = 1.100

Allocation of cases

Valid cases	601
Cases with invalid codes on variables in the model	3,422
Total cases	*4,023*

(CONT.)

suggests that we predict 45 percent of the variance from our complete list of predictors. This appears to be a far better ability to make predictions for delinquent behavior than what we had achieved when we predicted the variability in educational outcomes. As you examine the *p* value information (showing values above the .05 cut-off limit), you will note that nine variables in our model appear to be redundant: Q41, Q7G, PAAB, Q27C, Q48AA, Q48AB, Q48AH, and Q48AI. We can safely eliminate each of these nine variables and re-run the equation. The new regression result is shown in Table 15.7.

When we re-examine our output with the shorter list of variables, we should note that we lost a very small ability to make predictions, only 1

Variables					
Role	Name	Label	Range	MD	Dataset
Dependent	**TOTDLINK**		.00-7.00		2
Independent	**GENDER**	GENDER 1-2			1
Independent	**Q7T**	BEING SUSPENDED FROM SCHOOL	1-3	9	1
Independent	**Q7O**	HAVING TO REPEAT A SCHOOL GRADE	1-3	9	1
Independent	**Q43**	ANYONE IN FAMILY USE HARD DRUGS	1-4	9	1
Independent	**PA**	PHYSICALLY ASSAULTED	0-1		1
Independent	**Q48AD**	FRIENDS: HIT/THREATENED TO HIT SOMEONE	1-4	9	1
Independent	**PTSDL**	LIFETIME PTSD DSM-IV	0-1		1
Independent	**Q48AG**	FRIENDS: SOLD HARD DRUGS	1-4	9	1
Independent	**Q28F**	NUMBER OF DAYS PAST YEAR GOTTEN DRUNK	0-366	999	1
Independent	**Q48AF**	FRIENDS: BROKEN IN TO STEAL SOMETHING	1-4	9	1

	Regression Coefficients				Test That Each Coefficient = 0	
	B	SE(B)	Beta	SE(Beta)	T-statistic	Probability
GENDER	-.507	.086	-.177	.030	-5.902	.000
Q7T	-.495	.102	-.147	.030	-4.859	.000
Q7O	-.320	.148	-.063	.029	-2.156	.032
Q43	-.358	.112	-.097	.030	-3.183	.002
PA	.521	.096	.174	.032	5.447	.000
Q48AD	-.605	.092	-.205	.031	-6.577	.000
PTSDL	.270	.126	.067	.031	2.148	.032
Q48AG	-.431	.105	-.135	.033	-4.090	.000
Q28F	.001	.000	.085	.030	2.862	.004
Q48AF	-.580	.102	-.191	.034	-5.684	.000
Constant	6.123	.423			14.470	.000

Color coding:	<-2.0	<-1.0	<0.0	>0.0	>1.0	>2.0	T
Effect of each variable:		Negative			Positive		

Multiple R = .665   R-Squared = .442   Std Error of Estimate = 1.075

Allocation of cases	
Valid cases	695
Cases with invalid codes on variables in the model	3,328
Total cases	*4,023*

TABLE 15.7

percent, as the adjusted R-square fell from .45 to .44. As we look over this much shorter list of predictors, we find that the following play significant roles in increasing the likelihood that someone will act delinquently: being a male, being a physical abuse victim, having school problems of being expelled or having to repeat a grade, frequently getting drunk and having other family members with drinking problems, and having friends that engage in delinquent actions. The bright colors shown in the SDA display are indicators that each of these factors is important to improving our ability to make this prediction.

LOGISTIC REGRESSION

Multiple regression analysis is an extremely helpful analysis tool when you have dependent variables that are essentially continuous, as we demonstrated with the years of schooling a person may have completed (ranging from none to twenty), or the number of delinquent infractions (ranging from none to seven). Yet, one would be hard pressed to apply this tool when one is dealing with a dichotomous dependent variable. If one were studying some dichotomous phenomena, such as mortalities (living vs. deceased), suicide attempts (having attempted suicide vs. never attempting it), or smoking behavior (being a current smoker vs. being a nonsmoker), or other such two-category phenomena, then one must resort to a different regression analysis method: *logistic regression*.

The logistic regression software at SDA does not enable users to gauge the strength of associated influences. (You will find this facility available in some commercial statistical software packages like SPSS, SAS or STATA when odds ratios are calculated.) Nevertheless, the SDA platform is still important and useful because it enables users to discover redundancies in multivariate modeling. We may find certain factors producing significant associations in bivariate cross-tabular tests. But when the factors are simultaneously considered in multivariate models, the associations may simply become redundant or coincidental to other, more important factors, that exert more powerful influences. In multivariate logistical regression modeling, one may discern that certain associations simply duplicate other variables already in our models. We will show this in the following description of how to use the SDA logistic regression procedure. It should be noted that the logistic regression procedure is presently not available with the crime and drug studies data sets from the ICPSR data archive. It is, however, available for all data sets at the Berkeley SDA archive and from the NACDA Center archive for research on aging at ICPSR.

We will begin this demonstration of logistic regression analysis by running two separate cross-tabular analyses with GSS survey data (http://sda. berkeley.edu/cgi-bin/hsda?harcsda+gss02). Our focus will be upon smoking. During the period from 1977 to 1994, GSS asked respondents whether they were current smokers. Although the differences were not very large, it was noted that 38 percent of African Americans reported themselves to be smokers compared to 35 percent of whites. With the large sample size of over 16,000 cases, this difference turned out to be a statistically significant one. In fact, during this same period, other studies found even greater differences showing African Americans more inclined to smoke than whites. The question that needs to be examined is whether race is indeed a correlate of smoking, or whether what we are observing is really a byproduct of a social class-related phenomena. Many studies find that the lower classes smoke to a greater extent than their middle and upper class counterparts. With African Americans more often positioned at the lower end of the social class continuum, it is altogether possible that what we are witnessing is simply a reflection of the class differences associated with smoking. Race could simply be a redundant or coincidental correlate.

To examine this question, begin by making two separate crosstabular tests of smoking (SMOKE), crosstabulated by race (use the following recode: race (r:1 "White"; 2 "Black")); then make a second crosstabulation of smoking by social class (CLASS). You will find that both tests put race and class as statistically significant bivariate correlates of smoking (see Tables 15.8 and 15.9).

You can also replicate these tests with the logistic regression procedure. From the main SDA menu (http://sda.berkeley.edu) choose the "Logit/Probit" option. Then enter smoke as the dependent variable. Next, enter race as the

Variables					
Role	**Name**	**Label**	**Range**	**MD**	**Dataset**
Row	**smoke**	DOES R SMOKE	1-2	0,8,9	1
Column	**race(Recoded)**	RACE OF RESPONDENT (1972-2000)	1-2		1

Frequency Distribution				
Cells contain: -Column percent -N of cases		**Race**		
		1 White	2 Black	*ROW TOTAL*
smoke	1: YES	**34.7** 4,763	**37.7** 825	*35.1* *5,588*
	2: NO	**65.3** 8,983	**62.3** 1,362	*64.9* *10,345*
	COL TOTAL	*100.0* *13,746*	*100.0* *2,187*	*100.0* *15,933*
Means		1.65	1.62	1.65
Std Devs		.48	.48	.48

Color coding:	<-2.0	<-1.0	<0.0	>0.0	>1.0	>2.0	Z
N in each cell:	Smaller than expected			Larger than expected			

Summary Statistics					
Eta* =	.02	Gamma =	-.07	Chisq(P) =	7.82 (p= 0.01)
R =	-.02	Tau-b =	-.02	Chisq(LR) =	7.75 (p= 0.01)
Somers' d* =	-.03	Tau-c =	-.01	df =	1

*Row variable treated as the dependent variable.

TABLE 15.8

Variables					
Role	Name	Label	Range	MD	Dataset
Row	**smoke**	DOES R SMOKE	1-2	0,8,9	1
Column	**class**	SUBJECTIVE CLASS IDENTIFICATION	1-5	0,8,9	1

Frequency Distribution							
Cells contain: -Column percent -N of cases		class					
		1 LOWER CLASS	2 WORKING CLASS	3 MIDDLE CLASS	4 UPPER CLASS	5 NO CLASS	*ROW TOTAL*
smoke	1: YES	**46.8** 398	**39.0** 2,754	**30.0** 2,114	**26.0** 133	**.0** 0	*34.9* *5,399*
	2: NO	**53.2** 452	**61.0** 4,301	**70.0** 4,933	**74.0** 379	**100.0** 1	*65.1* *10,066*
	COL TOTAL	*100.0* *850*	*100.0* *7,055*	*100.0* *7,047*	*100.0* *512*	*100.0* *1*	*100.0* *15,465*
Means		1.53	1.61	1.70	1.74	2.00	1.65
Std Devs		.50	.49	.46	.44	.00	.48

Color coding:	<-2.0	<-1.0	<0.0	>0.0	>1.0	>2.0	Z
N in each cell:	Smaller than expected		Larger than expected				

Summary Statistics					
Eta* =	.11	Gamma = .21	Chisq(P) =	199.28	(p= 0.00)
R =	.11	Tau-b = .11	Chisq(LR) =	199.31	(p= 0.00)
Somers' d* = .10		Tau-c = .11	df =	4	

*Row variable treated as the dependent variable.

TABLE 15.9

first, and only, independent variable. Table 15.10 shows that the *p* value shows a significant relationship between race and smoking.

Now, do a second logistic analysis. This time enter **smoke** as the dependent variable and **race** and **class** as independent variables. When you run this analysis, you will note that race is no longer a statistically significant correlate of smoking (see Table 15.11). Thus, with the logistic regression procedure we have found that race is simply duplicating the influence of social class in the prediction of smoking.

Finally, we will evaluate a more elaborate multivariate model of potential correlates of smoking. There is another mix of interrelated correlates to smoking, any or all of which could be separate or duplicative influences on smoking. Each has been shown in earlier research to have some associations with smoking. Education is one factor, with more highly educated respondents less likely to smoke than the less well educated. Occupation is another, with white-collar and professional workers having been repeatedly shown to be less likely to smoke than manual and blue-collar workers. Class is still another correlate of smoking, with middle and upper class members less likely to smoke than members of the lower classes. Any one of these factors could have an overshadowing

Variables					
Role	Name	Label	Range	MD	Dataset
Dependent	**smoke(Recoded)**	DOES R SMOKE	0-1		1
Independent	**race(Recoded)**	RACE OF RESPONDENT (1972-2000)	1-2		1

Logit Coefficients			Test That Each Coefficient = 0	
	B	SE(B)	T-statistic	Probability
race	-.133	.048	-2.796	.005
Constant	.768	.057	13.503	.000

Color coding:		<-2.0	<-1.0	<0.0	>0.0	>1.0	>2.0	T
Effect of each variable:		Smaller than average			Larger than average			

Log Likelihood = -10,318.961   Pseudo R-sq = .000

LR Chi-sq(1) =   7.752   p =   .005

Recode for 'smoke'
0 = 1; 1 = *-*

Recode for 'race'
1 = 1 "White"; 2 = 2 "Black"

TABLE 15.10

Variables					
Role	Name	Label	Range	MD	Dataset
Dependent	**smoke(Recoded)**	DOES R SMOKE	0-1		1
Independent	**race(Recoded)**	RACE OF RESPONDENT (1972-2000)	1-2		1
Independent	**class**	SUBJECTIVE CLASS IDENTIFICATION	1-5	0,8,9	1

Logit Coefficients			Test That Each Coefficient = 0	
	B	SE(B)	T-statistic	Probability
race	-.057	.050	-1.140	.255
class	.363	.027	13.508	.000
Constant	-.206	.094	-2.187	.029

Color coding:		<-2.0	<-1.0	<0.0	>0.0	>1.0	>2.0	T
Effect of each variable:		Smaller than average			Larger than average			

Log Likelihood = -9,640.995   Pseudo R-sq = .010

LR Chi-sq(2) =   195.680   p =   .000

Recode for 'smoke'
0 = 1; 1 = *-*

Recode for 'race'
1 = 1 "White"; 2 = 2 "Black"

TABLE 15.11

influence on smoking over the rest, or they could each exert separate influences on smoking. In a multivariate logistic regression test, we can examine which of all possible conclusions would be the most appropriate one to make.

Another potential source of confusion about correlates to smoking can be found in examining gender and smoking. Early studies of smoking showed men to be more likely to smoke than women. But in recent years the gender gap has been narrowing, with men and women becoming more equally matched in their smoking behavior. Do gender differences still remain when we take the period of time into account? In more recent years, smoking itself has declined; yet is this merely a reflection of men's declining interest in smoking or does the period of time exert an independent influence on smoking? Another piece in this puzzle are military veterans, who have been found to be more likely to smoke than non-veterans. But is this another confounder helping to create another illusion about gender and smoking, when veteran status, more than gender is the stronger correlate? Only by placing all these potential confounders into a multivariate logistic regression model will we be able to see which exert independent influences on smoking.

In the next logistic regression, we will include all of the potential correlates that we have mentioned in a single regression model. We will enter smoking (**SMOKE**) as the dependent variable and each of the following as independent variables (note the recoded language):

- *white collar vs. blue collar occupation*   occ(r:1-400; 401-986)
- *gender*   **sex**
- *social class*   **class**
- *race differences*   race(r:1; 2)
- *veteran status*   vetyears(r:0; 1-3)
- *educational attainments*   educ(r:0-12; 13-20)
- *survey year*   year(r:1977-1984; 1985-1994)

After you enter each of these variables, press **Run** to run the logistic regression test. The results are shown in Table 15.12. The test shows that each of the presumed correlates, with the exception of race, have statistically significant *p* values, showing that they make independent contributions to the variability of smoking. Thus, every hypothesized correlate, except race, has a contribution to smoking outcomes: gender, occupational differences, social class differences, veteran status, educational differences and the time period difference before and after 1984.

In conclusion, we can say that, after we have identified and tested our bivariate hypotheses with crosstabular statistical tests, we should be ready to seek a more advanced state of knowledge of causal relationships, from which we will be able to prioritize causal influences and search for redundancies in our conceptual models. We have to recognize that in the world we inhabit events happen because of a multiplicity of causal influences, and that causal influences interact with one another. Our analytic models must permit us to handle the fact that a variety of different events

Logit Coefficients			Test That Each Coefficient = 0	
	B	SE(B)	T-statistic	Probability
race	-.089	.058	-1.537	.125
class	.246	.033	7.556	.000
occ	-.171	.044	-3.843	.000
sex	.444	.040	10.994	.000
educ	.365	.045	8.069	.000
year	.299	.040	7.549	.000
Constant	-1.311	.177	-7.406	.000

Color coding:	<-2.0	<-1.0	<0.0	>0.0	>1.0	>2.0	T
Effect of each variable:	Smaller than average			Larger than average			

Log Likelihood = -7,484.220   Pseudo R-sq = .030

LR Chi-sq(6) =   469.417   p =   .000

TABLE 15.12

impinge on one another simultaneously and influence the outcomes of our scientific interests. In this chapter, we have used regression models to help us handle these complexities. Multiple regression models can be used when we have continuous dependent variables of interest and logistic regression with dichotomous dependent variables. In the next, and final, chapter you will try to apply these new analytic tools to solve several complex research problems.

Chapter 16

Multiple and Logistic Regression

In this final chapter, we will draw on several different subjects covered in earlier parts of this book to provide a set of questions and research activities on complex multivariate analyses. If you have read Chapter 15, you should be ready to complete the following set of multiple choice questions and the larger scale analysis projects that are offered here.

1. If you were engaged in a study of the many different and sometimes overlapping influences affecting whether a person had ever driven an automobile, which would be the best statistical analytic tool to use?
   a. Multiple regression analysis
   b. Logistic regression analysis
   c. Comparison of means tests
   d. Three-way crosstabulations

2. If you were engaged in a study of different, and sometimes overlapping, influences affecting a person's feelings of depression, which would be the best statistical analytic tool to use, considering that you had a ten-item list of highly inter-correlated symptoms of depression as your primary dependent variable?
   a. Multiple regression analysis
   b. Logistic regression analysis
   c. Comparison of means tests
   d. Three-way crosstabulations

3. You are doing an exploratory analysis of a 20-item scale of post-traumatic stress disorder, comparing responses in two similar adjacent communities, one of which experienced devastating tornados, the other of which was spared. Which would be the best statistical analytic tool to use in this analysis?
   a. Multiple regression analysis
   b. Logistic regression analysis
   c. Comparison of means tests
   d. Three-way crosstabulations

Doing a multiple regression analysis is usually one of the very last steps in a lengthy screening process of identifying potential correlates to a dependent variable. The regression analysis usually uncovers redundancies in the model of causal influences and identifies variables that simply duplicate influences of other variables already in the model.

Let us assume that you are doing an analysis of the correlates associated with problem gambling. We will use the data from the 1999 National Gambling Commission Survey of the American adult population as our source material (available online from **www.icpsr.umich.edu/cgi-bin/SDA/ hsda?samhda+gibs1**).

We will assume you have done a literature review of previous studies of problem gambling and have identified the following factors as correlates to problem gambling (we have included the necessary recode syntax in this list):

- *gambling availability*   lotstate
- *race differences*   raceth(d:2-4)
- *marital status differences*   marital (r:1,4;2,3)
- *household income differences*   income
- *gender differences*   a1_
- *age differences*   a2_r
- *differences in educational attainments*   a7_
- *being suspended or expelled from schools*   a10_
- *frequent geographic mobility*   a14_
- *the importance of faith*   a12_
- *mental health problems*   j3
- *a history of depression*   j23
- *being arrested*   h2
- *higher drug uses such as greater use of alcohol*   k1_
- *greater use of marijuana*   k2_
- *greater use of cocaine*   k3_
- *greater use of stimulants*   k4_
- *greater use of tranquillizers*   k5_

In your preliminary analysis, you will complete a series of cross-tabulations to see if each of these 18 variables have a bivariate association with the dependent variable. In this preliminary screening we will enter the following recode for the variable "Ever experienced gambling problems?" **everprob(r:0;1;2-10)**. Later, in our multiple regression model, we will apply the complete 11-point scale without any recoding. As we find potential correlates that fail to pass the .05 significance test, we can safely discard them from further consideration in the multivariate modeling. Be sure to turn the weight option to "No weight."

4. Which of the following crosstabular analyses found the presumed correlate *not* significantly associated with having ever experienced problem gambling?
   a. Gambling availability
   b. Gender differences
   c. Educational attainments
   d. Age difference
   e. All of the above

5. Which of the following crosstabular analyses found the presumed correlate *not* significantly associated with having ever experienced problem gambling?
   a. Importance of faith
   b. Number of times moved and being suspended or expelled from schools
   c. A history of depression
   d. Marital status differences, married or cohabiting vs. divorced or never married
   e. All of the above

6. Which of the following crosstabular analyses found the presumed correlate *not* significantly associated with having ever experienced problem gambling?
   a. Racial differences
   b. Being arrested
   c. Self-identified mental health problems
   d. Drug use
   e. Income differences

7. Which of the following drug use variables showed statistically significant associations with having ever experienced problem gambling?
   a. Recent alcohol use
   b. Marijuana and stimulants
   c. Cocaine and tranquillizer use
   d. All of these drugs showed significant associations with problem gambling
   e. None of these drugs showed significant associations with problem gambling

After examining the bivariate relationships between gambling problems (EVERPROB) and other independent variables, your next task is to run a multiple regression. In the multiple regression analysis, you enter only those remaining significant correlates as your independent variables. To do so:

1. Go to www.icpsr.umich.edu/cgi-bin/SDA/hsda?samhda+gibs1.
2. Select "Multiple regression" and click **Start**.
3. Enter **everprob** in the "Dependent" variable box.
4. Do *not* apply the recode for "gambling problems" in this analysis.
5. Enter all the remaining significant correlates in the independent variable boxes.
6. Click **Run Regression**.

Now answer the following questions:

8. Which of the following variables remained significant when all significant bivariate correlates were run against ever having gambling problems?
   a. Gambling availability
   b. Gender differences
   c. Age differences
   d. Educational attainments

9. In the multiple regression analysis of all remaining significant correlates, which remained significant when all significant bivariate correlates were run against ever having gambling problems?
   a. Racial differences
   b. Being arrested
   c. Self-identified mental health problems
   d. Income differences
   e. b and c only

10. In the multiple regression analysis of all remaining significant correlates, which remained significant when all significant bivariate correlates were run against ever having gambling problems?
   a. Drug use
   b. Being sad or depressed
   c. The importance of faith
   d. School suspensions and expulsions

11. Of all remaining significant correlates to problem gambling in the multivariate model, what was the one with highest beta weight value?
   a. −0.08
   b. −0.12
   c. 0.10
   d. 0.53

12. What does the R-square show about all significant correlates of ever experiencing problem gambling in this multi-variate model?
   a. It shows that the significant correlates explain a very substantial amount of the variance in gambling problems.
   b. It shows that the significant correlates explain a modest amount of the variance in gambling problems.
   c. It shows that the significant correlates explain very little, less than 5 percent, of the variance in having gambling problems.
   d. None of the above.

The next section examines the correlates of voting behavior. We'll use GSS data for the exercises. The dependent variable, **vote00**(r: 2 "Not voted"; 1 "Voted"), shows whether one voted in the 2000 presidential election. Again, we will assume that you have done a literature review of previous studies of voting behavior and have identified the following factors as correlates to voting:

- *homeownership differences*   **dwelown**(r:1 "Own"; 2 "Rent")
- *racial differences*   **racecen1**(r:1 "White";2-16 "Non-white")
- *marital status differences*   **marital**
- *personal income differences*   **rincom98**(r: 1-17"Low"; 18-23"High")
- *gender differences*   **sex**
- *age differences*   **age**(r: 18-29; 30-44; 45-59; 60-89)
- *differences in educational attainments*   **educ**(r: 0-11; 12; 13-15; 16; 17-20)
- *social class differences*   **class**
- *self employed or works for someone else*   **wrkslf**
- *occupational prestige differences*   **prestg80**(r:*-30 "Lowest"; 31-40 "Low"; 41-50 "Medium"; 51-* "High")

- *political view differences*   polviews(r: 1-3 "Liberal"; 4 "Moderate"; 5-7 "Conservative")
- *type of city*   xnorcsiz
- *born in the United States*   born

In your preliminary analysis you will complete a series of crosstabulations to see if each of these 13 variables has a bivariate association with the dependent variable. As we find potential correlates failing to make the .05 significance test, we can safely discard these from further consideration in the multivariate modeling. Be sure to turn the weight option to "No weight."

13. Which of the following presumed correlates is *not* significantly associated with voting in the 2000 presidential election?
    a. Homeownership
    b. Race
    c. Marital status
    d. City size
    e. All of the above are correlated with voting
14. Which of the following presumed correlates is *not* significantly associated with voting in the 2000 presidential election?
    a. Gender
    b. Age
    c. Education
    d. Social class
    e. All of the above are related to voting in the 2000 election
15. Which of the following presumed correlates is *not* significantly associated with voting in the 2000 presidential election?
    a. Work status (self-employed or works for someone else)
    b. Occupational prestige
    c. Political views
    d. Personal income differences
    e. a and d only
16. What is the relationship between one's country of birth (whether in the United States or abroad) and voting in the 2000 presidential election?
    a. Those born in the United States were less likely to vote
    b. Those born in the United States were more likely to vote
    c. Unclear results
    d. The relationship between country of birth and voting was not statistically significant
    e. None of the above

After examining the bivariate relationships between voting behavior (**VOTE00**) and other independent variables, the next task is to run a logistic regression. In the logistic regression analysis, you enter only those remaining significant correlates as your independent variables. To do so, go to **http://sda.berkeley.edu/cgi-bin/hsda?harcsda+gss02**. Select "Logit/Probit regression" and click **Start**. Enter **vote00** in the "Dependent" variable box. Then enter all the remaining significant correlates in the independent variable boxes. Make sure you enter **vote00(1-2)** in the "Selection filter(s)" box to exclude those who were ineligible to vote in the 2000 election. Then click **Run Logit/Probit**.

17. Which of the following variables remained significant when all significant bivariate correlates were run against voting in the 2000 presidential election?
    a. Homeownership
    b. Race
    c. Marital status
    d. Personal income
    e. b and c only
18. Which of the following variables remained significant when all significant bivariate correlates were run against voting in the 2000 presidential election?
    a. Gender
    b. Age
    c. Education
    d. Social class
    e. b, c, and d
19. In the logistic regression analysis of all remaining significant correlates, which ones remained significant when all significant bivariate correlates were run against voting in the 2000 presidential election?
    a. Personal income
    b. Occupational prestige
    c. Political views
    d. Homeownership
    e. a and d only
20. What does the *pseudo* R-square show about all significant correlates of voting in the 2000 presidential election in this multivariate logistic regression model?
    a. It shows that the significant correlates explain a very substantial amount of the variance in voting behavior (about one half of the variation of the dependent variable).
    b. It shows that the significant correlates explain a modest amount of the variance in voting behavior (about one-fifth of the variation of the dependent variable).
    c. It shows that the significant correlates explain very little (i.e. less than 5 percent) of the variance in voting in 2000 election.
    d. None of the above.

Our final multiple regression exercise examines binge drinking from the 2002 National Survey on Drug Use and Health (**www.icpsr.umich.edu/cgi-bin/SDA/hsda?samhda+03903-0001**). The question asks respondents the number of days on which they had five or more drinks during the past 30 days (**DR5DAY**). The answer choices range from 0 to 30. We will assume you have done a literature review of previous studies of binge drinking and have identified the following factors as correlates to the dependent variable:

- *age*   catage
- *race*   newrace2(r: 1 "Non-Hispanic white"; 2-7 "Non White")

- *gender*   irsex
- *education*   ireduc2(r:1-7 "Less than high school"; 8 "High school"; 9-11 "Some college")
- *ever smoked a cigarette*   cigever
- *ever used marijuana*   mjever
- *ever used methamphetamine*   methdes
- *ever used cocaine*   cocever
- *neighborhood's attitude toward adult drinking daily*   snaaldly(r: 1 "Neutral"; 2-3 "Disapprove")
- *number of friends who drink alcohol*   snfdalc(r: 1 "None"; 2 "Few"; 3 "Most"; 4 "All friends")
- *church attendance*   snrlgsvc
- *total family income*   income

In your preliminary analysis, you will complete a series of cross-tabulations to see if each of these 13 variables has a bivariate association with the dependent variable. As we find potential correlates failing to make the .05 significance test, we can safely discard these from further consideration in the multivariate modeling. To get started:

1. Go to the 2002 National Survey on Drug Use and Health site at www.icpsr.umich.edu/cgi-bin/SDA/hsda?samhda+03903-0001.
2. Select "Frequencies or crosstabulation" and click **Start**.
3. Be sure to turn "Weight Option" to "No weight" and to select "Statistics" and "Question text" from "Other options."
4. For all bivariate analysis, type **dr5day(r: 0 "None"; 1-3 "1-3 days"; 4-6 "4-6 days"; 7-30 "7-30 days")** into the dependent variable field.

Now answer the following questions:

21. Which of the following crosstabular analyses found the presumed correlate to be *not* significantly associated with binge drinking?
    a. Age
    b. Race
    c. Gender
    d. Education
    e. All of the above are correlated with binge drinking
22. Which of the following crosstabular analyses found the presumed correlate to be *not* significantly associated with binge drinking?
    a. Ever smoked before
    b. Ever used marijuana
    c. Ever used methamphetamine
    d. Ever used cocaine
    e. All of the above are correlated with binge drinking
23. Which of the following crosstabular analyses found the presumed correlate to be *not* significantly associated with binge drinking?
    a. Neighborhood's attitude toward daily adult drinking
    b. Number of friends who drink alcohol
    c. Church attendance
    d. Family income
    e. All of the above are correlated with binge drinking

After examining the bivariate relationships between binge drinking (DR5DAY) and other independent variables, your next task is to run a multiple regression. In the multiple regression analysis, you enter only those remaining significant correlates as your independent variables. To do so:

1. Go to **www.icpsr.umich.edu/cgi-bin/SDA/hsda?samhda+03903-0001**.
2. Select "Multiple regression" and click **Start**.
3. Enter **dr5day** in the "Dependent" variable box.
4. Do *not* apply the recode for binge drinking in this analysis.
5. Then enter all the remaining significant correlates in the "Independent" variable boxes.
6. Click **Run Regression**.

You are now ready to answer the final set of questions:

24. Which of the following variables remained significant when all significant bivariate correlates were run against binge drinking?
    a. Age
    b. Race
    c. Gender
    d. Education
    e. All of the above are correlated with binge drinking
25. Of all the correlates in the multiple regression equation, which produced the highest beta weight against binge drinking (DR5DAY)?
    a. Age
    b. Education
    c. Gender
    d. Being a cigarette smoker
    e. None of the above
26. Which of the following variables remained significant when all significant bivariate correlates were run against binge drinking?
    a. Neighborhood's attitude toward adult drinking daily
    b. Number of friends who drink alcohol
    c. Church attendance
    d. Family income
    e. All of the above are correlated with binge drinking
27. Of all remaining significant correlates to binge drinking in the multivariate model, what was the strongest beta weight value?
    a. −0.19
    b. −0.12
    c. 0.10
    d. 0.99
28. What does the R-square show about all significant correlates of binge drinking in this multi-variate model?
    a. It shows that the significant correlates explain a very substantial amount of the variance in binge drinking
    b. It shows that the significant correlates explain a modest amount of the variance in binge drinking (R-square is higher than .15)
    c. It shows that the significant correlates explain very little (i.e. less than 5 percent) of the variance in binge drinking
    d. None of the above

ESSAY QUESTIONS

16–A Has the racial disparity in educational attainment waned over the past few decades? Answer this question by using the GSS data. Go to http://sda.berkeley.edu/cgi-bin/hsda?harcsda+gss02 and select "Comparison of means." Enter **educ** in the "Dependent" variable Box, **race** in the "Row" Box and **year** in the "Column" Box. Select "ANOVA Stats" from "Other Options." What is the trend?

16–B Use the above procedure for ANOVA analysis and investigate family income differences and family size. Enter **childs** as the dependent variable and the recoded variable **income98(r:1-10 "less than 15K";11-16"15K-35K";17-19"35-60K";20-21"60-90K";22-23 "90K and higher")** in the "Row" Box. Also be sure to type **year (2002)** in the "Selection Filter(s)" Box. Explain why there is an association between family size and family income differences. Consult some of the earlier research literature on this hypothesis and compare your 2002 based results with others' past findings.

16–C Use the above procedure for ANOVA analysis and investigate the class differences (**CLASS**) in the number of hours per day spent watching TV (**TVHOURS**). Be sure to type **year (2002)** in the "Selection Filter(s)" Box. Discuss you findings and present SDA output tables.

16–D Review prior literature on homeownership (**DWELOWN**). Identify the key determinants and run a logistic regression using the GSS 2002 data. Type **dwelown(d:1)** in the Dependent variable Box and **year (2002)** in the "Selection Filter(s)" Box. Discuss you findings and present SDA output tables.

16–E Follow the instructions given in Chapter 7 to create a new variable for traditional gender roles (**TRADSEXR**). Once you have created this variable, use it as a dependent variable in a multiple regression analysis. Consider any demographic, or other, factors that might be related to people's support for modern (or traditional) gender roles for women (e.g. age, education, a woman's work status, among others) and put together a multivariate model of the results and test it. Present all output tables and your interpretation of the results.

CHAPTER PROJECT

In the 1998 General Social Survey, respondents were asked whether they attended any dance or ballet performance during the past year (**DANCE**); whether they went to a stage play (**DRAMA**); whether they went to a classical music or opera performance (**GOMUSIC**); whether they made any art of crafts objects (**MAKEART**); whether they took part in any music, dance or theatrical performance (**PERFORM**); whether they played any musical instruments (**PLYMUSIC**); whether they attended any popular music performances (**POPMUSIC**); whether they read any works of fiction (**READFICT**); whether they saw any films in a movie theatre (**SEEMOVIE**); and whether they went to any art museums or galleries (**VISITART**). In this exercise, you will need to form an index of arts participation from each of these ten variables. After creating the index, perform bivariate and multiple regression analyses of the demographic, and other, correlates to arts participation.

You can select your independent variables from the GSS SDA website by going to http://sda.berkeley.edu/cgi-bin/hsda?harcsda+gss02 and clicking **Browse codebook**. Present all tables documenting your findings and conclusions. Be sure to type **year(1998)** in the "Selection Filter(s)" Box in order to limit the analysis to the 1998 data. To create the index:

1. Go to http://sda.berkeley.edu/cgi-bin/hsda?harcsda+gss02.
2. Select "Compute a new variable" and click **Start**.
3. Enter **artparti = dance + drama + gomusic + makeart + perform + plymusic + popmusic + readfict + seemovie + visitart** in the "EXPRESSION TO DEFINE THE NEW VARIABLE" Box.
4. Select "Yes" for the "Replace that variable, if it already exists?" option.
5. Click **Start Computing**.
6. If you are not sure how to construct an arts performance index, see Figure 16.1.

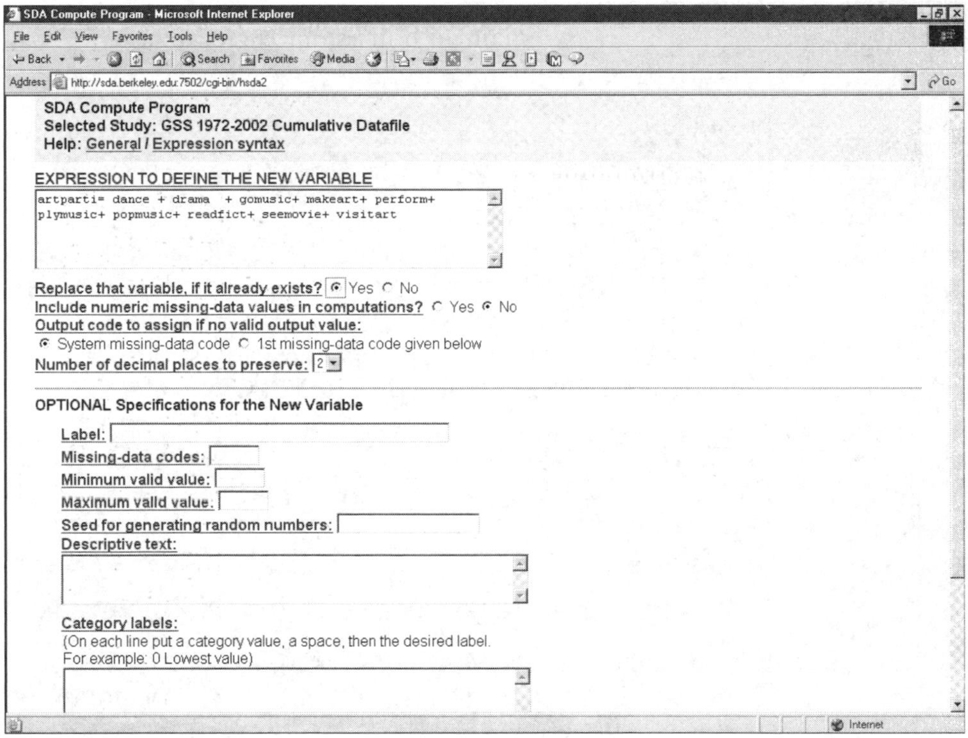

FIGURE 16.1

SYNTAX GUIDE

1999 NATIONAL GAMBLING COMMISSION SURVEY RECODES

Please note that all recodes can also be copied and pasted from either **www.ncc.edu/users/feigelb/sda.htm** or **www.ablongman.com/feigelman3e**. If you type the recode syntax in, make sure that you type *exactly* what is shown below.

everprob(r:0;1;2-10)

> *Note: Only use this recode for bivariate analyses. For regression analyses, simply use EVERPROB.*

marital(r:1,4;2,3)

raceth(r:1 "White"; 2-4 "Non-white") and where specified raceth (d: 2–4)

No recode needed: A1_; A2_R; A7_; A10_; A12_; A14_; INCOME; J3; J23, H2; K1_; K2_; K3_; K4_; K5_; LOTSTATE

GENERAL SOCIAL SURVEY

Go to: http://sda.berkeley.edu/cgi-bin12/hsda?harcsda+gss02
Select "Frequencies or crosstabulation"
Click **Start**

General Social Survey Recodes

Please note that all recodes can also be copied and pasted from either www.ncc.edu/users/feigelb/sda.htm or www.ablongman.com/feigelman3e. If you type the recode syntax in, make sure that you type *exactly* what is shown below.

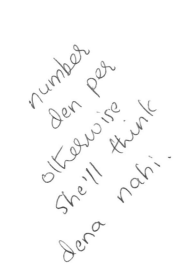

age(r: 18-29; 30-44; 45-59; 60-89)

dwelown(r:1 "Own"; 2 "Rent")

educ(r: 0-11; 12; 13-15; 16; 17-20)

income98 (r:1-10 "less than 15K"; 11-16 "15K-35K"; 17-19 "35-60K"; 20-21 "60-90K"; 22-23 "90K and higher")

polviews(r: 1-3 "Liberal"; 4 "Moderate"; 5-7 "Conservative")

prestg80(r:*-30 "Lowest"; 31-40 "Low"; 41-50 "Medium"; 51-* "High")

racecen1(r:1 "White";2-16 "Non-white")

rincom98(r: 1-17"Low"; 18-23"High)

vote00(r: 2 "Not voted"; 1 "Voted")

No recode needed: BORN; CLASS; DANCE; DRAMA; GOMUSIC; MAKEART; MARITAL; PERFORM; PLYMUSIC; POPMUSIC; READFICT; SEEMOVIE; SEX; TVHOURS; VISITART; WRKSELF; XNORCSIZ

2002 NATIONAL SURVEY ON DRUG USE AND HEALTH

Go to: www.icpsr.umich.edu/cgi-bin/SDA/hsda?samhda+03903-0001
Select "Run Frequency or crosstabulation"
Click **Start**

2002 National Survey on Drug Use and Health Recodes

Please note that all recodes can also be copied and pasted from either www.ncc.edu/users/feigelb/sda.htm or www.ablongman.com/feigelman3e. If you type the recode syntax in, make sure that you type *exactly* what is shown below.

dr5day(r: 0 "None"; 1-3 "1-3 days"; 4-6 "4-6 days"; 7-30 "7-30 days")
   Note: Only use this recode for bivariate analyses. For regression analyses, simply use DR5DAY

ireduc2(r:1-7 "Less than high school"; 8 "High school"; 9-11 "Some college")

newrace2(r: 1 "Non Hispanic white"; 2-7 "Non White")

snaaldly(r: 1 "Neutral"; 2-3 "Disapprove")

snfdalc(r: 1 "None"; 2 "Few"; 3 "Most"; 4 "All friends")

No recode needed: CATAGE; CIGEVER; COCEVER; INCOME; IRSEX; METHDES; MJEVER; SNRLGSVC